Praxis Educational Leadership:

Administration and Supervision (5412) Exam Study Guide 2024-2025

Master Strategic, Instructional, and Organizational Leadership with Detailed Content Review, Test-Taking Strategies, and Full-Length Practice Tests for Future School Leaders

Test Treasure Publication

COPYRIGHT

All content, materials, and publications available on this website and through Test Treasure Publication's products, including but not limited to, study guides, flashcards, online materials, videos, graphics, logos, and text, are the property of Test Treasure Publication and are protected by United States and international copyright laws.

Copyright © 2024-2025 Test Treasure Publication. All rights reserved.

No part of these publications may be reproduced, distributed, or transmitted in any form or by any means, including photocopying, recording, or other electronic or mechanical methods, without the prior written permission of the publisher, except in the case of brief quotations embodied in critical reviews and certain other noncommercial uses permitted by copyright law.

Permissions

For permission requests, please write to the publisher, addressed "Attention: Permissions Coordinator," at the address below:

Test Treasure Publication

Email: support@testtreasure.com

Website: www.testtreasure.com

Unauthorized use or duplication of this material without express and written permission from this site's owner and/or author is strictly prohibited. Excerpts and links may be used, provided that full and clear credit is given to Test Treasure Publication with appropriate and specific direction to the original content.

Trademarks

All trademarks, service marks, and trade names used within this website and Test Treasure Publication's products are proprietary to Test Treasure Publication or other respective owners that have granted Test Treasure Publication the right and license to use such intellectual property.

Disclaimer

While every effort has been made to ensure the accuracy and completeness of the information contained in our products, Test Treasure Publication assumes no responsibility for errors, omissions, or contradictory interpretation of the subject matter herein. All information is provided "as is" without warranty of any kind.

Governing Law

This website is controlled by Test Treasure Publication from our offices located in the state of California, USA. It can be accessed by most countries around the world. As each country has laws that may differ from those of California, by accessing our website, you agree that the statutes and laws of California, without regard to the conflict of laws and the United Nations Convention on the International Sales of Goods, will apply to all matters relating to the use of this website and the purchase of any products or services through this site.

Contents

Introduction	1
Brief Overview of the Praxis Educational Leadership Exam and Its Importance	5
Detailed Content Review	9
Study Schedules and Planning Advice	16
Frequently Asked Questions	20
1. Chapter 1: Strategic Leadership	25
2. Instructional Leadership	52
3. Chapter 3	79
4. Ethical Leadership	105
5. Organizational Leadership	134
6. Community Engagement Leadership	162
7.1 Full-Length Practice Test 1	191
7.2 Answer Sheet - Practice Test 1	215
8.1 Full-Length Practice Test 2	229
8.2 Answer Sheet - Practice Test 2	253
Test-Taking Strategies	267
Additional Resources	273

Final Words	280
Explore Our Range of Study Guides	283

INTRODUCTION

Welcome to the **Praxis Educational Leadership: Administration and Supervision (5412) Study Guide 2024-2025**—your ultimate companion for preparing and excelling in one of the most significant milestones of your educational leadership journey. Whether you aspire to become a school principal, instructional leader, or educational supervisor, this guide is meticulously crafted to help you succeed on the Praxis 5412 exam and advance your career in educational leadership.

Why This Study Guide?

The Praxis 5412 exam is a critical step in validating your expertise and readiness to lead schools and educational systems effectively. With a focus on areas such as **Strategic Leadership, Instructional Leadership, Climate and Cultural Leadership, Ethical Leadership, Organizational Leadership,** and **Community Engagement Leadership**, this exam assesses your ability to apply theoretical knowledge to practical challenges in education. This study guide is designed to demystify the exam process and equip you with the tools, strategies, and confidence needed to excel.

What You'll Find Inside

This study guide offers a comprehensive approach to your exam preparation, featuring:

1. **Detailed Content Review:**
   Each section of the Praxis 5412 exam is broken down into manageable topics, with clear explanations and examples to deepen your understanding.

2. **Test-Taking Strategies:**
   Learn proven techniques to manage time effectively, reduce stress, and navigate complex questions with ease.

3. **Customizable Study Schedules:**
   Whether you have weeks or months to prepare, our flexible study plans help you stay organized and focused.

4. **Practice Tests with Explanations:**
   Two full-length practice exams featuring 200 questions, complete with detailed answer explanations, simulate the real exam experience.

5. **Additional Resources:**
   Explore recommended online tools, academic references, and further reading to enhance your preparation.

6. **Motivational Insights:**
   Stay inspired with practical advice and encouragement as you work toward your goals.

Who Is This Study Guide For?

This guide is designed for aspiring educational leaders, including:

- Future **school principals** and **assistant principals**

- Educational supervisors and administrators

- Instructional leaders and curriculum coordinators
- Anyone pursuing certification in educational leadership through the Praxis 5412 exam

Our Commitment to Your Success

At **Test Treasure Publication**, we believe that preparation is the key to success. That's why we've created this study guide with one goal in mind: to empower you to achieve your professional aspirations. With clear explanations, practical examples, and a focus on exam readiness, this guide provides everything you need to excel.

How to Use This Guide

1. **Familiarize Yourself with the Exam:** Begin by understanding the structure, content areas, and format of the Praxis 5412 exam.

2. **Study Each Section:** Dive into the detailed reviews for each leadership domain, focusing on areas where you need the most improvement.

3. **Take Practice Tests:** Use the full-length practice exams to assess your knowledge, identify gaps, and refine your test-taking strategies.

4. **Stay Consistent:** Follow the study schedules to maintain a steady and productive pace throughout your preparation.

A Note of Encouragement

Preparing for the Praxis 5412 exam is a challenge, but it is also an opportunity to showcase your skills and commitment to educational excellence. This study guide is more than a resource—it's a roadmap to your success. Stay focused, work diligently, and remember that your journey as a leader in education starts here.

Good luck, and we wish you great success on your Praxis 5412 exam and beyond!

Brief Overview of the Praxis Educational Leadership Exam and Its Importance

The **Praxis Educational Leadership: Administration and Supervision (5412)** exam is a standardized test designed to assess the knowledge and skills of aspiring school leaders. This exam evaluates your ability to manage and lead schools effectively, address challenges, and foster a positive learning environment. It is an essential step for obtaining certification as a principal, assistant principal, or other leadership roles in education.

Exam Pattern and Structure

The Praxis 5412 exam is computer-based and consists of the following:

Category	Details
Format	Computer-Delivered
Number of Questions	120 multiple-choice questions
Time Allowed	2 hours (120 minutes)
Question Types	Selected-response questions
Content Areas	Six domains of educational leadership:
	- Strategic Leadership
	- Instructional Leadership
	- Climate and Cultural Leadership
	- Ethical Leadership
	- Organizational Leadership
	- Community Engagement Leadership
Score Range	100 to 200
Passing Score	Varies by state (typically between 146 and 160)
Test Dates	Offered year-round by appointment

Administered By

The **Educational Testing Service (ETS)** administers the Praxis 5412 exam. ETS is a trusted organization that develops and delivers assessments to measure proficiency and readiness in various professional fields.

Importance of the Praxis 5412 Exam

The Praxis 5412 exam serves as a critical gateway for individuals pursuing careers in educational leadership. Its significance lies in:

1. **Validating Leadership Skills:**
    The exam evaluates your ability to lead, manage, and support effective teaching and learning environments.

2. **Meeting Certification Requirements:**
    Most states in the United States require passing the Praxis 5412 exam as

part of the certification process for school administrators.

3. **Advancing Professional Goals:**
Achieving a passing score demonstrates your readiness to take on key responsibilities in shaping educational policies and practices.

4. **Building Confidence:**
Preparing for and succeeding in the exam equips you with the knowledge and confidence to excel in leadership roles.

Key Topics Covered

The Praxis 5412 exam assesses six primary domains of leadership:

1. **Strategic Leadership** - Developing and implementing vision and goals.

2. **Instructional Leadership** - Enhancing curriculum, instruction, and assessment practices.

3. **Climate and Cultural Leadership** - Building a supportive and inclusive school environment.

4. **Ethical Leadership** - Upholding integrity, fairness, and ethics.

5. **Organizational Leadership** - Managing resources, operations, and policies.

6. **Community Engagement Leadership** - Fostering relationships with families and the community.

Scoring and Results

- **Raw Score:** Calculated based on the number of correct answers.

- **Scaled Score:** Converted to a range between 100 and 200 for consistency.

- **Passing Scores:** Vary by state; consult your state's licensing board for specific requirements.

- **Score Reports:** Typically available within 10–15 business days after the test date.

Why Take the Praxis 5412 Exam?

The Praxis 5412 exam is not just a certification requirement but a benchmark for your readiness to lead in a dynamic educational environment. Passing this exam demonstrates your ability to make data-driven decisions, manage resources effectively, and create a thriving learning culture for students and staff alike.

DETAILED CONTENT REVIEW

The **Praxis Educational Leadership: Administration and Supervision (5412) Study Guide 2024-2025** is designed to provide in-depth coverage of the six key domains of educational leadership evaluated in the Praxis 5412 exam. Below is a comprehensive review of each section, breaking down the essential knowledge and skills you need to excel.

1. Strategic Leadership

Strategic leadership focuses on creating and communicating a vision, setting goals, and fostering a culture of continuous improvement.

Key Topics:

- **Vision and Mission Development:**
    - Crafting and articulating a clear, compelling vision for the school.
    - Aligning the vision with the school's goals and priorities.

- **Strategic Planning:**
    - Conducting a needs assessment using data.
    - Setting measurable goals and benchmarks for success.

- **Change Management:**
  - Leading change initiatives effectively.
  - Building stakeholder buy-in for new programs and policies.

- **Decision-Making:**
  - Using data-driven strategies to address challenges and allocate resources effectively.

2. Instructional Leadership

Instructional leadership emphasizes supporting teachers, improving instructional practices, and enhancing student learning outcomes.

Key Topics:

- **Curriculum Design and Alignment:**
  - Aligning curriculum with state standards and learning objectives.
  - Promoting cross-curricular connections and vertical alignment.

- **Instructional Strategies:**
  - Supporting evidence-based teaching methods.
  - Encouraging differentiated instruction to meet diverse student needs.

- **Assessment and Accountability:**
  - Using formative and summative assessments to measure progress.

- Analyzing data to identify trends and inform instructional improvements.

- **Professional Development:**
    - Designing and implementing effective teacher training programs.
    - Encouraging peer collaboration and mentorship.

3. Climate and Cultural Leadership

This domain focuses on creating a safe, inclusive, and supportive environment for students and staff.

Key Topics:

- **School Climate and Culture:**
    - Establishing high expectations for behavior and performance.
    - Promoting respect, equity, and inclusivity in the school community.

- **Conflict Resolution and Mediation:**
    - Addressing and resolving disputes among students, staff, and families.
    - Encouraging restorative justice practices.

- **Social-Emotional Learning (SEL):**
    - Supporting programs that foster empathy, resilience, and interpersonal skills.

- **Staff Morale and Collaboration:**
  - Building a positive work environment that values teamwork and professional growth.

4. Ethical Leadership

Ethical leadership is about upholding integrity, fairness, and equity while making decisions that benefit all stakeholders.

Key Topics:

- **Professional Ethics and Conduct:**
  - Adhering to ethical standards in educational leadership.
  - Demonstrating fairness and transparency in decision-making.

- **Confidentiality and Privacy:**
  - Protecting sensitive student and staff information.
  - Understanding legal requirements related to data privacy.

- **Equity and Fairness:**
  - Addressing systemic inequities and advocating for underserved populations.
  - Ensuring fair access to opportunities and resources for all students.

- **Ethical Decision-Making:**
  - Balancing competing interests to make decisions in the best interest

of the school community.

5. Organizational Leadership

This domain emphasizes resource management, operational efficiency, and policy implementation.

Key Topics:

- **Resource Allocation:**
    - Managing budgets to prioritize critical needs.
    - Ensuring equitable distribution of resources across programs.

- **Operational Management:**
    - Overseeing daily school operations, including safety protocols and scheduling.
    - Streamlining administrative processes to improve efficiency.

- **Human Resource Management:**
    - Hiring, retaining, and supporting highly qualified staff.
    - Conducting performance evaluations and providing constructive feedback.

- **Policy Development and Implementation:**
    - Designing and enforcing policies aligned with state and district regulations.

6. Community Engagement Leadership

Community engagement leadership focuses on building relationships with families, local organizations, and other stakeholders to support student success.

Key Topics:

- **Parent and Family Engagement:**
  - Establishing strong communication channels with families.
  - Hosting events and workshops to involve families in the educational process.

- **Community Partnerships:**
  - Collaborating with local businesses, non-profits, and government agencies.
  - Leveraging community resources to enhance school programs.

- **Public Relations:**
  - Communicating the school's successes and needs to the community.
  - Managing crises effectively and maintaining trust with stakeholders.

- **Advocacy and Outreach:**
  - Promoting the school's mission and vision to external audiences.
  - Encouraging community involvement in decision-making processes.

Table: Summary of Key Domains and Responsibilities

Domain	Key Responsibilities
Strategic Leadership	Developing vision, strategic planning, and leading change initiatives.
Instructional Leadership	Supporting curriculum, improving instruction, and analyzing assessment data.
Climate & Cultural	Building an inclusive, supportive school culture and resolving conflicts.
Ethical Leadership	Upholding ethical standards, equity, and transparency in decision-making.
Organizational Leadership	Managing resources, policies, and operational efficiency.
Community Engagement	Fostering family and community partnerships, advocacy, and outreach.

This **Detailed Content Review** ensures you understand the breadth and depth of topics covered in the Praxis 5412 exam. By mastering these areas, you'll be well-prepared to demonstrate your knowledge and skills in educational leadership.

Study Schedules and Planning Advice

Preparing for the **Praxis Educational Leadership: Administration and Supervision (5412)** exam requires a strategic and consistent study plan. This section provides customizable study schedules and practical planning advice to help you organize your time effectively, maximize your focus, and build confidence as exam day approaches.

Creating Your Study Schedule

Below are three study plans tailored to different preparation timelines. Choose the one that best suits your needs based on how much time you have before the exam.

1. Four-Week Intensive Study Plan

Ideal for those with limited time before the exam but who can dedicate focused study hours daily.

Day(s)	Focus Area
Week 1 (Days 1–7)	- Familiarize yourself with the exam structure and content.
	- Study **Strategic Leadership** (focus on vision, mission, and strategic planning).
	- Begin practice questions for this section.
Week 2 (Days 8–14)	- Study **Instructional Leadership** and **Climate and Cultural Leadership**.
	- Review assessment strategies and classroom management practices.
	- Take a practice test to assess progress.
Week 3 (Days 15–21)	- Study **Ethical Leadership** and **Organizational Leadership**.
	- Focus on operational management and professional ethics.
	- Continue with targeted practice questions.
Week 4 (Days 22–28)	- Study **Community Engagement Leadership** and review weaker areas.
	- Take the second full-length practice test and analyze your performance.
	- Review notes and fine-tune test-taking strategies.

2. Eight-Week Balanced Study Plan

Best for individuals with moderate time availability who want to cover all topics thoroughly.

Week	Focus Area
Week 1 & 2	- Study **Strategic Leadership** and complete practice questions.
Week 3 & 4	- Study **Instructional Leadership** and **Climate and Cultural Leadership**.
Week 5 & 6	- Study **Ethical Leadership** and **Organizational Leadership**.
Week 7	- Study **Community Engagement Leadership** and begin full-length practice tests.
Week 8	- Take additional practice tests, review weaker areas, and reinforce key concepts.

3. Twelve-Week Comprehensive Study Plan

Perfect for those who want an in-depth review with ample time for reinforcement and practice.

Week	Focus Area
Weeks 1–2	- Familiarize yourself with the exam format and study **Strategic Leadership** in depth.
Weeks 3–4	- Study **Instructional Leadership** and **Climate and Cultural Leadership**.
Weeks 5–6	- Study **Ethical Leadership** and **Organizational Leadership**.
Weeks 7–8	- Study **Community Engagement Leadership** and take mini-practice tests for each domain.
Weeks 9–10	- Take the first full-length practice test and analyze your performance.
Weeks 11–12	- Focus on weaker areas, take the second practice test, and finalize your test-taking strategy.

Planning Advice for Effective Studying

1. Set SMART Goals

Your study goals should be **Specific, Measurable, Achievable, Relevant,** and **Time-bound**. For example:

- Complete the "Strategic Leadership" section in two days.
- Answer 50 practice questions by the end of the week.

2. Create a Dedicated Study Environment

Choose a quiet, organized, and distraction-free space where you can focus on your preparation.

3. Use Active Learning Techniques

- Take notes in your own words to reinforce understanding.
- Highlight key points in the study guide.
- Summarize each section after studying it.

4. Incorporate Practice Questions Daily

Practice questions not only test your knowledge but also familiarize you with the exam format. Review detailed explanations for both correct and incorrect answers to deepen your understanding.

5. Schedule Regular Review Sessions

- Revisit previously studied sections weekly to reinforce retention.
- Use flashcards or summary notes for quick reviews.

6. Balance Study and Rest

Avoid burnout by scheduling breaks during study sessions. Use the **Pomodoro Technique**: study for 25 minutes, then take a 5-minute break.

7. Simulate Exam Conditions

Take full-length practice tests under timed conditions to build stamina and confidence for the actual exam.

8. Stay Consistent

Consistency is key. Set aside dedicated study time each day and stick to your schedule.

9. Seek Support

Join study groups, engage with online forums, or seek guidance from mentors to clarify doubts and share resources.

Frequently Asked Questions

This section addresses some of the most common questions about the **Praxis Educational Leadership: Administration and Supervision (5412)** exam to help you navigate the preparation process with confidence.

General Exam Questions

Q1: What is the Praxis Educational Leadership: Administration and Supervision (5412) exam?

The Praxis 5412 exam is a standardized test designed to assess the knowledge and skills required for effective educational leadership. It evaluates your ability to manage schools, support teaching and learning, and lead a positive school culture. Passing this exam is often a requirement for certification as a principal, assistant principal, or other school leadership roles.

Q2: Who administers the Praxis 5412 exam?

The exam is administered by the **Educational Testing Service (ETS)**, a trusted organization that develops and delivers professional assessments.

Q3: What are the eligibility requirements to take the Praxis 5412 exam?

Eligibility requirements vary by state. Typically, candidates need to have completed a graduate degree in educational leadership or a related field and meet state-specific certification prerequisites. Check your state's licensing board for detailed requirements.

Q4: How long is the exam, and how many questions are there?

The Praxis 5412 exam is **120 minutes** long and contains **120 selected-response questions**. You'll need to pace yourself, answering approximately one question per minute.

Q5: What is the passing score for the Praxis 5412 exam?

Passing scores vary by state but typically range between **146 and 160**. Check your state's certification requirements for the exact passing score.

Preparation Questions

Q6: How should I prepare for the Praxis 5412 exam?

Effective preparation involves:

- Studying this guide's **Detailed Content Review** for all six leadership domains.

- Practicing with **full-length practice tests** to simulate the exam experience.

- Following the **Study Schedules and Planning Advice** provided in this book.

- Using additional resources like online tools and ETS materials.

Q7: What topics are covered in the Praxis 5412 exam?

The exam assesses six primary domains:

1. Strategic Leadership

2. Instructional Leadership

3. Climate and Cultural Leadership

4. Ethical Leadership

5. Organizational Leadership

6. Community Engagement Leadership

Each domain tests your knowledge and skills in specific aspects of school leadership.

Q8: How much time should I dedicate to studying?

The amount of study time depends on your familiarity with the content and your schedule.

- **4 Weeks:** Study 2–3 hours daily, focusing on high-impact areas.
- **8 Weeks:** Study 1–2 hours daily for a balanced approach.
- **12 Weeks:** Study 5–8 hours weekly for a comprehensive review.

Follow the **customizable study schedules** provided in this guide to maximize your preparation.

Q9: How many practice tests should I take?

At a minimum, take two full-length practice tests:

1. **Midway through your preparation** to identify strengths and weaknesses.
2. **Two weeks before the exam** to build confidence and refine your test-taking strategy.

Q10: Are there additional resources available to supplement my study?

Yes, several online resources and tools can complement this study guide:

- ETS's official Praxis study materials

- Educational leadership forums and study groups
- Videos and webinars focused on test-taking strategies and leadership concepts

This guide also includes recommendations for trusted online resources.

Test-Taking Questions

Q11: Can I skip questions during the test and come back to them later?
Yes, the computer-based test allows you to skip and return to questions. Use this feature strategically to manage your time efficiently.

Q12: Are all questions weighted equally?
Yes, every question carries the same weight, so answer all questions, even if you have to guess.

Q13: What should I bring to the test center?
Bring the following items:

- A valid, government-issued photo ID (e.g., driver's license or passport).
- Your **admission ticket**, if required by your test center.

Personal items like cell phones, watches, and study materials are not permitted in the testing area.

Q14: Can I take breaks during the exam?
Breaks are not allowed during the 2-hour test, so ensure you are well-rested and focused before starting.

Q15: When will I receive my scores?
Scores are typically available **10–15 business days** after the test date. You can access them through your ETS account.

Post-Test Questions

Q16: What happens if I don't pass the exam?
If you don't pass, you can retake the exam. ETS allows retakes after a **28-day waiting period**. Use your score report to identify weak areas and focus on improving them before your next attempt.

Q17: How can I use my score for certification?
Submit your score to your state's licensing board as part of your application for certification. ETS allows you to designate score recipients during registration.

Q18: Is my Praxis 5412 score valid in other states?
Many states accept Praxis scores as part of their certification requirements. However, check with individual state boards for reciprocity details.

Q19: How long are my scores valid?
Praxis scores are typically valid for **10 years** from the test date, though this may vary by state.

Q20: Can I appeal my test scores?
ETS allows for score verification upon request. If you believe there was an error in scoring, you can request a review for an additional fee.

1

Chapter 1: Strategic Leadership

Strategic Planning Process

Strategic planning, in the context of educational leadership, constitutes a systematic and deliberate process through which schools and educational institutions define their desired future and chart a course for achieving it, thereby serving as a critical framework for school improvement and long-term success. This proactive approach enables educational leaders to anticipate future challenges and opportunities, allocate resources effectively, and align all organizational efforts towards shared goals. The process of strategic planning is not merely an exercise in documentation, but a dynamic and ongoing cycle of assessment, planning, implementation, and evaluation that fosters a culture of continuous improvement. Effective strategic planning is characterized by a deep understanding of the school's current context, a clear vision of its preferred future, and a comprehensive plan for bridging the gap between the two. It is a vital practice for creating schools that are responsive, effective, and sustainable in the rapidly changing landscape of education.

The strategic planning process is not monolithic, but rather a sequence of carefully designed steps, each critical to the development of a robust and effective strategic plan. These components encompass the articulation of a shared vision and mission, the diligent analysis of the internal and external environment, the establishment of clear and measurable goals, and the formulation of detailed action plans. These steps are not isolated activities, but rather are interconnected components that contribute to a cohesive and impactful strategic direction for an educational institution.

The initial phase of strategic planning involves the development of a compelling vision and mission. The vision statement serves as an inspirational declaration of the school's ideal future, painting a picture of where the institution aspires to be in the long term. The creation of an effective vision statement requires a collaborative effort that engages all stakeholders in the educational community, including teachers, administrators, students, parents, and community members. This process encourages a unified understanding of the school's purpose and fosters a shared sense of ownership in its success. A strong vision statement should be aspirational, concise, and memorable, articulating the core values and ambitions of the educational institution. For instance, a school might envision a future where "all students achieve their full potential in a supportive and innovative learning environment." This type of statement provides a clear direction and inspires all members of the school community to work towards a common aim.

The mission statement, complementary to the vision, provides a clear and concise explanation of the school's present purpose and ongoing activities. It defines the school's core function, its primary target population, and its fundamental approach to education. Effective mission statements should be specific, actionable, and easily understood by all stakeholders, offering a roadmap for daily operations and decision-making. The mission statement should reflect the unique context and values of the school, and it should align with the broader goals of the educational system. For example, a school's mission might be: "To provide a rigorous and inclusive education that fosters critical thinking, creativity, and civic responsibility." Such a mission guides the school's programs and practices, ensuring they consistently align with its overarching objectives. These vision and mission statements, together, provide a powerful framework for the entire strategic planning process, providing both direction and motivation for the school community.

Following the formulation of the vision and mission, the strategic planning process proceeds to environmental scanning, a critical phase dedicated to gathering comprehensive information about the factors that impact the school both internally and externally. Internal analysis examines the school's strengths and weaknesses, exploring aspects such as the quality of teaching, the effectiveness of programs, the level of student achievement, and the availability of resources. This phase requires a rigorous evaluation of the school's performance, often using data-driven methods to pinpoint areas of excellence and those that require improvement. External analysis, on the other hand, concentrates on the broader environment in which the school operates. This includes political, economic, social, technological, environmental, and legal factors that could influence the school. It also requires evaluating competitive forces, demographic shifts, and community needs. The systematic analysis of these internal and external forces allows for a well-informed assessment of the school's position and informs the strategic choices that follow.

A widely recognized method for conducting environmental analysis is the SWOT analysis, which examines the school's Strengths, Weaknesses, Opportunities, and Threats. This framework allows educational leaders to identify key internal capabilities and limitations while also assessing the external factors that could either benefit or hinder the school's progress. For example, a school might identify "experienced teachers" as a strength and "limited funding" as a weakness, while "community partnerships" could be an opportunity, and "changing educational standards" a potential threat. Such a detailed analysis enables the school to leverage its strengths, address its weaknesses, capitalize on opportunities, and mitigate threats.

Gathering stakeholder input is also a crucial aspect of environmental scanning. This involves collecting perspectives from a wide variety of stakeholders, including students, teachers, parents, staff, and community members, using surveys, interviews, focus groups, and public forums. The inclusion of diverse viewpoints ensures that the strategic plan is comprehensive and relevant to the needs of the entire school community. The information gathered helps to establish a common understanding of the school's context and allows for the identification of priorities and concerns that should be addressed in the strategic plan.

Once a thorough environmental scan is completed, the next stage of strategic planning involves goal setting and action planning. This stage involves the establishment of clear, measurable goals and the creation of concrete action plans to achieve these objectives. SMART goals, which are Specific, Measurable, Achievable, Relevant, and Time-bound, are highly recommended for educational institutions. A SMART goal, for instance, might be: "To increase the percentage of students achieving proficiency in reading by 15% within the next three years." This clarity enables targeted efforts and effective monitoring of progress. Each goal should be supported by a detailed action plan that specifies the strategies, activities, timelines, resources, and responsible individuals. The action plan should outline the steps necessary to implement each strategy and should be flexible enough to accommodate changes or unforeseen challenges.

Strategic planning documents should be carefully structured and should include an executive summary, the school's vision and mission statements, an overview of the environmental scan results, the established goals and objectives, detailed action plans, and metrics for evaluating progress. These documents should be regularly reviewed and updated to ensure their continued relevance and efficacy. The implementation of these plans requires strong leadership, commitment from all stakeholders, and a culture that supports continuous improvement. A collaborative approach in the creation and implementation of the plan ensures buy-in from all parties and promotes success.

In real-world scenarios, successful strategic planning implementations demonstrate that it is not only essential to have a well-crafted plan, but also to be ready for adjustments when the needs of a school change or when new issues arise. For example, a school that implemented a comprehensive literacy program may find that initial data indicates a lower-than-expected rate of progress among English language learners. The strategic planning process allows for the iterative adjustments of plans to address unexpected challenges.

Common pitfalls in strategic planning include a lack of stakeholder involvement, vague or unmeasurable goals, inadequate environmental analysis, and failure to monitor and evaluate progress regularly. To avoid these pitfalls, it's imperative to engage a broad spectrum of stakeholders, set clear and measurable objectives, undertake thorough analyses, and establish robust monitoring and evaluation systems. Additionally, failing to allocate necessary resources and neglecting to adapt the plan to changing circumstances can undermine its success. Strategic planning in educational leadership requires not just a structured plan, but also the capacity to be flexible and adjust course when necessary. The process should be seen as a living document that is continuously reviewed, revised, and improved, ensuring that it serves as an effective tool for guiding school improvement and enhancing student outcomes.

Data-Driven Leadership

Data-driven decision making has become an indispensable element of effective educational leadership in the contemporary educational landscape, demanding that school leaders move beyond intuition and rely on empirical evidence to guide their actions and policies. This shift towards data-informed practices signifies a departure from traditional, often subjective, methods of school administration, instead advocating for the systematic collection, analysis, and interpretation of data to improve educational outcomes and optimize resource allocation. The use of data provides a transparent and accountable framework for assessing the effectiveness of educational initiatives, ensuring that decisions are based on demonstrable facts rather than assumptions or personal preferences.

The foundation of data-driven leadership lies in the systematic and rigorous collection and analysis of various types of educational data. This data can broadly be categorized into academic, behavioral, and demographic information, each providing unique insights into different aspects of the educational environment. Academic data includes standardized test scores, classroom assessment results, grades, and graduation rates. This type of data provides a critical perspective on student learning and academic progress, enabling leaders to identify areas where students are excelling and areas where additional support may be necessary. Behavioral data encompasses information related to student attendance, disciplinary incidents, and engagement in school activities. This type of data can highlight patterns of behavior that may be impacting student learning or the overall school climate, allowing leaders to proactively address issues related to student well-being and school safety. Demographic data includes information about students' backgrounds, such as race, ethnicity, socioeconomic status, and special education needs. This data provides crucial insights into the diversity of the student population and enables leaders to identify and address disparities in educational opportunities and outcomes for different groups of students. The combination of these data sets allows for a holistic and comprehensive understanding of the educational context.

The methods and tools used for data collection are varied and must be chosen carefully to ensure the integrity and reliability of the data. Common data collection methods include standardized assessments, such as state-mandated tests or national benchmarks, which provide standardized metrics of student achievement. Classroom assessments, including quizzes, tests, and projects, offer a more granular view of student progress within specific courses. Surveys, administered to students, teachers, and parents, provide valuable qualitative insights into their experiences and perspectives. Observation protocols, used by school leaders and instructional coaches, offer detailed information about teaching practices and classroom environments. Data management systems, such as student information systems (SIS) and learning management systems (LMS), facilitate the collection, storage, and organization of data. These systems integrate various types of data into centralized databases that can be accessed and analyzed by school leaders and educators. The selection of appropriate data collection methods and tools is essential for ensuring that the data are accurate, reliable, and valid, and that they provide meaningful insights into the educational environment.

Once data has been collected, educators need to utilize basic statistical analysis techniques to transform raw data into actionable information. Descriptive statistics, such as mean, median, mode, and standard deviation, provide summaries of central tendencies and variability within the data, allowing educators to understand the overall performance of student groups. Inferential statistics, such as t-tests and ANOVA, enable educators to make comparisons between groups and to draw conclusions about the significance of differences. Correlation analysis helps educators to understand the relationships between different variables, such as the relationship between attendance and academic achievement. Regression analysis can be used to predict future outcomes based on current data. These statistical techniques equip educators to identify meaningful trends and patterns in the data, enabling them to make data-informed decisions about curriculum, instruction, and support services. For instance, if statistical analysis reveals a significant achievement gap between different student groups, the educational leader might focus on specific interventions targeted at closing that gap, with the analysis guiding the allocation of resources and targeted support.

The use of data for decision-making is a critical component of data-driven leadership, requiring educational leaders to effectively interpret data to inform strategic decisions about instruction, resource allocation, and program evaluation. Interpreting student achievement data involves analyzing trends and patterns to identify areas of strength and areas requiring improvement. For instance, longitudinal data can be used to track student progress over time and to identify subgroups of students who may need additional support. Analysis of assessment data can reveal gaps in the curriculum or areas where instructional practices may need to be adjusted to improve student outcomes. Leaders must analyze data with an understanding of its limitations, recognizing that data is only one piece of the puzzle, and that contextual factors also play a significant role in educational success.

In addition, analyzing trends and patterns within the data is crucial to making data-informed decisions. By examining trends over time, leaders can identify patterns in student performance, behavior, and engagement, which can inform the development of targeted interventions and support services. Patterns in attendance data might reveal periods where there is lower attendance, which might be related to specific events. Leaders also utilize data to identify inequities within the system, allowing them to proactively address these disparities and ensure that all students have access to high-quality educational opportunities. The use of data to identify patterns and trends can lead to preventative and proactive measures, rather than reactive solutions.

Making evidence-based decisions means that school leaders base their decisions on what the data indicates, rather than relying on assumptions, anecdotes, or personal preferences. This approach requires leaders to understand the nuances of data analysis, to critically evaluate data sources, and to be open to adjusting their practices when the data suggests the need for change. Leaders who employ evidence-based decision-making actively seek out relevant data, analyze it objectively, and use the results to make choices about curriculum, instruction, and resource allocation. The results, in turn, should be consistently monitored and evaluated to ensure that the chosen strategies are achieving the desired outcomes.

Data communication is a critical component of data-driven leadership, requiring leaders to effectively communicate data findings to various stakeholders, including teachers, students, parents, and community members. Effective data communication involves creating clear and concise data visualizations that are easily understood by diverse audiences. Bar graphs, pie charts, and line graphs can effectively illustrate trends, patterns, and comparisons within the data, which should be customized to the needs and interests of the audience. Furthermore, data visualizations should be accompanied by clear and concise narrative explanations that provide context and highlight the key takeaways from the data.

Presenting data to different stakeholders requires leaders to tailor their message to the audience's needs and interests. When presenting data to teachers, leaders may focus on the implications for instruction and classroom practices, whereas when presenting data to parents, leaders may emphasize student progress and outcomes. The use of data stories can be a particularly effective way to engage stakeholders, using narratives to illustrate how data can lead to positive change. Data stories should highlight real-life examples of how data has been used to inform decisions and improve educational outcomes. These stories should connect the data to the lives of the students and teachers, helping stakeholders understand the significance of the data and how it informs the school's direction.

Successful school leaders use data to improve student outcomes, allocate resources effectively, monitor program effectiveness, and guide professional development. For example, a school leader may analyze student achievement data to identify a specific subject area where students are struggling, and then allocate resources to provide additional support in that area. This could involve hiring additional teachers, purchasing new materials, or providing tutoring services. Leaders also use data to monitor the effectiveness of programs and initiatives, by tracking student outcomes, using data to assess whether these programs are achieving the desired results, and adjusting the programs accordingly. The utilization of data for evaluating effectiveness allows educational leaders to ensure that investments in specific initiatives are providing a return in the form of enhanced student outcomes. Furthermore, data can also be used to guide professional development activities, by identifying areas where teachers may need additional training or support.

For example, hands-on data analysis exercises using realistic school scenarios, can be used to give practical training. Consider a scenario where a school principal receives data showing a decline in math scores among middle school students. Educators are then given access to data and asked to explore possible contributing factors, analyze trends within the data, and develop potential intervention strategies. This exercise can be structured to ensure educators are using and discussing not only the numbers, but also the context, including student attendance, socioeconomic factors, and teaching methodologies. The exercise may also require educators to discuss data, consider different points of view, and communicate their findings using visuals that they have generated. These exercises are designed to enhance their abilities to interpret data and develop evidence-based action plans.

Through such detailed analysis and interpretation, educators develop skills in using data to make sound decisions. The emphasis on data-driven leadership is not just about using data but about cultivating a culture of inquiry, where decisions are informed by evidence, where adjustments are made based on analysis, and where the focus remains consistently on improvement. This focus on data-driven leadership empowers educators to become more effective agents of positive change in the lives of their students, while contributing to the overall success of their schools.

Change Management

Change management theory provides a framework for understanding and navigating the complexities of organizational transformation, and its application within educational settings is particularly crucial given the dynamic nature of societal needs and pedagogical advancements. Educational institutions are not static entities; they must continually evolve to meet the diverse needs of their students, adapt to advancements in technology, and respond to shifts in educational policy. The implementation of change in schools, therefore, requires a strategic and thoughtful approach, one that recognizes the potential for disruption, resistance, and the need for collaborative effort. Within this context, change management theory offers valuable insights into how to initiate, implement, and sustain transformative efforts within educational communities.

The process of change in educational organizations is multifaceted, often involving several different types of organizational shifts, each presenting unique challenges and requiring tailored strategies. Transformational change, for instance, represents a fundamental shift in the organization's mission, values, or culture. This type of change is often necessary when educational institutions need to respond to major societal shifts or systemic issues. For example, a move from a traditional, teacher-centered approach to a more student-centered, personalized learning model could be viewed as a transformational change, affecting not just instructional methods but also the overall ethos of the school. Incremental change, on the other hand, involves making small, gradual adjustments to existing systems and processes, which may be implemented to enhance existing programs or address specific issues. For instance, the addition of a new elective course or the revision of a grading policy would be considered incremental changes. Finally, remedial change becomes necessary when an organization is facing significant issues or underperforming in key areas, requiring corrective measures. This type of change may occur when standardized test scores are consistently low or when there are systemic issues with student discipline or attendance. Understanding the nature of the change being implemented—whether it is transformational, incremental, or remedial—is crucial for selecting appropriate change strategies and anticipating potential challenges.

Implementing change within educational settings typically involves several stages, each requiring specific strategies and considerations. Kurt Lewin's three-stage model—unfreezing, changing, and refreezing—is a foundational framework for understanding the change process. The unfreezing stage involves preparing the organization for change by creating a sense of urgency and addressing any resistance or concerns. This may include identifying problems, communicating the need for change, and developing a vision for the future. The changing stage involves implementing the proposed changes, often requiring significant adjustments in processes, roles, and relationships. During this phase, school leaders need to provide clear direction, offer support and training, and actively involve stakeholders in the implementation process. The refreezing stage involves stabilizing the changes and embedding them into the organization's culture, which may necessitate the establishment of new routines, policies, and structures. Continuous monitoring and evaluation are also crucial at this stage to ensure the changes are having the intended effect and to make any necessary adjustments.

One of the most significant challenges in implementing change within schools is resistance, which can manifest in various forms, including passive compliance, active opposition, or outright sabotage. Resistance often stems from a variety of factors, such as a fear of the unknown, a lack of understanding about the need for change, or concerns about the impact of change on job security or working conditions. Teachers, for example, may resist new instructional technologies if they fear it will increase their workload or if they lack the necessary training to use it effectively. Furthermore, school staff may resist changes they were not involved in developing, leading to a sense of disempowerment and disengagement. School leaders must anticipate and proactively address potential resistance by engaging stakeholders in the change process, listening to their concerns, and providing opportunities for feedback and participation. This will help in creating a supportive environment for the change.

Effective leadership is crucial to successfully implementing and sustaining change within schools, and school leaders play a critical role in managing the complex dynamics of change. One essential leadership strategy is building buy-in and support among stakeholders. This involves communicating the vision for change, explaining why the change is necessary, and clearly articulating the expected benefits. Furthermore, involving teachers, staff, students, and parents in the planning and implementation process can foster a sense of ownership and commitment to the change. Collaborative decision-making, wherein all relevant parties are empowered to contribute, also ensures that the changes are relevant and useful. Furthermore, by fostering a sense of collective responsibility, school leaders can transform what may initially appear to be external impositions into collaborative opportunities for growth.

Communication is a key component of effective change management, as it ensures that all stakeholders are aware of the reasons for change, their roles in the process, and the expected outcomes. Transparent, consistent, and timely communication can reduce uncertainty and anxiety, as well as proactively address any emerging concerns. Multiple communication channels—including meetings, emails, newsletters, and online platforms—should be utilized to reach different audiences. It is important to avoid jargon, which may confuse non-technical stakeholders, and to convey the message in plain language that is easily accessible. Furthermore, leaders need to listen carefully to the questions and concerns raised by stakeholders, responding honestly and openly.

Managing stakeholder expectations is also important when undertaking change initiatives in schools. This means that leaders must be realistic about the timeframe for change and the resources needed to support it. Change should be viewed as an ongoing process, and leaders should celebrate small successes and acknowledge setbacks. Furthermore, leaders should manage any anxiety among staff by providing opportunities for reflection and discussion. Finally, managing expectations also requires leaders to acknowledge that not all change initiatives will be successful, and that some adjustment or revision may be needed. This transparent approach builds trust and encourages a culture of continuous improvement.

Several frameworks can guide the implementation of change in educational settings, and John Kotter's 8-Step Change Model provides a systematic process for initiating and managing change. This model begins with creating a sense of urgency by highlighting the need for change and mobilizing support for the initiative. The second step is forming a powerful coalition of change agents, which should be a team of individuals who are committed to the change and who have influence within the school community. The third step is developing a vision for the future and communicating it effectively to stakeholders. The fourth step is empowering others to act on the vision, which may involve delegating tasks and providing resources to support the change. The fifth step is planning for and creating short-term wins, which provide momentum and demonstrate progress. The sixth step is consolidating improvements and producing more change, which may involve expanding the scope of the change and addressing additional issues. The seventh step is institutionalizing new approaches, which involves embedding the changes into the culture of the school. The final step is anchoring new approaches in the culture, which requires a reinforcement of the changes and a continued emphasis on improvement. By following this model, school leaders can systematically move from the initial recognition of a need for change to the establishment of new organizational practices.

Lewin's Change Management Model, with its unfreeze, change, and refreeze stages, offers a more simplified yet equally effective framework for managing change in education. The unfreeze stage focuses on making stakeholders aware of the need for change, while creating an environment that is conducive to the transition. For example, if school leaders wish to shift toward digital learning, they may need to demonstrate to staff members how it will improve their teaching, reduce their administrative burden, and increase student engagement. The change stage then introduces new systems, practices, and behaviors, with a focus on providing staff with adequate training and support during the transition. Finally, the refreeze stage solidifies the changes by incorporating them into everyday practices. This stage might involve establishing policies to reinforce digital learning practices, providing continued professional development, and monitoring the progress of the school. This approach of systematically working through these stages enables schools to integrate changes smoothly, and to ensure their long-term effectiveness.

The ADKAR model, which focuses on individual change management, also provides a useful perspective for understanding and addressing change within educational environments. ADKAR is an acronym that represents Awareness, Desire, Knowledge, Ability, and Reinforcement. Awareness involves creating an understanding among stakeholders about the need for change. Desire involves motivating them to support and participate in the change. Knowledge involves providing staff with information about how to implement the change, including the procedures, techniques, and skills required. Ability refers to providing staff with the skills and resources to implement the change effectively. Reinforcement involves ensuring that the change becomes ingrained in the school's culture and that staff members are regularly recognized for their contributions. The model recognizes that individual readiness is key to the success of any change initiative, thereby highlighting the importance of targeted support and empowerment.

Successful school change initiatives provide valuable case studies for understanding how to effectively implement change in educational contexts, such as the implementation of curriculum reforms, which is often a major undertaking for schools. A school implementing a new, standards-aligned curriculum, for instance, needs to carefully plan and communicate the changes to teachers, administrators, and parents. This may include providing professional development to help teachers adjust to the new content, pedagogy, and assessment methods. It also requires gathering feedback from teachers during the implementation to make any necessary adjustments, while ensuring that all of the stakeholders understand the reasoning behind the change and how it will benefit students.

Technology integration within schools also represents another major area of change. A school introducing a one-to-one laptop program or adopting a new learning management system needs to provide adequate training and support for teachers and students. Furthermore, it may involve changing teaching and learning practices to effectively incorporate the new technology. Furthermore, it is critical that a school ensures that all students have equal access to the technology and the support they need to use it effectively, and to provide equitable opportunities.

Finally, efforts aimed at cultural transformations, such as creating a more inclusive and equitable school climate, demand a deep understanding of the existing school culture and the factors that contribute to disparities or exclusion. Such transformation often involves school-wide professional development that addresses issues such as diversity, equity, and inclusion. The change also requires school leadership to address policies and practices that may perpetuate inequalities and to cultivate a climate of respect and empathy. Such transformations require sustained efforts, with continual reflection and adaptation to ensure the change remains relevant to a continuously evolving student body.

Despite careful planning, school change initiatives often face challenges that must be addressed to ensure their success. A common challenge is resistance to change, which can be overcome through effective communication, stakeholder engagement, and opportunities for feedback. Another challenge is insufficient resources, such as time, funding, or staff, and school leaders must allocate resources strategically, seeking external funding when needed. In addition, effective change management also requires continuous evaluation to ensure initiatives are having the intended effects and to make any necessary adjustments. By continually assessing their progress, schools can develop the capacity to respond to new challenges and to ensure the long term effectiveness of their programs.

School leaders should also utilize practical tools and templates for planning and executing change initiatives. These may include change management plans that clearly outline the goals, strategies, and timelines of the change initiatives. Communication plans, which specify the different stakeholders and communication methods to be used, may also be beneficial. Finally, evaluation templates, which assist in monitoring progress and making any necessary adjustments, provide a systematic approach to managing change. By implementing such tools and structures, schools can ensure the effective and long-lasting integration of changes that are critical to their ongoing development.

Resource Allocation

Resource allocation within educational institutions represents a critical function that directly influences the achievement of strategic objectives and the overall effectiveness of the learning environment. The process of effectively distributing resources necessitates a comprehensive understanding of various resource types, strategic allocation methodologies, and optimization techniques to ensure that financial, human, physical, and temporal assets are deployed to maximize positive impacts on student outcomes. Fundamentally, resource allocation is not merely about distributing funds or materials but rather about strategically aligning all available resources with the educational goals and priorities of the institution.

The resources available to educational organizations are diverse, encompassing financial, human, physical, and temporal dimensions. Financial resources, often the most scrutinized, include public funding, grants, private donations, and revenue from auxiliary services. These funds underpin all operations, from salaries and benefits to program development and facility maintenance. Human capital, referring to the educators, administrators, support staff, and volunteers, constitutes another critical resource, and their expertise and dedication are crucial in shaping the educational experiences of students. Physical resources encompass the school facilities, including classrooms, libraries, laboratories, and athletic fields, all of which need to be properly maintained and equipped. Furthermore, time, often an overlooked resource, is an essential factor in determining how much can be accomplished, given that both instructional time and planning time are finite, and their effective utilization has a direct impact on educational outcomes. Each of these resource types must be carefully evaluated and judiciously allocated to meet the unique needs of the institution and its students.

Effective resource allocation strategies begin with a thorough needs assessment to identify the most critical areas requiring support. Methods for assessing needs vary, encompassing quantitative measures like student performance data, attendance rates, and dropout statistics, as well as qualitative data collected from surveys, focus groups, and community feedback. This data-driven process allows leaders to identify disparities, evaluate the effectiveness of current programs, and prioritize interventions. The information derived from such assessments must then inform budget allocations, utilizing priority-based budgeting approaches that align financial distributions with strategic priorities established through a transparent and collaborative process. In this process, equity considerations become essential, and resources should be distributed in a manner that addresses disparities and provides additional support to students with greater needs, such as those from disadvantaged backgrounds, special education students, or English language learners. Such an equity-focused approach ensures that resources are used to level the playing field and provide all students with the opportunity to succeed.

Optimization techniques also play a pivotal role in the strategic management of resources. A cost-benefit analysis can help educational leaders assess the relative value of different programs and interventions, weighing the costs against the projected benefits for students, for example, when considering adopting new software. This technique requires a comprehensive understanding of both direct costs, such as equipment and salaries, and indirect costs, like staff training and implementation. Efficiency measures must be continually evaluated, with the purpose of streamlining processes and eliminating waste. Moreover, the sharing of resources and collaboration among different schools or districts can lead to greater efficiencies and better program outcomes. Resource sharing might involve consolidating services, such as transportation or purchasing, or sharing specialized personnel, such as speech therapists or curriculum specialists, leading to cost savings and also improved service delivery. The strategic deployment of optimization techniques creates the conditions for improved efficiency and maximizes the educational impact of available resources.

Practical application of resource allocation principles is evident in different budget models and staffing distribution plans. One common approach is zero-based budgeting, where each budget line must be justified each year, promoting a careful review of expenditures and alignment with current priorities. Another model, formula-based budgeting, uses student enrollment or other metrics to determine the allocation of funds, ensuring that each school receives equitable resources based on their student needs. Staffing distribution, also a crucial aspect of resource allocation, involves strategic decisions about teacher assignment, support staff allocation, and administrator responsibilities. In this respect, factors such as the level of experience, specific expertise, and the needs of the students are all relevant. Schools may implement team-teaching models to leverage the skills of different educators, or they might provide additional support staff for students with special needs. Finally, facility utilization plans are crucial for optimizing the usage of physical resources and may encompass schedules for classroom usage, library hours, and athletic field access. These strategic approaches demonstrate the practical application of resource management theory within educational institutions.

Consider, for instance, a school district implementing a needs-based budget allocation model. After conducting a thorough needs assessment, they determine that several schools with high populations of students from low-income families are underperforming academically. Using this information, they reallocate additional resources to these schools, funding additional tutoring, instructional materials, and professional development opportunities for their educators. This could mean a shift of funds away from less critical areas of other schools, to address the inequalities between the districts. Additionally, in terms of staff allocation, a school district may recognize that some schools have higher populations of students with special needs, and would therefore reallocate more special education teachers or support staff to those particular schools. These kinds of adjustments also create opportunities for resource sharing, for example, if two adjacent schools share a common library or athletic field, optimizing their facilities resources and reducing duplication. Furthermore, an evaluation of facility utilization might reveal that some classrooms are underutilized. The school may then decide to relocate some programs to those classrooms, or use them for after school activities, thus maximizing their physical resources. These examples illustrate the importance of using strategic resource allocation to improve education outcomes.

Another example of a practical resource allocation scenario involves a school that is trying to integrate more technology into its curriculum. They conduct a needs assessment, and find that while some teachers are using digital tools, others lack the necessary training or the resources. In this case, they would need to determine the total cost of implementing the technology, including the purchase of devices, software, and teacher training. Following that, they would allocate resources based on priority and availability of funding, perhaps starting with pilot programs that can demonstrate the benefits of new technology before expanding to the entire school. Another consideration could be how to integrate the technology into existing curricula, which may also affect staff time allocation and professional development resources. This holistic approach to technology integration serves as a practical illustration of how resources can be allocated to support innovation and improve educational practices.

To further understand the complexities of resource allocation, consider a scenario where a school must decide how to allocate a grant of $100,000 to support struggling readers. The school's options are to hire a reading specialist, purchase new literacy software, or provide small group tutoring. A cost-benefit analysis could be conducted for each option: hiring a specialist would cost around $70,000 including salary and benefits, literacy software licenses may cost $20,000 for the entire school, and funding small group tutoring sessions would cost approximately $50 per student per month. By carefully evaluating the potential impacts of each option, and considering the cost effectiveness of the approach, the school can make a sound decision that maximizes the educational outcomes of the students and the effective use of the resources. The analysis may also include the time needed to train teachers on new software, the availability of tutoring support, and the long term sustainability of each approach. This detailed analysis is critical in identifying the best way to allocate available funding.

Another important aspect of resource allocation involves time as a resource. Consider a school that wishes to increase instructional time for students without extending the school day. They might decide to shorten transition times between classes, adjust the schedule to allow longer blocks of instruction, or reorganize the time given to non-instructional tasks, such as lunch and recess. They might also consider using technology and online resources to deliver content in a more efficient manner or to offer personalized learning, freeing up instructional time. Effective time management and creative scheduling can allow a school to maximize instructional time within the existing framework. Similarly, teacher planning time can also be carefully managed. For example, team planning meetings, the use of shared online resources, and efficient communication systems can reduce the workload on teachers, allowing them to focus more on lesson planning and student engagement, thereby optimizing the use of the time resource.

In conclusion, effective resource allocation within educational institutions requires a strategic approach that considers all available resources, including financial, human, physical, and temporal assets. Furthermore, a successful allocation strategy includes a needs-based assessment, priority-based budgeting, and a deep understanding of equity considerations, as well as a rigorous approach to resource optimization. Through a practical application of budgeting models, staffing plans, and facility utilization plans, educational leaders can make well-informed decisions that maximize student learning outcomes and promote overall school effectiveness.

Performance Monitoring

Performance monitoring systems in educational leadership serve as a crucial mechanism for driving continuous improvement by providing data-driven insights into the effectiveness of educational programs and practices. These systems allow educational leaders to assess the progress of their initiatives, identify areas of success and challenge, and make informed decisions about resource allocation and strategic adjustments, thereby fostering a culture of accountability and ongoing development. A robust performance monitoring system includes several essential components that collectively contribute to its effectiveness in enhancing educational outcomes.

One of the fundamental components of a performance monitoring system is the establishment of clear and relevant performance metrics. These metrics, often referred to as Key Performance Indicators (KPIs), function as measurable values that demonstrate the effectiveness of educational strategies and processes. In the educational context, KPIs can be broadly categorized into academic performance measures, operational efficiency metrics, and school climate indicators. Academic performance metrics often focus on student achievement and growth, encompassing standardized test scores, graduation rates, college enrollment rates, and course completion rates. These indicators provide direct feedback on the effectiveness of the instructional strategies and curriculum and are crucial in gauging the academic success of students across different demographics. Operational efficiency metrics, on the other hand, assess how well the school system manages resources and implements administrative processes. This category includes measures such as budget utilization, resource allocation efficiency, teacher-student ratios, and facilities utilization rates. Operational efficiency metrics evaluate how well the educational system is functioning, identifying areas where resources could be better utilized. School climate indicators reflect the social and emotional environment of the school, encompassing measures of student attendance, disciplinary incidents, parental involvement, and staff satisfaction. These indicators are vital for creating a positive and supportive school environment, which significantly impacts student learning outcomes and overall well-being, thereby providing a holistic view of the school's functioning.

A well-designed performance monitoring system requires not only relevant metrics but also effective systems for collecting, analyzing, and reporting data. Data collection frameworks must be carefully designed to ensure that data is gathered in a consistent and reliable manner. This involves specifying the data points to be collected, the methods of collection (e.g., surveys, assessments, observations), and the frequency of data gathering. These frameworks also define procedures for data entry, storage, and management. Progress tracking tools are another essential element of the monitoring system, and they convert raw data into usable information. These tools utilize data visualizations such as charts, graphs, and dashboards to illustrate progress towards goals, and are designed to identify trends and patterns in the collected data. Dashboards, in particular, provide a visual summary of key performance indicators, enabling leaders to quickly assess the current status and identify areas needing attention. Reporting mechanisms are used to communicate the findings to various stakeholders including teachers, administrators, parents, and community members. These mechanisms can take the form of regular reports, presentations, or online portals, and are crucial for ensuring that all relevant parties are informed about the progress of the school and understand their roles in supporting its improvement.

The final critical component of a performance monitoring system is the evaluation and adjustment process. Regular review processes are essential to assess the effectiveness of interventions and strategies, and these reviews should be conducted at scheduled intervals to ensure consistent evaluation of the data. Feedback loops are critical for sharing information and insights gathered through data analysis. These loops allow educators to provide feedback on the implementation of programs and identify areas that require improvement, which encourages a process of continuous learning. Feedback loops also ensure that the process remains dynamic, and flexible in responding to emerging trends or difficulties. Corrective action planning is a structured process for addressing any deviations from established goals. This includes the development of detailed plans that specify the steps needed to remediate challenges. These corrective action plans might involve adjustments to teaching methods, resource allocation, or professional development programs. These adjustments require a thorough understanding of the data and a clear strategic intent.

Practical implementation of performance monitoring systems involves several key steps that educational leaders must navigate to ensure effectiveness. The first step involves setting up the system. The process should start with a comprehensive needs assessment to identify the areas that require monitoring. The specific needs and priorities of the school or district will shape the selection of relevant KPIs. Once KPIs have been selected, the next step is to establish clear, measurable targets. These targets should be ambitious but achievable. Another crucial step is establishing data collection protocols. This requires selecting appropriate data collection methods, such as standardized assessments, classroom observations, and surveys. These protocols must ensure the validity and reliability of the data. Another crucial component is choosing an appropriate monitoring software or platform, which can automate data collection, analysis, and reporting. These platforms can streamline processes, reduce the administrative burden, and enhance the efficiency of the performance monitoring system, and are an invaluable tool for modern leaders.

Creating effective dashboards is an essential part of the performance monitoring process. Dashboards should visually represent key performance indicators, and the design should ensure that the most important information is immediately visible. These dashboards should be designed to allow for easy navigation and should enable users to quickly drill down into the data for more detailed analysis, and should also be customizable for various stakeholders. The creation of dashboards requires selecting the most relevant data visualizations, for example, bar graphs, line graphs, or pie charts. Dashboards should also include clear labels, annotations, and explanatory text to enhance understanding. Finally, these dashboards should be regularly updated with the latest data, to ensure that the information is current and relevant.

Conducting performance reviews is a vital component of the evaluation and adjustment process, and these reviews should be conducted on a regular basis, involving all relevant stakeholders. The purpose of the reviews is to analyze the performance data, identify areas of success and challenges, and determine the necessary adjustments to the plan. These reviews should focus on constructive feedback, emphasizing collaboration and continuous improvement, and provide opportunities for stakeholders to share insights, ask questions, and contribute to the decision-making process. Performance reviews are an opportunity to identify the root causes of performance issues, and address any systemic problems that may be affecting the overall functioning of the school. Furthermore, these reviews are also an opportunity to celebrate successes, recognize achievements, and reinforce positive behaviors, which helps in fostering a positive and collaborative work environment.

To understand the practical application of performance monitoring, it is beneficial to review several case studies. Consider a school district that implemented a comprehensive performance monitoring system that focuses on student achievement metrics. They selected key indicators including standardized test scores in reading and math, graduation rates, and college enrollment rates. They developed a system for data collection using school databases and student assessments, and created dashboards to visualize the progress of each school in the district. Through regular performance reviews, they identified significant gaps in achievement across several schools. The system provided evidence that allowed the district leadership to reallocate resources, providing additional tutoring, instructional materials, and professional development to the struggling schools. As a result, the district saw an improvement in standardized test scores and graduation rates over a three-year period, which indicates the effectiveness of the data-driven approach.

Another case study involves a school implementing a performance monitoring system focused on operational efficiency. This school tracked metrics such as budget utilization, resource allocation, and facilities management. Data was gathered by analyzing financial records and conducting facilities audits. Performance reviews were held monthly with department heads to discuss progress and address any issues. This monitoring system revealed that resources were not being allocated effectively; for instance, several departments were overspending, while other departments had unutilized funds. The school made data-driven changes to its budget, reallocating resources to more critical areas, and streamlining its financial processes. Over time, this resulted in more efficient use of the school's budget, which allowed for reinvestment in additional academic programs, demonstrating the practical value of operational performance monitoring.

A third example involves a school district that established a performance monitoring system centered on school climate. They used metrics such as student attendance, disciplinary incidents, parent involvement, and teacher satisfaction.

These data were collected through student attendance records, incident reports, surveys, and focus group discussions. The data was presented through dashboards accessible to all stakeholders. A comprehensive evaluation revealed that certain schools had high rates of disciplinary incidents and low levels of parental engagement. The leadership teams at those schools worked to improve the communication systems with parents and develop school programs that would help improve student behavior. Over a one-year period, these schools saw a noticeable decrease in disciplinary incidents and increased parent participation.

The success of these case studies reinforces the importance of performance monitoring systems in educational leadership. The practical application of performance metrics, monitoring systems, and regular evaluation processes demonstrate that data-driven decision-making can lead to significant improvements in educational outcomes, operational efficiency, and overall school climate. Moreover, these examples underscore the critical need for continuous evaluation and adaptation to maintain the effectiveness of the monitoring systems and ensure that they continue to meet the evolving needs of the school community. Therefore, performance monitoring systems are not just a tool for measuring outcomes, but a catalyst for ongoing development.

2

INSTRUCTIONAL LEADERSHIP

Curriculum and Instruction

Curriculum development and instructional leadership form the bedrock of effective education, requiring a systematic and thoughtful approach to ensure that students receive the highest quality learning experiences. At the heart of curriculum development lies the complex task of transforming broad educational goals into specific, actionable learning plans that cater to diverse student populations and prepare them for future success. Effective instructional leadership, primarily demonstrated by the principal, ensures that curriculum planning translates into robust teaching practices and positive student outcomes. The process begins with a meticulous alignment of curriculum with state and national educational standards, which are typically designed to specify learning objectives and competencies across various subjects. This alignment is not a mechanical task; it demands a deep understanding of the standards and the ability to interpret them in a manner that is both faithful to their intent and appropriate for the context of a specific school. This means considering the particular learning needs of the students, the availability of resources, and the professional expertise of the teachers.

Integrating diverse learning needs into the curriculum involves a careful analysis of the student body, encompassing variations in learning styles, prior knowledge, and socio-cultural backgrounds. An inclusive approach ensures that all students have access to learning experiences that meet their unique needs, such as students with disabilities, English language learners, and those who are gifted and talented. Differentiation, therefore, becomes crucial; this is the process of adjusting instruction, content, and assessment to accommodate different learning profiles. This can include modifying learning tasks, providing supplemental materials, or offering alternative modes of assessment. The curriculum must not only acknowledge these differences, but also celebrate the diversity of the student population as a valuable resource for learning and growth.

The sequential and coherent organization of content is another critical aspect of curriculum design. Content must be structured in a way that builds logically from one topic to the next, ensuring a clear progression of learning. A well-sequenced curriculum allows students to connect new knowledge to what they have learned before, thereby reinforcing learning and facilitating deeper understanding. Vertical alignment, which ensures that curriculum content progresses seamlessly across grade levels, is crucial for preventing repetition and learning gaps. This alignment requires a detailed understanding of curriculum standards at all grade levels and active collaboration among teachers across grades. Horizontal alignment, which ensures that content across different subjects is consistent at the same grade level, is equally essential. When students learn about related concepts across different courses, it can enhance their ability to integrate knowledge and make connections.

Assessment alignment is the final major component of effective curriculum planning. Assessments should be aligned with the curriculum's learning objectives and should provide valuable information on student learning and progress. This includes both formative assessments, which help guide instruction by providing ongoing feedback to students and teachers, and summative assessments, which evaluate learning at the end of a unit or term. Using different forms of assessment ensures that the evaluation methods accurately capture the range of learning expected in the curriculum. Valid and reliable assessment is the cornerstone of evaluating the effectiveness of curriculum and instructional practice.

Principals, as instructional leaders, play a crucial role in guiding curriculum selection and implementation. They should be familiar with different curricula and learning resources and should be able to evaluate their quality and appropriateness for the school's student population. The principal ensures that the selected curriculum is in alignment with both the state standards and the school's specific mission and goals. This requires a deep understanding of the curriculum and the pedagogical approaches it promotes and involves a collaborative decision-making process with teachers to find the most suitable fit. Principals support teachers by creating a collaborative professional culture where teachers feel comfortable discussing their needs, sharing their knowledge, and collaborating to improve instructional strategies. Principals' support is not limited to selecting curriculum; it also encompasses the provision of resources, training, and professional development opportunities to assist teachers in effectively implementing the curriculum.

Furthermore, a principal's role in ensuring vertical and horizontal alignment is significant. They must establish structures and processes that foster communication between teachers across different grade levels and departments. This requires the principal to organize regular meetings, professional learning communities, and planning sessions that encourage teachers to collaboratively map their curriculum and assess their efficacy. The principal should monitor curriculum effectiveness by implementing a system of regular review and feedback. Monitoring data on student achievement, teacher feedback, and parent feedback is vital in evaluating the success of a curriculum. These monitoring systems must also allow for adaptability and flexibility; curriculum and instruction should be revised on a regular basis, based on data and feedback to ensure that it meets the needs of students and continues to reflect the most up to date knowledge in the field.

Successful curriculum implementation requires the application of specific strategies that can ensure the smooth transition from planning to practice. Curriculum mapping, for example, is a tool that allows teachers to chart out their curriculum and identify areas of overlap, gaps, or inconsistencies. In addition, professional development is a fundamental element to help teachers understand curriculum standards and learn new instructional techniques, allowing them to adapt the curriculum in a way that is relevant to their students. Collaborative planning is another essential strategy. By working together, teachers can share their expertise and develop a more cohesive instructional approach. Teachers can learn from each other's experiences, create shared resources, and develop assessment tools that align with common instructional goals.

However, common challenges can arise during curriculum development and implementation. One significant challenge is teacher resistance. Teachers might resist changes to the curriculum if they feel that it imposes more work, restricts their professional autonomy, or does not adequately meet the needs of their students. Overcoming this requires active engagement of teachers in the curriculum development process and communicating the benefits of the changes. Another challenge is the lack of resources. Implementing a new curriculum can require financial investments in new materials, technology, and professional development opportunities. Principals must advocate for these resources and manage them efficiently. They need to engage stakeholders to generate support and allocate resources in a way that supports the implementation of the curriculum.

Furthermore, the lack of time is another significant obstacle. Teachers often have heavy workloads, and dedicating time to curriculum development can be challenging. Principals can address this by providing dedicated time for curriculum planning, reducing non-instructional burdens, and creating collaborative planning teams that facilitate the sharing of workload. Other typical challenges include misaligned or insufficient assessment systems, and inadequate or infrequent monitoring of curriculum effectiveness. If assessment data is not properly utilized to modify instructional strategies, teachers may not see the practical value in the curriculum changes. To avoid these challenges, principals must develop a culture of data-driven decision-making.

Practical tools for curriculum mapping and instructional planning are essential for principals to support their teaching staff. Curriculum mapping tools, whether they are in paper or digital form, help teachers visualize the flow of their curriculum and ensure proper sequencing and alignment. These maps should include information about learning objectives, standards, key skills, and assessment strategies. Principals can also assist teachers with instructional planning by providing access to lesson plan templates that promote effective teaching strategies. This could involve templates that incorporate differentiated instruction, collaborative learning activities, and diverse assessment methods. These templates serve as valuable frameworks for educators when planning lessons aligned with curriculum goals.

Instructional leadership involves a combination of support, mentorship, and strategic planning to improve the quality of instruction throughout a school. Principals as instructional leaders must be advocates for effective teaching practices, facilitating professional development opportunities, and working collaboratively with teachers to create a culture of continuous improvement. Creating opportunities for peer observation and teacher-led professional development can also foster a sense of community and allow teachers to learn from each other's experiences. They must create an environment in which teachers are empowered to grow professionally, utilize data to make informed decisions about instruction, and engage with curriculum in a creative and meaningful way. By ensuring that the curriculum is relevant, well-organized, and responsive to the needs of all students, principals contribute significantly to the success of their schools. By addressing these topics, educational leaders can ensure their schools provide an equitable and effective education for all learners.

Teacher Evaluation

Effective teacher evaluation systems are fundamental for fostering professional growth and ensuring high-quality instruction in educational settings. A well-structured evaluation process incorporates multiple components, each designed to provide a holistic view of a teacher's practice and identify areas for improvement. These components typically include observation protocols and rubrics, pre- and post-observation conferences, diverse evidence collection methods, and clearly defined performance criteria and standards. Together, these elements form a framework that facilitates constructive feedback, targeted professional development, and ultimately, enhanced student outcomes.

Observation protocols and rubrics serve as the foundation for fair and consistent evaluation practices. Protocols dictate the structured procedures for conducting observations, including the frequency and duration of visits, as well as the focus of each observation. A well-designed observation protocol should provide clarity on the specific aspects of teaching that will be evaluated, allowing both the observer and the teacher to approach the process with shared expectations. These protocols often align with established teaching standards, such as those developed by professional organizations or state education agencies, ensuring a common understanding of effective teaching practices. Rubrics, on the other hand, detail the criteria for evaluating teacher performance. Typically, rubrics contain a set of specific dimensions, often corresponding to the aspects of instruction highlighted in the observation protocol. Each dimension is described through a series of performance levels, ranging from unsatisfactory to exemplary, providing clear benchmarks for evaluating teacher performance within each area. For example, a rubric might assess lesson planning, instructional delivery, classroom management, and student engagement, detailing specific behaviors and practices associated with each level. This clarity ensures that evaluations are objective, valid, and equitable, which are crucial for the credibility of the evaluation system.

Pre- and post-observation conferences are integral to the evaluation process, serving as critical opportunities for dialogue and reflection. The pre-observation conference, typically occurring a day or two prior to the observation, is a chance for the teacher and the evaluator to discuss the upcoming lesson. During this conference, the teacher should provide a brief summary of the lesson plan, explain the learning objectives, and highlight any specific strategies that will be used. This allows the evaluator to gain context, better understand the lesson's purpose and design, and focus on specific aspects of the instruction during the observation. Additionally, the pre-observation conference allows the teacher to clarify any questions they may have about the observation process, reducing anxiety and encouraging a collaborative approach to evaluation. The post-observation conference, conducted soon after the observation, is equally critical. This conference serves as an opportunity for the evaluator to provide specific feedback, based on the observed lesson and the evaluation rubric. The feedback should be specific, descriptive, and focused on observable behaviors, avoiding vague or subjective comments. The post-observation conference is also a forum for the teacher to reflect on their performance, ask clarifying questions, and discuss potential strategies for improvement. Both pre- and post-observation conferences should be structured in a way that fosters open dialogue and shared problem-solving, making the evaluation process not just an assessment but a supportive learning opportunity for the teacher.

Evidence collection methods should extend beyond classroom observations to encompass multiple sources of data, providing a more comprehensive view of teacher effectiveness. While classroom observations remain a critical component of teacher evaluation, relying solely on this method may not capture the full scope of a teacher's impact. Collecting evidence from different sources ensures a more balanced and accurate evaluation, mitigating the biases and limitations inherent in any single method. For example, student learning data, derived from both standardized assessments and classroom-based assignments, can provide valuable insights into the impact of a teacher's instruction. If student learning outcomes show significant growth over time, this can be a strong indicator of effective teaching practice. Additionally, student surveys can provide feedback on the classroom environment and instructional methods from the student's perspective. Teacher self-reflections, which are written or oral responses from the teacher regarding their professional growth, can also be included in the evaluation process. These reflections can demonstrate the teacher's capacity for self-analysis and their commitment to continuous improvement. Lesson plans, sample student work, and peer feedback can further supplement observations, providing a holistic view of a teacher's contributions to the school community. This multi-faceted approach to evidence collection ensures that evaluation is based on a range of data points, reducing subjectivity and promoting a fair evaluation process.

Performance criteria and standards must be clearly defined and communicated to all teachers, providing a framework against which performance can be consistently evaluated. These criteria should be directly tied to the school's mission, values, and educational goals, aligning teacher practice with school-wide priorities. Effective performance standards should outline specific knowledge, skills, and dispositions expected of effective teachers, focusing on key areas such as planning, instruction, assessment, professional development, and collaboration. They should also encompass professional responsibilities, including communication with parents and collaboration with colleagues. For example, standards might detail expectations regarding the design of differentiated lessons, the utilization of effective instructional strategies, the analysis of student data to inform instruction, or the contributions to school-based initiatives. Performance standards should not be vague or generic; instead, they should articulate specific, observable behaviors associated with high-quality teaching. These standards also provide a basis for constructive feedback and support teacher development, enabling teachers to understand where they are excelling and where they need to improve.

When teachers have a clear understanding of performance expectations, they are better positioned to set professional goals and strive for continuous growth.

Conducting meaningful classroom observations involves more than just passively observing a lesson; it requires the evaluator to actively engage with the instruction and analyze the specific teaching practices. The observer must be thoroughly familiar with the observation protocol and the evaluation rubric, allowing them to focus on predetermined aspects of teaching. During the observation, the evaluator should take detailed, objective notes, recording specific behaviors and instances rather than making broad, subjective judgments. These notes should serve as a concrete basis for feedback, providing specific examples of observed practices. Effective observations also entail the use of data-gathering techniques that help capture nuances in instruction, such as tracking student engagement, noting the types of questions asked, and observing the teacher's interaction with diverse groups of students. An effective observer should also be attuned to the classroom environment, analyzing how it contributes to student learning and development. Finally, a meaningful observation is not an isolated event; instead, it is part of a larger cycle of planning, teaching, observing, and reflection, designed to continuously improve the quality of instruction.

Providing constructive feedback is an art that requires sensitivity, skill, and a focus on growth. Feedback should be timely, specific, and focused on observable behaviors and actions, avoiding vague or general praise. It is crucial that the evaluator starts by recognizing and reinforcing the teacher's strengths and areas of success, which sets a positive tone and builds trust. After highlighting strengths, the evaluator can then move on to areas for improvement. Constructive feedback should always be framed as areas for growth and should be accompanied by specific examples from the observation or data collection. For example, instead of simply stating that a lesson was disorganized, the evaluator might say, "During the lesson, the transitions between activities were unclear, and several students were confused about the next steps. It may be helpful to provide clearer verbal or visual cues during activity changes." Feedback should be presented in a manner that encourages reflection and self-assessment, helping teachers to understand the rationale behind suggested improvements. Effective feedback also includes strategies and resources to support growth, enabling the teacher to act on the feedback. The tone of feedback should be collaborative and supportive, creating a space where teachers feel safe to ask questions and discuss concerns, thereby reinforcing the teacher's dedication to development.

Developing improvement plans requires a collaborative effort between the teacher and the evaluator, focusing on targeted actions and strategies for growth. An improvement plan is not a punitive measure, but rather a personalized road map for professional development. The plan should be directly tied to the feedback provided in the post-observation conference and should incorporate specific, measurable, achievable, relevant, and time-bound (SMART) goals. The process begins with the teacher and evaluator identifying specific areas of focus, based on the evaluation data. The plan should then outline specific activities that the teacher will undertake to address areas for improvement, which could include professional development workshops, peer observations, coaching, or modifications to their curriculum or instruction. The improvement plan should also establish a timeline for implementation, with regular check-ins to monitor progress and make necessary adjustments. The evaluator's role is to support the teacher throughout the implementation of the plan, providing guidance, resources, and additional feedback, and creating a culture of growth by creating an environment that is supportive and encourages professional growth.

Documenting teacher growth is a crucial step in ensuring accountability and supporting continuous improvement, which is vital for building an effective school environment. Documentation must be thorough and systematic, including all observation data, feedback from conferences, evidence from multiple sources, and progress on improvement plans. This documentation should serve as a record of a teacher's performance, illustrating the journey of their growth and their dedication to continuous development. Documenting teacher growth not only serves an evaluation function, but it also provides a valuable resource for individual development and school-wide improvement. The documented progress can help teachers identify patterns of professional learning, showing which techniques or approaches have been most effective and where they might further their growth. For the school, the documented data provides a broad perspective on teacher effectiveness, enabling the identification of areas that may require additional professional development for staff and guiding decisions related to resource allocation. The documentation process should be organized in a manner that is easily accessible for both teachers and administrators, facilitating transparency and promoting ongoing dialogue on teacher quality. Finally, this data should be utilized in a constructive way to support teachers' individual growth and to enhance the overall effectiveness of the school.

Effective feedback conversations are characterized by open dialogue, shared reflection, and a focus on growth. A typical conversation might start by the evaluator asking the teacher to share their reflections on the lesson they taught, providing an opportunity for the teacher to initiate self-assessment. The evaluator then provides specific feedback, including observed strengths and areas for growth. This is accomplished by using the data from the lesson and focusing on observable and specific actions. The feedback should be constructive, focusing on actions that the teacher can change and improve. The conversation should also focus on potential action steps, encouraging the teacher to identify concrete strategies to address specific challenges. The evaluator should support the teacher in this process, providing suggestions and resources for improvement. In challenging evaluation situations, where a teacher may be defensive or resistant, the evaluator must maintain a calm and professional demeanor, focusing on the data and the performance standards. The conversation must center on specific facts and behaviors, avoiding personal attacks or subjective opinions. The evaluator should actively listen to the teacher's concerns and provide opportunities for dialogue and clarification, creating a space where the teacher feels respected and supported. In the most challenging situations, the evaluator may need to involve other school leadership or human resources personnel to ensure a fair and supportive evaluation process, making sure that every teacher is treated fairly and their professional development is at the forefront.

Using evaluation data to inform professional development and school improvement is essential for continuous progress, as this allows schools to target resources and initiatives where they are most needed. Data gathered from teacher evaluations, including trends in teacher performance, common areas for improvement, and indicators of effective practice, should inform the design and implementation of professional development programs. For example, if data reveals that many teachers need support in differentiating instruction, a school might organize workshops on differentiation strategies and techniques. Evaluation data can also inform decisions about school-wide goals and initiatives, enabling leaders to identify systemic needs and develop interventions to address these challenges. The use of evaluation data can also facilitate discussions among staff about effective teaching practice and encourage a culture of shared learning and professional development. By utilizing evaluation data in this manner, schools can ensure that their professional development efforts are targeted, effective, and aligned with the school's overall mission, creating a continuous improvement cycle that benefits both teachers and students, making sure the school is the best that it can be.

Professional Development

Effective professional development programs are essential for fostering continuous improvement and enhancing instructional practices within educational settings, necessitating a systematic approach that begins with a thorough needs assessment and culminates in ongoing evaluation and refinement. The initial step in creating a robust professional development program involves identifying areas where teachers require additional support or expertise, and this process requires the utilization of various data sources to determine specific needs. Data such as student performance data, classroom observation reports, teacher self-assessments, and feedback from stakeholders can provide valuable insights into the strengths and weaknesses of current instructional practices. These data sources can be triangulated to create a comprehensive picture of the professional development needs of the school or district. The data analysis should focus on identifying recurring themes or patterns of need rather than isolated incidents. Following the comprehensive needs assessment, goals must be set, which should be clearly defined, measurable, achievable, relevant, and time-bound (SMART), aligning with both the school's overall strategic plan and the specific professional growth needs of educators. Such goals might include improving teachers' proficiency in utilizing technology, implementing differentiated instruction strategies, or enhancing classroom management techniques.

Research-based professional learning models, informed by empirical studies and best practices in the field, provide a framework for the design and implementation of effective professional development. These models emphasize sustained, job-embedded learning opportunities rather than isolated workshops or seminars. For instance, the Learning Forward standards for professional learning outline characteristics of effective professional development, such as job-embeddedness, active learning, coherence, and data-driven decision-making. Cognitive apprenticeship models, which focus on modeling expert practices and providing scaffolding, also demonstrate positive effects in teacher growth. Mentoring and coaching models, similarly, provide individualized support and guidance to teachers, promoting both instructional and professional development. These models are not static; instead, they are continuously adapted and refined based on research and best practices, ensuring that the professional learning programs remain current and effective.

Professional Learning Communities (PLCs) represent a collaborative approach to professional development, which emphasizes shared inquiry and collective learning among educators. In a PLC, teachers work together to analyze student data, discuss instructional strategies, and develop lesson plans, which fosters a sense of shared responsibility for student learning. Through collaborative inquiry, teachers not only enhance their skills but also contribute to a culture of continuous improvement, making their professional growth more effective and meaningful. A key component of effective PLCs is the presence of a dedicated facilitator, who is essential for guiding the group process, ensuring focus, and promoting productive discourse. PLCs should also be provided with protected time for meetings and planning, as well as resources to facilitate their work, underscoring the importance of institutional support for collaborative professional learning.

Mentoring and coaching programs provide individualized support and guidance to teachers, with a focus on enhancing instructional practices and promoting professional growth. Mentoring typically involves pairing experienced educators with novice teachers, while coaching may focus on a specific area of instructional practice. Effective mentoring programs incorporate a structured approach, including regular meetings, observation of teaching practices, and feedback sessions that are focused on actionable steps. Similarly, coaching models often include cycles of goal setting, observation, reflection, and feedback, providing a systematic and supportive framework for growth. Both mentoring and coaching programs should be designed to address the unique needs of individual teachers, ensuring that the support is tailored to the particular contexts in which they work and that such support promotes practical skills in the classroom.

Designing targeted professional development activities involves selecting appropriate delivery methods and resources to address specific needs and goals, and this can be achieved using a variety of formats, such as workshops, seminars, online courses, and collaborative projects. Workshops are useful for introducing new concepts or skills, whereas seminars provide an opportunity for in-depth discussion and exploration of specific topics. Online courses can offer flexibility and access to a wide range of resources, which makes it easier for teachers to learn and study at their own pace. Collaborative projects encourage teachers to work together, develop innovative practices, and share their experiences. Whatever the form, professional development activities should be interactive and engaging, and should utilize a variety of strategies, such as modeling, role-playing, case studies, and group work. Activities should be designed to encourage reflection, allowing teachers to connect new knowledge with their current practice.

Implementing job-embedded learning opportunities is essential for ensuring that professional development translates into meaningful changes in classroom practices, and this approach emphasizes integrating learning into the daily routines of educators. Job-embedded learning can take many forms, such as peer observation, collaborative lesson planning, action research, and instructional coaching. Peer observation, for example, allows teachers to observe and learn from one another, whereas collaborative lesson planning encourages teachers to work together to develop engaging and effective lessons. Action research involves teachers engaging in systematic inquiry to solve problems in their own classrooms, promoting a culture of continuous improvement through individual learning and analysis. Instructional coaching provides individualized support and guidance to teachers as they integrate new strategies and techniques in their practice. Job-embedded learning opportunities should be supported by school leaders and integrated into the regular school day, ensuring that teachers have the time and resources necessary to engage in these activities.

Evaluating program effectiveness is crucial for determining the impact of professional development on teacher practice and student outcomes, and this is achieved by using a variety of methods to assess the efficacy of professional development activities. Data sources such as teacher surveys, classroom observation data, and student assessment results can provide insights into the impact of professional development on both teacher behavior and student learning. Teacher surveys can provide valuable feedback about their perceptions of the professional development activities, whereas classroom observation data can reveal whether teachers are implementing new strategies and techniques in their classrooms. Student assessment results can be utilized to determine whether the professional development has had a positive impact on student learning outcomes. The data analysis should focus on identifying patterns of growth and areas where further refinement is necessary. The evaluation process should be iterative, allowing educators to use the findings to improve and enhance the professional development program.

Supporting continuous improvement requires ongoing monitoring of teacher performance and consistent refinement of professional development strategies, and this entails the creation of a continuous improvement cycle, where data collected during the evaluation process is used to inform the development and refinement of professional development activities. The cycle should begin with a comprehensive needs assessment, which is followed by the development and implementation of targeted professional development activities. The program is then evaluated using multiple data sources, which is followed by the refinement of activities based on evaluation results. This cycle should be repeated regularly, which will ensure that the professional development program remains responsive to the needs of teachers and students. School leaders must also actively promote a culture of continuous improvement, where professional growth is seen as an ongoing process rather than an isolated event.

Practical examples of successful professional development initiatives can provide guidance and inspiration for educators seeking to improve their own programs. For instance, a school that uses a mentoring program has been shown to improve retention rates among new teachers and positively impact instructional practices. Another school may have implemented a school-wide project-based learning initiative, where teachers receive extensive training and support in project-based learning techniques. These kinds of initiatives serve as examples of effective professional development programs. Another example would be using action research teams within schools, where the teachers work together to tackle specific challenges, which encourages data-driven decision making and collaborative problem-solving. Such successful initiatives often share common elements, including a strong focus on needs assessment, the use of research-based professional learning models, job-embedded learning opportunities, and a culture of continuous improvement.

Overcoming common implementation challenges in professional development programs requires proactive planning and ongoing support. One common challenge is resistance from teachers, which can often be overcome by involving teachers in the planning and design of professional development activities. This involvement can help create a sense of ownership, and by doing so, it makes it more likely that teachers will be committed to the process. Another challenge is time constraints, which can be addressed by providing protected time for professional development and incorporating it into the regular school day. Resource limitations can also hinder the effectiveness of professional development programs, but careful prioritization of resources and collaborative partnerships can help to address these issues. It is also essential to ensure that the program is aligned with the school's strategic plan and vision, which helps to ensure support and commitment at all levels.

Templates and planning tools can assist educators in creating comprehensive professional development plans, and these can include checklists for conducting needs assessments, planning templates for professional development activities, and evaluation tools for measuring effectiveness. A professional development plan template might include sections for identifying needs, setting goals, selecting activities, and establishing a timeline. An evaluation tool, on the other hand, might include a checklist for observing teachers in the classroom, survey questions for assessing teachers' perceptions, and a rubric for analyzing student work samples. These planning tools should be readily available and easily accessible to teachers and administrators, which ensures that the planning process is efficient and effective. The use of templates and tools should be flexible and adaptable to the specific contexts of individual schools and districts. By utilizing such resources, educators can create professional development plans that are both comprehensive and effective.

Student Assessment

Student assessment, a cornerstone of instructional leadership, serves as a vital mechanism for gauging student learning, informing pedagogical decisions, and driving school improvement initiatives. Formative assessments, integrated into the daily flow of instruction, furnish teachers with ongoing feedback about student comprehension, enabling timely modifications to teaching methods and addressing learning gaps as they arise. These assessments, which can range from informal questioning and quick quizzes to more structured tasks, serve to enhance the learning process by providing teachers with immediate insights into student understanding and enabling them to adjust their instruction accordingly. Summative assessments, in contrast, occur at the conclusion of a unit, course, or academic period, offering a comprehensive evaluation of student mastery of learning objectives. These evaluations, such as end-of-term examinations or final projects, provide a snapshot of overall student achievement and serve as benchmarks for evaluating the efficacy of educational programs, and the data from such assessments can be used to identify larger trends and potential areas for improvement at the school or district level.

Standardized tests, designed to evaluate student performance against common benchmarks, represent another key aspect of student assessment. These tests, often administered at the state or national level, furnish valuable data for comparing student achievement across various populations and geographic areas, and they also provide data on how schools and districts are meeting educational standards, which is crucial for accountability and improvement. However, standardized tests often face criticism for their limited capacity to capture the full spectrum of student learning, particularly in areas like creativity, problem-solving, and critical thinking. It is important for educational leaders to recognize both the benefits and the limitations of standardized assessments, and to use the data from these tests alongside other forms of assessment for a more holistic perspective on student performance. In this regard, performance-based assessments, which require students to demonstrate their skills and knowledge through complex tasks, offer an alternative to traditional testing methods. These assessments often include projects, presentations, performances, and portfolios, and their design allows students to apply their learning in real-world contexts, which can promote deeper learning and engagement. Such performance based tasks also provide educators with insights into the application of student learning, and allow the teachers to evaluate student ability to think critically and use different skills in their work.

Authentic assessments, which are closely aligned with real-world tasks and situations, represent a significant development in student assessment methodology. These evaluations necessitate that students apply knowledge and skills in authentic contexts, offering a more genuine picture of their abilities and are frequently used in disciplines such as the arts and sciences, which are aimed at assessing student understanding beyond simple factual recall. The use of authentic assessments often increases student engagement because of its relevance, and such assessments also promote the application of higher-level thinking skills, which are critical for student success in the modern world. This approach offers a more student-centered approach to assessment by allowing them to showcase what they know through practical application rather than simple memorization or recall.

Analyzing assessment data is paramount for effective instructional leadership, requiring school administrators and teachers to move beyond merely collecting data to interpreting and utilizing it for instructional improvement. Data analysis involves several key steps, including organizing assessment results in a manner that allows for easy access and comparison. This may include aggregating data across various student groups, identifying patterns and trends, and using statistical analysis to uncover relationships between student background, instructional practices, and achievement. Data should not only identify areas of deficiency but also highlight the strengths and weaknesses of existing instruction. Once data has been analyzed, it can be used to inform instructional decisions, such as identifying students who may require additional support, evaluating the efficacy of current teaching methods, or determining the appropriate placement of students in different programs. Assessment data also informs the development of professional development activities for teachers, ensuring they are focused on areas of need, and fostering a culture of continuous improvement in the educational context.

A balanced assessment system, comprising both formative and summative assessments, standardized testing, and performance-based and authentic assessments, is essential to provide a holistic perspective on student learning. This systematic approach ensures that no single assessment type disproportionately influences educational decisions, which can be detrimental to many students. The balance also allows for a comprehensive understanding of student abilities and learning styles, supporting a more individualized and equitable approach to instruction. Creating such a system requires a clear understanding of the purposes of assessment, alignment with educational standards, and integration with curriculum development and instructional planning. Moreover, establishing a balanced assessment system requires ongoing communication and collaboration among teachers, administrators, and other educational stakeholders.

Ensuring assessment validity and reliability is essential for maintaining the integrity and effectiveness of assessment systems. Validity pertains to the degree to which an assessment measures what it intends to measure, and this requires the careful alignment of assessment items with learning objectives and curriculum standards. Reliability, conversely, refers to the consistency and stability of assessment results over time and across different administrations, which can be achieved through consistent procedures in data collection, scoring, and reporting. Moreover, attention should be paid to issues of bias and fairness in assessment design, and careful consideration must be given to the impact of assessment on various student groups. This consideration will help make the system as a whole, more equitable and fair.

Practical applications of assessment data in school improvement planning are numerous, and can be used to identify trends and patterns in student performance, for example, which is critical for focusing improvement efforts on specific areas. Analysis of assessment data can highlight gaps in the curriculum, areas of instruction that are not effective, and can identify specific students who need extra help, such as students with learning disabilities. Assessment data is an important component of resource allocation as well, and it can guide decisions on budgeting, staffing, and the implementation of new programs, ensuring that resources are used in an effective manner. The data should also be used to evaluate the success of various school initiatives and to identify how to make sure the school is moving forward in the right direction.

Furthermore, assessment data facilitates data-driven instructional decisions, ensuring that educators have the information they need to adapt their teaching to meet student learning needs. Data from formative assessment, for example, may indicate areas where students are struggling, enabling teachers to modify their instruction and provide more targeted intervention. Summative assessment data might inform decisions about curriculum revision or the allocation of instructional time. Data-driven instructional leadership also necessitates that educators have the professional development to analyze data and use it effectively, and this often includes training in assessment methods, data analysis techniques, and strategies for differentiating instruction. This can also include helping teachers analyze what they have been teaching, and how it can be improved, by using data.

Providing support for teachers in developing effective classroom assessment practices is another crucial component of instructional leadership. This involves helping educators to implement varied assessment methods, analyze student results, and use data to inform their instructional decisions. Professional development activities should emphasize the importance of creating a culture of learning where assessment is seen as a tool for improvement. The goal is to help teachers develop their own assessment literacy, enabling them to become more confident and adept at assessing student learning, and then using the data to enhance their teaching. This type of teacher support ensures that classroom assessment is not merely a means of assigning grades, but a tool for promoting student learning.

Strategies for improving teacher assessment skills include ongoing professional development in assessment, peer coaching, and mentoring programs, all of which support teachers in the implementation of new practices. Professional development should focus on the practical aspects of assessment, such as designing valid and reliable assessments, analyzing data, and adjusting instruction based on assessment findings. Peer coaching allows teachers to observe each other's teaching and assessment practices, which can lead to valuable insights and new methods for assessing students. Mentoring, on the other hand, can provide teachers with the individualized support they need to refine their assessment skills and improve their instructional practices.

In summary, student assessment is integral to effective instructional leadership, which uses assessment data to inform decisions at all levels, and ensuring that assessment practices are valid, reliable, and aligned with instructional goals. Leaders should promote a culture of data-driven decision-making, where assessment data is used to improve educational programs, support teacher development, and promote student achievement. By doing so, educators can create a school environment that prioritizes student learning and continuous improvement.

Technology Integration in Education

Technology integration in education represents a paradigm shift in how teaching and learning occur, necessitating a strategic and well-planned approach to ensure that its potential benefits are fully realized. This integration transcends the mere introduction of devices into the classroom; it requires a comprehensive framework that encompasses digital learning environments, effective technology tools, blended learning strategies, and a strong commitment to digital citizenship. The successful implementation of technology in education demands not only the presence of hardware and software, but also careful evaluation, robust teacher support, equitable access, and reliable methods for measuring effectiveness.

Digital learning environments are the foundation for technology integration, and include the creation of virtual spaces where students can access resources, interact with their peers, and engage with content in a dynamic manner. These environments often incorporate learning management systems (LMS), online collaboration tools, and interactive whiteboards, all of which combine to promote active learning experiences. The effectiveness of a digital learning environment is directly related to its accessibility, user-friendliness, and ability to support diverse learning styles, which requires careful consideration of the specific needs of the students and the educational objectives. The design and implementation of digital learning environments should also align with curriculum goals and foster an environment of collaboration and critical thinking, encouraging students to become active participants in their educational journey.

Educational technology tools and platforms span a vast array of software applications, hardware devices, and digital resources, each designed to enhance particular aspects of the learning experience. These tools range from interactive simulations that provide students with immersive experiences to adaptive learning platforms that tailor content and pacing to individual student needs. Effective use of these tools demands careful selection, based on their alignment with curricular objectives, their pedagogical effectiveness, and their capacity to engage students. Educators should focus on integrating tools that promote creativity, critical thinking, and problem-solving skills, rather than using technology merely as a substitute for traditional teaching methods. Moreover, digital platforms must be carefully evaluated for their efficacy, accessibility, and suitability for the learning goals at hand, ensuring that they support student learning and do not become a distraction.

Blended learning strategies combine online and face-to-face instruction to provide a flexible, personalized educational experience for all students. These strategies can involve various models, such as the rotation model, where students cycle through different learning activities, some of which are digital, and the flipped classroom model, where students engage with content online at home and use class time for deeper discussion and application of knowledge. The efficacy of blended learning depends heavily on the strategic design of both the online and offline components of the course, ensuring that they are integrated seamlessly and support one another in promoting student learning. Implementing blended learning requires a significant shift in pedagogical practices, emphasizing active learning strategies, student engagement, and personalized instruction, all of which provide more student focused learning activities.

Digital citizenship and safety are indispensable components of technology integration in education, underscoring the importance of educating students on responsible and ethical online behavior. This includes teaching students about privacy, cyberbullying, intellectual property, and the appropriate use of digital media, as well as promoting digital literacy, equipping students with the skills they need to navigate online environments safely and effectively. Educators must proactively address these issues by providing clear guidelines for online behavior, modeling appropriate use of technology, and integrating digital citizenship into the curriculum, thus ensuring that students are well-prepared for participating in the digital world. Furthermore, schools need to implement robust safety protocols to protect students from online threats and ensure a positive and inclusive online learning environment.

The process of evaluating educational technology should be rigorous and systematic, focusing on the pedagogical effectiveness, usability, and accessibility of the various tools. This evaluation should also include assessments of the technology's capacity to improve student learning outcomes, as well as consideration of its alignment with curriculum goals and standards. Data from student performance, feedback from teachers, and assessments of the technology's impact on student engagement should be considered, which will ensure that technology integration enhances, rather than detracts from the quality of education. Evaluation should also be an ongoing activity, allowing for adjustments and improvements to the selection and implementation of technology.

Supporting teachers in technology integration requires comprehensive professional development that is focused, practical, and ongoing. This support should be designed to help teachers become confident and proficient users of technology, as well as empower them to integrate technology effectively into their teaching practices. Professional development initiatives should emphasize pedagogical best practices, practical application of technology, and strategies for assessing the effectiveness of technology use in the classroom. Moreover, such training should be ongoing and sustained, rather than one-time workshops, which will help ensure teachers remain up-to-date with the latest technological tools and trends, as well as providing them with mentorship and collaborative support.

Ensuring equitable access to technology requires careful consideration of the diverse needs and circumstances of all students, meaning that schools should strive to eliminate the digital divide by providing all students with access to devices, reliable internet connectivity, and the necessary technical support. This may involve providing laptops or tablets to students from low-income families, setting up community Wi-Fi hotspots, or offering training on how to use digital resources. Moreover, schools should be mindful of students with disabilities, ensuring that digital learning materials are accessible to everyone by providing alternative formats and assistive technologies. Equitable access to technology is not merely about providing hardware; it's about creating an inclusive learning environment that benefits all students, which can be achieved by removing barriers to learning.

Measuring technology effectiveness is essential for understanding the impact of technology on student learning and for making informed decisions about future investments in technology. This measurement should involve both quantitative data, such as student assessment results, and qualitative data, such as teacher and student feedback. Data should be used to assess the effectiveness of different technology tools, the impact of blended learning strategies, and the effectiveness of professional development for teachers. Furthermore, a holistic and thoughtful approach to evaluation is needed that takes into account the diverse contexts and goals of different schools, thus ensuring that technology is contributing positively to the overall goals of the educational system.

Successful technology integration initiatives often include a strong emphasis on collaboration, community building, and ongoing support, and by focusing on these areas, schools can ensure technology adoption is both effective and embraced by all stakeholders. For example, initiatives involving the implementation of online collaboration tools have seen significant improvements in student engagement and collaborative problem-solving skills. Such initiatives highlight the importance of a clear implementation strategy, ongoing professional development for teachers, and a focus on student needs. Another example is the use of adaptive learning platforms that have shown to improve student learning by providing individualized instruction tailored to the unique needs of each student. The key to the success of these programs lies in the selection of the right technology tools, the effective training of teachers, and a strong focus on student learning outcomes.

Common implementation challenges in technology integration include resistance from teachers, inadequate infrastructure, and lack of funding, among many other issues. Overcoming teacher resistance requires strong leadership, clear communication, and targeted professional development that addresses specific concerns and needs. Overcoming infrastructure challenges may require collaboration with local government and the community to ensure all students have reliable access to internet and technology. Securing sufficient funding might include grants, partnerships with businesses, and innovative budget allocation strategies. Addressing these challenges requires a holistic and thoughtful approach that involves all stakeholders, ensuring a smooth and effective transition to technology-rich learning environment.

Future trends in educational technology include artificial intelligence (AI), virtual and augmented reality (VR/AR), and personalized learning, all of which are poised to transform teaching and learning in the future. AI-powered systems can provide personalized learning experiences, automate routine tasks, and offer valuable insights into student learning patterns, while VR/AR technologies can provide immersive and engaging educational experiences that were previously impossible. Personalized learning platforms can adapt instruction to individual student needs, providing more targeted support and opportunities for growth. The implications for instructional leadership in this space are profound, requiring that school leaders are prepared to embrace these new tools and strategies, by implementing appropriate infrastructure, and supporting teachers in using them effectively. This new landscape requires a commitment to continuous learning, innovation, and strategic planning, all of which will promote the best possible environment for student learning.

3

School Culture Development

School culture, the deeply ingrained patterns of behavior, values, and beliefs that shape the daily experiences of students and staff, represents a critical determinant of a school's success. It comprises the unspoken norms, the accepted traditions, and the collective mindset that permeates the institution, influencing everything from student achievement to teacher morale. At its core, school culture is defined by the shared understanding of "how we do things around here," reflecting both the formal policies and the informal interactions among all stakeholders. This encompasses not only the explicit mission and goals but also the implicit values and beliefs that guide actions and decisions within the school community. A thriving school culture fosters a sense of belonging, encourages collaboration, and promotes a positive learning environment where every member feels valued and supported. In contrast, a toxic school culture can lead to disengagement, conflict, and a decline in academic performance. Consequently, a detailed analysis of a school's existing culture, alongside specific strategies for transforming and maintaining a positive environment, is of paramount importance.

Several key elements collectively construct the culture of an educational institution, each playing a crucial role in shaping the overall school climate. Shared values and beliefs form the bedrock of any culture, dictating the ethical standards, priorities, and guiding principles that shape the school's actions. When these values are clearly articulated, consistently reinforced, and embraced by all members of the community, they create a cohesive identity and foster a sense of purpose. Traditions and rituals are the regular practices and events that give a school its unique character and identity, contributing to the overall sense of community and belonging. From weekly assemblies to annual celebrations, these rituals reinforce cultural norms and provide occasions for shared experiences that strengthen the bonds among students and staff. The behavioral expectations, both formal and informal, dictate how individuals interact with one another, shaping the social climate of the school. Clearly defined rules, fair disciplinary procedures, and consistently enforced expectations are essential for creating a safe, respectful, and productive learning environment. These expectations extend to staff-student interactions, staff-staff collaborations, and the overall tone of the school. The physical environment of a school also impacts its culture by reflecting its values and priorities. Clean, well-maintained facilities, vibrant and engaging learning spaces, and welcoming communal areas create a positive atmosphere. Spaces that promote interaction, creativity, and inclusivity signal a commitment to creating an environment that supports both learning and personal well-being. By systematically analyzing these key elements, educational leaders can gain valuable insights into the strengths and weaknesses of their school's culture, and devise appropriate strategies for improvement.

Assessing the existing school culture is a critical first step in any effort to foster positive change. This process requires the employment of appropriate assessment tools and methods designed to capture the complexities of school climate and culture. Cultural assessment tools range from quantitative surveys to qualitative methods like focus groups and interviews, enabling leaders to gather a diverse set of perspectives. Surveys can collect valuable data on stakeholder perceptions of school values, practices, and overall satisfaction. Focus groups and interviews provide rich, descriptive data, allowing for in-depth exploration of specific issues and concerns. Observations of daily interactions and school activities can help to identify implicit norms and patterns of behavior that may not be revealed through other means. This comprehensive approach to cultural assessment ensures that all stakeholders, including students, staff, parents, and community members, have opportunities to share their perspectives. Identifying areas of strength and improvement is equally important. Analysis of assessment data helps to pinpoint the elements of school culture that are functioning effectively and areas where improvements are needed. By comparing data from various sources, leaders can gain a comprehensive understanding of school culture. Strengths should be highlighted and celebrated, while areas needing improvement should be carefully addressed. It is important to approach the assessment with a constructive mindset, emphasizing the opportunity for growth and development rather than focusing on blame or criticism. It is also essential to recognize that different stakeholders may have different perceptions, and their diverse perspectives should be carefully considered.

Transforming and maintaining a positive school culture necessitates a series of deliberate strategies and committed leadership. Leadership practices play a pivotal role in shaping the culture of an educational institution. Effective leaders model desired behaviors, communicate a clear vision, and actively engage in culture-building activities. They are proactive in reinforcing positive values, consistently applying school policies, and creating a sense of shared purpose. These leaders are also accessible and responsive to the needs of their staff and students, fostering a culture of open communication and mutual respect. Leaders must also be open to feedback and willing to adapt their approaches based on the needs of the school. Staff involvement and buy-in are also crucial components. When staff members feel valued, respected, and empowered, they are more likely to contribute to a positive school culture. Creating opportunities for staff collaboration, promoting professional development, and recognizing their contributions are important steps in fostering staff engagement. Empowered staff also promote a more positive school environment through their own actions. The inclusion of student voice and participation is essential for a holistic and thriving school culture. When students feel that they are heard, their contributions are valued, and their perspectives are considered, they are more likely to engage in positive behaviors and contribute to a collaborative environment. Schools can involve students by including them in decision making, and by providing them with channels for expressing their concerns and ideas. Celebrating achievements and milestones is critical for reinforcing positive school culture. Recognizing academic successes, athletic achievements, community service projects, and acts of kindness promotes a sense of accomplishment and fosters pride in the school. Celebrations create opportunities for the entire school community to come together, strengthen bonds, and reinforce the values and principles that underpin the school culture. Regular celebrations of school milestones encourage a culture of appreciation and provide a positive atmosphere for future growth.

Specific case studies of schools that have successfully transformed their culture provide insights into the strategies used and the outcomes achieved. One notable example is a school that adopted a restorative justice approach to discipline, which replaced punitive measures with conflict resolution techniques. This approach reduced disciplinary referrals, fostered a culture of empathy, and improved student relationships. The school leaders proactively trained teachers in restorative practices, provided ongoing support, and created a culture that valued dialogue and reconciliation. The implementation required extensive planning, continuous evaluation, and unwavering commitment from all stakeholders. Another case study highlights the success of a school that focused on building a collaborative professional learning community (PLC). By creating time for teachers to meet and share best practices, the school improved instructional strategies, elevated teacher morale, and achieved improved academic outcomes. The leadership played a crucial role in facilitating the PLC meetings, fostering a culture of trust and mutual support, and ensuring that learning was the priority. The outcomes of these case studies are not limited to enhanced student performance;

they also encompass higher teacher satisfaction, increased parent engagement, and a stronger sense of community. These examples demonstrate that successful cultural transformation is the result of sustained effort, clear communication, and a commitment to continuous improvement. Each school's experience illustrates that the process of transformation is not always easy but that positive change is achievable with planning, dedication, and commitment.

To assist schools in their culture-building efforts, several practical tools and templates can be utilized. The creation of a comprehensive school culture plan is essential. This plan should start with a clear vision for the desired school culture, include specific, measurable, achievable, relevant, and time-bound (SMART) goals, and outline actionable steps for achieving these goals. Templates for communication plans can ensure that all stakeholders are informed about the culture-building initiatives and that progress is communicated clearly and transparently. Templates for surveys and feedback forms can be used to monitor progress and gather ongoing input. Surveys can be designed to assess key indicators of school culture, such as student and staff morale, parent engagement, and the level of respect and inclusivity within the school. Feedback from surveys can be used to adjust strategies. Regular review of the school culture plan should be an ongoing practice. Furthermore, methods for measuring cultural transformation over time are crucial for evaluating the effectiveness of culture-building initiatives. This involves setting clear, measurable benchmarks and regularly collecting data to assess progress toward these benchmarks. Data collection methods may include surveys, focus groups, observations, and analysis of school records. Progress must be communicated to all stakeholders, which reinforces accountability and transparency. It is important to acknowledge that cultural transformation is a continuous process that requires ongoing attention and effort. Consistent monitoring, evaluation, and adjustments are essential for creating a positive and enduring school culture. By providing the necessary tools and templates, the process becomes more manageable and successful.

Cultural Competency

Cultural competency in the educational context is defined as the ability of educators and school personnel to effectively interact with and understand students, families, and colleagues from diverse cultural backgrounds, acknowledging and respecting their values, beliefs, and traditions. This competency transcends mere tolerance, requiring instead a proactive and informed approach that embraces cultural differences as assets, contributing to a richer and more equitable learning environment. Its significance in modern diverse schools cannot be overstated, given the increasing heterogeneity of student populations in terms of race, ethnicity, socio-economic status, religion, language, and sexual orientation. Schools, therefore, must move beyond surface-level acknowledgments of diversity towards building an inclusive and equitable culture where all students feel valued, respected, and empowered to succeed. Cultural competency is crucial for addressing systemic inequities and implicit biases that may inadvertently impact student learning outcomes, promoting social justice, and preparing students to navigate an increasingly globalized world.

The development of cultural competency is multi-faceted, encompassing several key components that must be cultivated both individually and collectively within the school community. The first component, cultural awareness and self-reflection, involves an introspective examination of one's own cultural background, values, biases, and assumptions. This process requires educators to critically analyze how their own cultural lens may impact their interactions with others from different cultural groups. Self-reflection exercises may include journaling, completing cultural self-assessments, and engaging in discussions with colleagues to identify and confront personal biases. The goal is not to eradicate all biases, but to develop a deeper understanding of their existence and potential impact, allowing for more conscious and intentional interactions. This foundation of self-awareness is critical for fostering a culture of empathy and respect within the school.

Secondly, the acquisition of knowledge of different cultural perspectives is essential. This involves learning about various cultural norms, beliefs, traditions, communication styles, and worldviews through research, professional development, and active engagement with diverse communities. This knowledge should be context-specific, recognizing that cultural groups are diverse and that individuals may not always adhere to generalized cultural norms. This understanding also involves acknowledging the historical and systemic factors that have shaped the experiences of different cultural groups, including the impacts of colonialism, discrimination, and oppression. Through gaining knowledge of diverse perspectives, educators can develop a more nuanced understanding of the unique needs and strengths of their students, allowing them to create more culturally relevant learning experiences.

Thirdly, the development of skills for cross-cultural communication is imperative. This component involves not only verbal communication but also non-verbal cues, such as body language and facial expressions, which may vary across cultures. Effective cross-cultural communication includes active listening, empathy, patience, and the ability to adapt one's communication style to suit different contexts and individuals. This requires an awareness of potential communication barriers, such as language differences, and a willingness to seek clarification and engage in dialogue with cultural sensitivity. In educational settings, this means being mindful of how cultural backgrounds may influence a student's participation, engagement, and learning preferences.

Finally, cultural responsiveness in practice entails the translation of cultural awareness, knowledge, and communication skills into actionable strategies and pedagogies. This includes creating inclusive curricula, developing culturally relevant instructional materials, and adapting teaching methods to accommodate diverse learning styles. Cultural responsiveness also means establishing culturally sensitive discipline policies and engaging families as partners in the educational process, recognizing the critical role they play in their children's education. This requires ongoing reflection, evaluation, and refinement of practices to ensure they are meeting the needs of all students, fostering equitable outcomes, and creating an inclusive school climate.

Developing cultural competency requires a multi-faceted approach involving the entire school community. For school leaders, this means creating a vision for cultural inclusivity and actively promoting and modeling culturally responsive practices. Leaders can facilitate professional development opportunities for staff on cultural competency, establish school-wide policies that promote equity, allocate resources for diversity initiatives, and regularly monitor progress towards cultural competency goals. They should also create mechanisms for feedback and ensure that all voices within the school are heard and valued, including those of students, staff, and community members from diverse backgrounds. Furthermore, leaders should actively work to address systemic barriers to equitable educational outcomes.

For teachers, cultural competency development requires ongoing reflection, self-evaluation, and engagement with diverse communities. Teachers can benefit from professional development on topics such as culturally responsive teaching, implicit bias, and second language acquisition. They should actively seek to understand the cultural backgrounds of their students and adapt their instruction to meet their unique needs. This includes incorporating diverse perspectives and materials into their lessons, differentiating instruction, and building relationships with students and families based on trust and respect. Teachers should also create inclusive classroom environments where all students feel welcome and empowered to participate. They should also critically analyze their own biases and assumptions and engage in reflective practice.

For support staff, including counselors, social workers, administrative staff, and paraprofessionals, cultural competency training is also essential. These staff members often interact with students and families from diverse backgrounds and are instrumental in creating a supportive and welcoming school climate. Training should focus on developing cross-cultural communication skills, recognizing the unique needs of diverse student populations, and addressing cultural biases that may exist within support services. Support staff should be trained to be culturally sensitive in their interactions, and they should actively work to build trust with students and families.

For students, cultural competency development can be achieved through a variety of means, including the integration of multicultural education into the curriculum, promoting cross-cultural interactions, and engaging in dialogue about diversity and social justice. Students can learn about different cultures through literature, history, and the arts. They can participate in school clubs, activities, and community service projects that expose them to diversity. Opportunities to interact with students from different cultural backgrounds can break down stereotypes and foster empathy. Creating opportunities for students to share their own cultural heritage can promote a sense of belonging and build a positive school climate.

Creating an inclusive curriculum and instruction requires a deliberate effort to integrate diverse perspectives, experiences, and histories into all areas of the curriculum. Teachers should go beyond surface-level diversity by incorporating multiple perspectives in each lesson and considering how different cultural groups have influenced various fields of knowledge. This includes examining power dynamics, challenging dominant narratives, and ensuring representation of marginalized voices. The curriculum should be adaptable and flexible, allowing students to connect with the content in meaningful ways based on their cultural backgrounds and experiences. The goal is not just to learn about different cultures, but to develop a deeper understanding of how culture shapes identity, beliefs, and experiences.

Addressing implicit bias is a critical step in promoting cultural competency. Implicit biases are unconscious attitudes and stereotypes that can affect our actions and decisions. Strategies for addressing implicit bias include self-assessment, engaging in conversations about bias, and implementing strategies to mitigate its impact. Schools should provide professional development that raises awareness of implicit bias and offers tools for mitigating its effects. Leaders and teachers can use data to examine disparities in student outcomes and then consider implicit biases that may be contributing to those disparities.

Promoting equity in school policies and procedures requires a systematic review of all policies and practices, ensuring they are fair, inclusive, and do not unintentionally discriminate against any group of students. This includes policies related to discipline, assessment, special education, gifted and talented programs, and extracurricular activities. Schools should collect and analyze data to identify and address any disparities in student outcomes and ensure all students have access to the resources and support they need to succeed. It also requires actively addressing systemic barriers and challenging inequalities that may exist within the educational system.

Celebrating diversity is an essential aspect of fostering a positive school climate. It is important to go beyond token celebrations and create an environment where diversity is valued and respected every day. Schools can celebrate cultural holidays and traditions, but they should also provide ongoing opportunities for students to share their cultural heritages, express their identities, and learn from one another. This includes creating events and activities that showcase the diversity of the school community and promoting cultural awareness and understanding. These celebrations can help to build community and promote inclusivity.

Several practical exercises and self-assessment tools can be used to support the development of cultural competency. Self-assessment questionnaires can help educators reflect on their own cultural awareness, biases, and practices. Role-playing scenarios can help individuals practice cross-cultural communication skills in a safe and supportive environment. Case studies can help educators analyze situations that may arise in diverse school environments. Reflective journaling and peer coaching can provide opportunities for ongoing professional growth and development. Tools such as the Intercultural Development Inventory (IDI) and the Cultural Competence Self-Assessment Checklist can also be beneficial.

Real-world examples demonstrate the impact of successful cultural competency initiatives in schools. A school district in California implemented a culturally responsive teaching framework that involved professional development for teachers, the development of culturally relevant curriculum materials, and engagement with the community. This initiative resulted in significant improvements in student achievement and a more inclusive school climate. Another school in New York adopted a restorative justice approach to discipline, which reduced disciplinary referrals and improved student relationships. This was coupled with professional development for staff on cross-cultural communication and implicit bias. Another school, with a large immigrant population, implemented a family engagement program that provided culturally sensitive resources and support for families. All three examples demonstrate that a dedicated approach to cultural competency enhances educational outcomes.

Social-Emotional Learning

Social-emotional learning (SEL) is a vital component of holistic education, focused on the development of skills that enable individuals to understand and manage emotions, set and achieve positive goals, feel and show empathy for others, establish and maintain positive relationships, and make responsible decisions;

it is not merely an adjunct to academic learning, but an essential element that underpins success in school, career, and life. The Collaborative for Academic, Social, and Emotional Learning (CASEL) framework identifies five core competencies that constitute the foundation of effective SEL: self-awareness, self-management, social awareness, relationship skills, and responsible decision-making. Self-awareness, the ability to accurately recognize one's own emotions, thoughts, and values and how they influence behavior, involves skills such as identifying emotions, recognizing personal strengths and weaknesses, and developing self-confidence; it is not about introspection alone, but about understanding the self within the context of interactions with others and the environment. Self-management, the ability to regulate one's emotions, thoughts, and behaviors effectively in different situations, includes skills such as impulse control, stress management, self-discipline, and goal setting; this competency is critical for effective learning and problem-solving. Social awareness, the ability to understand the perspectives of and empathize with others, including those from diverse backgrounds and cultures, entails skills such as perspective-taking, showing empathy, appreciating diversity, and understanding social and ethical norms for behavior; this component moves beyond an understanding of the self to an understanding of others and the interconnectedness of communities. Relationship skills, the ability to establish and maintain healthy and rewarding relationships with diverse individuals and groups, includes skills such as effective communication, active listening, collaboration, and negotiation; these skills are fundamental for building positive and productive learning communities. Finally, responsible decision-making, the ability to make constructive choices about personal behavior and social interactions based on ethical standards, safety concerns, and social norms, involves skills such as problem identification, analyzing situations, ethical decision-making, and evaluating outcomes; this element is what enables students to move beyond reactivity to proactive, informed choices.

Implementing SEL effectively requires a multifaceted approach that integrates SEL across all aspects of the school environment, going beyond isolated lessons or programs, and calls for a systemic implementation strategy that permeates the school's culture and practices. Classroom integration of SEL involves incorporating SEL activities and strategies into daily instruction, such as using literature to explore emotions, conducting collaborative problem-solving sessions, and establishing class meetings to foster a sense of community; this approach also means teachers serving as SEL models, demonstrating self-awareness, empathy, and effective communication. School-wide SEL initiatives, such as creating positive behavior support systems, promoting inclusive practices, and developing a school climate plan, are critical for ensuring a consistent and supportive environment for all students; such initiatives demonstrate a school's commitment to SEL as a core value. Staff professional development in SEL is essential to prepare teachers and other school personnel to effectively implement SEL strategies and integrate SEL into their interactions with students, including trainings in SEL competencies, culturally responsive teaching, and trauma-informed practices; ongoing professional development is necessary to ensure that staff remain current with best practices and can effectively address the diverse needs of their students. Family engagement in SEL is critical for extending SEL principles beyond the school, fostering consistency between home and school, with strategies including parent workshops, family activities focused on SEL competencies, and communication tools that keep parents informed about SEL goals and progress; meaningful family engagement involves the active participation of families in the SEL process and acknowledgment of their critical role in student success.

The selection and implementation of SEL curricula must be thoughtful and grounded in research and best practices, aligning curriculum goals with the school's overall mission and objectives. Schools should choose SEL curricula that are evidence-based, culturally relevant, and developmentally appropriate for their students, ensuring that the selected programs are comprehensive and cover all five core SEL competencies. Implementation should include initial training for teachers, ongoing support and coaching, and regular evaluation of curriculum effectiveness to allow for necessary modifications and enhancements. The assessment of SEL competencies is complex, going beyond traditional academic assessments, encompassing direct observation, behavior ratings, self-reports, and student work samples; tools such as behavior checklists and teacher observation scales provide qualitative and quantitative data on the development of SEL competencies. Creating supportive learning environments is essential for fostering SEL, including establishing positive relationships between students and teachers, providing opportunities for collaboration and peer interaction, and creating a physically and emotionally safe school climate; a trauma-informed approach that acknowledges the potential impact of trauma on learning and behavior is critical. Addressing trauma and mental health in schools involves providing mental health support services, training staff on trauma-informed practices, and creating a culture of care and understanding; this also includes partnering with community mental health agencies to ensure that students have access to needed resources.

Examples of successful SEL programs demonstrate positive impacts on academic achievement, behavior management, school climate, and student well-being. The implementation of Second Step, a well-researched SEL curriculum, has shown significant gains in students' social-emotional skills, with improvements observed in behavior and academic performance; such programs need to be implemented with fidelity and sustained over time for maximum impact. Collaborative problem-solving programs, such as restorative practices, have been effective in reducing disciplinary referrals and improving school climate by addressing underlying causes of conflict and fostering positive peer relationships. School-wide initiatives that promote mindfulness and stress management have been linked to improvements in student well-being and a more positive and focused learning environment, which highlights the importance of attending to students' emotional and mental health. When SEL competencies are integrated across the curriculum and daily practices, students not only experience growth in emotional skills, but also increased engagement in learning.

The evaluation of SEL program effectiveness requires the use of comprehensive measurement tools and strategies to allow educators to understand the impact of their efforts. Data collected on SEL implementation should include multiple measures, such as attendance, discipline referrals, student grades, surveys and interviews with students and staff; data analysis must be used to identify areas of strength and areas of need, and provide insights for program improvements. Progress monitoring is essential to track student growth and identify areas where additional support is needed, with regular assessment of SEL competencies to inform program adjustments and refine program implementation strategies. Using data to inform decision-making is also essential to ensure that SEL programs are responsive to the needs of students and contribute to the overall improvement of the school environment, which allows for a continuous cycle of program evaluation and enhancement.

Safety and Discipline

School safety and positive discipline form the bedrock of an effective learning environment, necessitating a proactive and comprehensive approach that addresses both preventative measures and responsive strategies. A robust framework for school safety encompasses several essential components, starting with physical security measures designed to safeguard the school campus. These measures include controlled access points, such as secured entrances with visitor management systems, perimeter fencing, and surveillance technology, like strategically placed security cameras, all of which deter unauthorized entry and provide visual monitoring of school grounds. Regular safety audits of the physical plant, including inspections of structural integrity and hazard assessments, are essential for identifying vulnerabilities and informing necessary upgrades or repairs, ensuring compliance with safety standards and mitigating risks. Emergency response protocols are critical for managing a range of situations, from medical emergencies to security threats, necessitating well-defined procedures for various scenarios, including lockdowns, evacuations, and sheltering in place. These protocols must be developed collaboratively, involving school administrators, faculty, staff, and local emergency responders, to create a coordinated and effective response system. Regular drills and training exercises, conducted at least annually, are essential to prepare students and staff for different emergencies, while also familiarizing them with the necessary procedures and communication protocols.

Threat assessment procedures are another essential aspect of school safety, involving a systematic approach to identifying individuals who may pose a risk to themselves or others, and addressing those concerns in a proactive and collaborative manner. Threat assessment teams, typically composed of school administrators, counselors, psychologists, and security personnel, are trained to identify warning signs and concerning behaviors, and conduct comprehensive assessments, analyzing the information collected to assess the level of risk and develop appropriate intervention strategies. Such interventions may include providing mental health support, implementing behavior management plans, or initiating law enforcement involvement, all with a goal to mitigate potential harm and promote safety. Crisis management planning is also a critical element, focusing on detailed strategies for responding to and managing significant incidents. A comprehensive crisis plan includes clear communication protocols, defined roles and responsibilities for team members, procedures for providing support to students and staff, and a plan for post-crisis recovery, outlining steps for returning to normal operations. Crisis planning should be a collaborative effort that includes drills and exercises to test the plan's effectiveness and make needed adjustments. Such preparedness helps schools respond efficiently and effectively during and after an emergency.

Modern approaches to school discipline move away from punitive strategies toward those that foster student growth and positive behavior. Restorative justice practices offer a more relational approach to discipline, focusing on repairing harm and rebuilding relationships through dialogues, facilitated meetings, and community conferencing. When harm is caused, restorative justice seeks to bring together those who have been harmed and those who caused harm, allowing them to engage in meaningful conversations and create solutions collaboratively, thereby addressing the underlying causes of misbehavior and promoting accountability and empathy. The emphasis is on restoring relationships, rather than punishment, to create a more inclusive and supportive school climate. Positive Behavioral Interventions and Supports (PBIS) is a proactive framework for promoting positive behavior, involving three tiers of intervention. The first tier, school-wide positive behavior support, involves creating clear expectations for behavior and teaching these expectations to all students, implementing a unified system for promoting positive conduct. The second tier, targeted interventions, provides support for students who are at risk of engaging in misbehavior, such as individualized behavior plans and small group interventions. The third tier, intensive interventions, provides comprehensive support for students with more significant behavioral challenges, involving collaboration with parents, mental health professionals, and other community resources. PBIS employs data-driven decision-making to monitor progress and adjust interventions as needed, to create an environment that supports positive student behavior and reduces the need for punitive discipline.

Alternative discipline strategies move beyond punitive methods, focusing on skill building and positive behavior change. Approaches include conflict resolution and peer mediation programs that teach students how to manage disagreements and conflicts peacefully, also promoting a sense of responsibility and problem-solving skills. Social skills training programs offer students direct instruction in appropriate behaviors, communication, and self-regulation, to build their emotional and social competencies. Check-in/check-out systems provide students with daily check-ins with a designated adult, to monitor behavior and offer support, while also building a positive relationship between the student and an adult at the school. Trauma-informed approaches to discipline recognize the impact of trauma on student behavior, modifying traditional disciplinary responses, and creating a system of care that avoids re-traumatization. This approach requires understanding the signs and symptoms of trauma, and implementing practices that are sensitive to students' needs, using interventions that focus on building relationships, promoting a sense of safety, and teaching coping skills.

Developing comprehensive safety plans involves a detailed and systematic process of assessing vulnerabilities, creating protocols, and implementing strategies, requiring collaboration among multiple stakeholders, including school administrators, faculty, staff, students, parents, and community partners. The plan should include protocols for different types of emergencies, a detailed communication system, and a plan for regular evaluation and updates. These plans should include procedures for medical emergencies, security threats, weather-related events, and other crises, with clear roles and responsibilities for all team members. Creating effective behavior management systems requires a multi-faceted approach that includes clear expectations, consistent consequences, and positive reinforcement, involving the development of a code of conduct that outlines expected behaviors and disciplinary actions for rule violations, as well as the implementation of a system for documenting and addressing behaviors in a consistent and fair manner. Staff training in safety protocols is an essential component of school safety. Training should include emergency response protocols, threat assessment procedures, and de-escalation techniques, providing staff with the knowledge and skills to handle safety concerns effectively, including training in CPR, first aid, and mental health first aid, to prepare staff to respond effectively in a range of situations. Building positive student-staff relationships is paramount for fostering a supportive and inclusive school climate that promotes positive student behavior, involving strategies such as mentoring programs, relationship-building activities, and restorative practices, all of which facilitate positive interactions and a sense of connection.

Case studies provide real-world examples of successful safety and discipline initiatives, illustrating transformations that have occurred when schools have shifted from punitive to supportive approaches. One such example is the implementation of restorative justice practices in a high school with a history of disciplinary issues, leading to a significant reduction in suspension rates, improved student relationships, and a more positive school climate. Another case study focuses on a school that successfully implemented PBIS, which resulted in fewer behavioral incidents, increased student engagement, and higher academic achievement. Through the use of data and collaboration with staff and community, the school built a consistent and supportive environment, which allowed for more time for instruction. Yet another example is a school that has adopted a trauma-informed approach, which has led to significant reductions in disciplinary referrals and increased understanding and empathy among school staff, creating a culture that supports the needs of students who have experienced trauma.

Assessment tools for evaluating safety measures and discipline policies are essential for continuous improvement, utilizing surveys, observations, and data collection, to gain insights into the effectiveness of safety measures and discipline practices. Regular analysis of these assessments allows for the identification of areas of strength and areas that require improvement, using data to inform decisions and implement changes. The process should involve both qualitative and quantitative data, to provide a holistic view of the effectiveness of the policies, with surveys and interviews providing valuable feedback from students, parents, and staff. Data on disciplinary incidents, suspensions, and expulsions should be analyzed regularly, to assess patterns and trends, and make necessary adjustments to school safety and discipline practices. This continuous process ensures that schools are prepared to manage a range of situations effectively and cultivate a positive and inclusive learning environment.

Family Engagement

Family engagement is a crucial element in fostering a positive school culture and enhancing student outcomes, necessitating a multifaceted approach that recognizes families as integral partners in the educational process. Effective family engagement extends beyond mere parental involvement, requiring a deep commitment to building collaborative relationships between schools and families, with the shared goal of supporting student success. When families are actively engaged, students tend to exhibit improved academic performance, reduced behavioral issues, and an overall more positive attitude toward school; conversely, when families feel disconnected or disengaged from their children's education, it can negatively impact student motivation and academic achievement. A comprehensive framework for family engagement must be inclusive, addressing the diverse needs and backgrounds of all families within the school community, recognizing that each family brings a unique set of strengths, challenges, and perspectives. This necessitates that schools adopt strategies that are flexible, adaptable, and responsive to the unique contexts of their communities.

Developing a comprehensive approach to family engagement requires a strategic plan that includes multiple layers of interaction, moving from basic communication to more collaborative partnerships. Communication methods and protocols form the foundation of family engagement, requiring schools to establish clear and consistent channels for sharing information and soliciting feedback. Effective communication should be bidirectional, ensuring that families receive timely updates about school events, student progress, and policy changes, while also providing opportunities for families to voice their concerns, share their perspectives, and contribute to the decision-making process. Various communication tools can be utilized to reach families, including newsletters, websites, social media platforms, email, text messaging, and phone calls, with consideration given to families' preferred language and communication preferences. Regular parent-teacher conferences are crucial for fostering open communication and allowing teachers and parents to collaboratively assess student progress, develop personalized learning strategies, and address any concerns. The timing and format of these conferences should be flexible, catering to the diverse schedules of working families, and providing translators or interpreters where necessary, to promote equitable access to communication. Additionally, schools should explore innovative ways to engage families, such as virtual meetings, online communication portals, and home visits, to ensure that all families feel informed and connected to their children's educational experiences. A system for responding to family inquiries and feedback in a timely manner is essential to building trust and demonstrating that school leaders value family input.

Opportunities for parent involvement represent another crucial component of a comprehensive family engagement framework. Schools should create diverse pathways for parents to participate in their children's education, ranging from volunteering in classrooms to serving on school committees, attending school events, and participating in family workshops. Volunteer opportunities may include assisting teachers in the classroom, chaperoning field trips, helping with school projects, or participating in fundraising activities, recognizing the varied time constraints and skills sets of parents. The creation of family-school partnerships fosters a sense of shared responsibility for student success, providing a platform for parents and teachers to collaborate on curriculum development, school improvement, and family engagement initiatives. Parent advisory councils offer opportunities for families to contribute to school policies and decision-making processes, ensuring that families' voices are heard and considered. Community outreach initiatives, such as family literacy programs, parenting skills workshops, and cultural events, are invaluable for fostering connections between the school and the broader community, leveraging community resources and expertise to benefit students and families. Schools should prioritize the creation of a welcoming school environment that is accessible and inviting to all families, providing resources and supports that are tailored to the diverse needs of the community.

Family education programs are vital to empowering families to support their children's academic success. These programs should be designed to enhance families' understanding of the curriculum, teaching strategies, and assessment methods, to empower them to assist their children with homework and home learning. Workshops on topics such as literacy, numeracy, technology, and social-emotional learning can provide families with the necessary knowledge and skills to reinforce learning at home. These sessions should be interactive and engaging, incorporating practical tips and strategies that families can implement immediately, and should take place at various times and in multiple locations to ensure accessibility. Additionally, schools can provide families with resources and materials, such as homework tips, online learning platforms, and access to educational websites and books, to support home learning. Culturally responsive workshops that address specific topics relevant to diverse communities can create inclusive and relevant learning opportunities. These programs should be offered in multiple languages and be accessible to all families, regardless of their backgrounds or levels of education, incorporating opportunities for families to connect with each other and build supportive networks.

Cultural bridging strategies are essential to ensure that families from diverse backgrounds feel welcome and valued within the school community. Schools should take a proactive approach to understanding the cultural norms, values, and beliefs of all families, using this knowledge to inform communication methods, school policies, and engagement practices. This entails providing training for teachers and staff on cultural competency and culturally responsive teaching practices, so that they are able to effectively engage with families from different cultural backgrounds, recognizing and respecting the diverse cultural perspectives and experiences that families bring to the table. Schools should make a concerted effort to incorporate culturally relevant materials and activities into the curriculum, celebrating the diversity of the school community. The use of bilingual staff and translated materials is crucial for removing language barriers and ensuring that all families have access to information about their children's education. In addition, schools can organize cultural events that celebrate the traditions and heritage of different communities, providing families with opportunities to share their culture with the wider school community.

Specific approaches to engaging diverse families are required to ensure equitable opportunities for participation and support, understanding that what works for one family might not work for another. Schools must take into account the unique circumstances and challenges faced by families, such as cultural differences, language barriers, work schedules, and transportation issues, tailoring engagement strategies accordingly. Employing bilingual staff and volunteer translators can help bridge language gaps and ensure that families from diverse language backgrounds are able to participate fully in school activities and access important information. Flexible meeting times and locations should be available, taking into account the needs of working families, while also offering childcare services and transportation assistance to ensure that all families have the ability to attend. It is also essential to recognize the varied forms of family structure and create engagement opportunities that are inclusive of all caregivers and family members. Moreover, schools should take a strengths-based approach, focusing on the assets and resources that families bring to the table, rather than deficits, working collaboratively with families to identify their needs, goals, and aspirations.

Overcoming language barriers is paramount to creating an inclusive and equitable school environment. Schools should provide interpretation and translation services, ensuring that families receive information in their preferred language, this should include documents, announcements, and communications with school staff. Bilingual staff members and volunteers can play a crucial role in bridging communication gaps, facilitating conversations between families and educators, and creating a more welcoming and inclusive atmosphere. Schools should also utilize technology to support multilingual communication, including translation apps, websites, and online platforms. Providing language classes for parents is yet another strategy for building relationships between families and the school, promoting cross-cultural communication, and facilitating language acquisition. Language should never be a barrier to family engagement, schools should commit to finding innovative ways to overcome linguistic challenges, ensuring that all families have equitable access to information and opportunities.

Supporting working families requires schools to acknowledge the time constraints and challenges faced by parents who work outside the home. Schools should be flexible in their scheduling, offering meetings and events at various times of the day, and providing options for remote participation through virtual meetings, online forums, and flexible appointment times. Providing childcare services can also remove a major barrier to participation, as many working families may struggle to find affordable care. Schools should also partner with community organizations and employers to provide support services, such as transportation assistance, after-school programs, and family resource centers. Recognizing the importance of family time, schools should strive to minimize the amount of time required for family engagement activities, offering condensed, focused events that are both meaningful and efficient. Flexible, responsive, and supportive approaches help to ensure that working families are able to be fully engaged in their children's education.

Building trust and relationships between schools and families is a foundational component of effective engagement, which necessitates open communication, mutual respect, and genuine collaboration. Schools should take the time to build personal connections with families, getting to know them as individuals and understanding their unique needs and aspirations, actively listening to families' concerns, valuing their perspectives, and treating them as equal partners in the educational process. Regular, informal interactions, such as school-wide events, parent support groups, and informal gatherings, are helpful for building strong relationships, with schools providing opportunities for families to connect with each other and build a sense of community. Establishing clear communication protocols and following up with families promptly are ways to build trust and establish reliability, showing families that their voices are heard and valued.

Several practical tools and resources can support effective family engagement initiatives, starting with a family needs assessment to gather data about family backgrounds, resources, and educational needs. This may include surveys, focus groups, and one-on-one interviews, to collect information about families' priorities and preferences, and to identify challenges that may hinder their participation. This assessment data will help schools develop targeted interventions and programs that meet the specific needs of their communities. Creating a welcoming school environment entails providing a comfortable, inclusive, and accessible space for families to gather, including designated family resource centers, comfortable waiting areas, and easily accessible communication materials. The physical environment of the school should reflect a commitment to diversity and inclusion, showcasing the cultures and heritage of all families within the school community. Developing family leadership opportunities, such as parent advisory councils and volunteer leadership roles, enables parents to become active agents of change, contributing their ideas and expertise to the school community. Providing training, resources, and support to parent leaders is critical to empowering them to make meaningful contributions to the school and community. Measuring engagement effectiveness using various data collection methods, such as surveys, observations, attendance records, and feedback sessions, is helpful for monitoring progress and making necessary adjustments to improve program implementation. This continuous process of assessment and adaptation is essential to ensure that engagement strategies are effective and responsive to the ever-changing needs of students and their families.

Successful case studies of schools with strong family engagement programs illustrate the positive impact of proactive and inclusive engagement practices, showcasing innovative approaches and highlighting positive outcomes. One school, for example, successfully implemented a two-way communication system, which includes multiple channels of communication, that allowed families to access information in their preferred language and also offer direct feedback to school staff. This led to increased levels of parent participation in school events and a stronger sense of community between parents and the school. Another school created a volunteer program that offered varied opportunities for parents to be involved in the classroom, that gave parents flexibility in their ability to participate, and that increased parent engagement while also providing additional support to teachers. A further example of a positive outcome is the case of a school that implemented family literacy nights where parents were empowered to support their children's learning at home, enhancing both family engagement and student achievement. These case studies underscore the importance of a deliberate approach to family engagement, with an emphasis on building relationships, creating welcoming environments, and providing ongoing support and resources to families.

Templates and tools for developing and implementing family engagement plans can provide practical guidance for school leaders, including step-by-step instructions, assessment tools, planning guides, communication protocols, and evaluation matrices, that help schools organize, manage, and evaluate family engagement initiatives. A comprehensive family engagement plan should clearly define goals and objectives, identify target populations, outline specific engagement strategies, assign responsibilities, establish timelines, and include protocols for ongoing evaluation and improvement. The use of templates, such as communication plans, meeting agendas, feedback forms, volunteer management tools, and family needs assessment surveys, can support effective planning and implementation. The inclusion of these tools will equip school leaders with the necessary resources to build effective and sustainable partnerships with families, ultimately ensuring that all families are engaged and empowered to support their children's educational journeys.

4

ETHICAL LEADERSHIP

Legal and Ethical Standards

Ethical leadership in education is fundamentally rooted in a comprehensive understanding of the legal and ethical standards that govern the operation of schools and the conduct of educational professionals. This necessitates not only a knowledge of the relevant laws and regulations, but also the capacity to apply these standards in complex and evolving scenarios, ensuring the rights and well-being of all students and staff are protected. Federal education laws, in particular, form a bedrock of these standards, laying out broad requirements that all states and school districts must adhere to. One of the most crucial of these is the Family Educational Rights and Privacy Act (FERPA), a federal law enacted to safeguard the privacy of student educational records. This law grants parents of students under 18, and students themselves over 18, the right to access their educational records, request amendments to records they believe are inaccurate or misleading, and exercise some control over the disclosure of personally identifiable information from these records. FERPA stipulates that school officials are not permitted to disclose a student's records to third parties without consent, with specific exceptions for school officials with legitimate educational interests, other schools to which a student is transferring, and in certain circumstances, to parents of dependent students. The practical implication of FERPA on school leadership is significant; principals, administrators, and teachers must be thoroughly trained on the parameters of what information is considered private and the procedures for both maintaining and releasing that information, ensuring that all communication and documentation practices respect the privacy of student educational records.

Another central piece of federal legislation is the Individuals with Disabilities Education Act (IDEA), which guarantees that all children with disabilities have access to a free and appropriate public education (FAPE). IDEA mandates that schools identify and evaluate students who may have disabilities, create individualized education programs (IEPs) tailored to meet the unique needs of each student, and provide special education and related services that support academic success. The scope of IDEA is extensive, covering various areas from early intervention services for infants and toddlers to transition services for older students, requiring that schools not only accommodate students with disabilities but also strive to ensure their participation and integration into the regular educational environment to the greatest extent possible. For educational leaders, compliance with IDEA requires a deep understanding of the legal processes and requirements surrounding special education, including the IEP process, procedural safeguards for parents, and the provision of least restrictive environments (LRE). School administrators are also expected to provide resources, training, and support to staff who work with students with disabilities, emphasizing the need for collaborative teamwork among educators, special education specialists, related service providers, and families. Furthermore, Title IX of the Education Amendments of 1972 stands as a critical federal law that prohibits sex-based discrimination in any educational program or activity that receives federal funding. Title IX encompasses a broad range of discriminatory behaviors, including sexual harassment, sexual assault, and unequal access to opportunities, affecting students and employees in all educational settings. Schools must establish clear policies and procedures to address complaints of discrimination and ensure that these policies are effectively implemented, creating an environment free from discrimination and harassment based on sex or gender. School leadership's role is to ensure that staff are well-trained on Title IX requirements and the investigation of complaints, implement grievance procedures, and prevent sex-based discrimination.

Section 504 of the Rehabilitation Act of 1973 is a civil rights law that prohibits discrimination based on disability in programs and activities that receive federal financial assistance, including public schools. Section 504 requires that schools provide reasonable accommodations to students with disabilities to ensure equal access to educational opportunities, similar to those provided to students without disabilities. Unlike IDEA, Section 504's definition of disability is broader and encompasses a wider range of students with physical or mental impairments that limit a major life activity. This also includes students with temporary disabilities. It also requires a 504 plan that explains the type of accommodations the student should have. Compliance with Section 504 requires educational leaders to be proficient in the identification of qualifying students, understand the development of 504 plans, and ensure these plans are implemented effectively in all aspects of the school environment. Furthermore, state-specific education laws provide a supplementary layer of standards that must be observed by school leadership. These state laws often expand upon the broad mandates of federal laws, establishing more detailed regulations and guidelines that are specific to the educational context of each state. For example, many states have laws that govern teacher licensure, student disciplinary actions, curriculum requirements, and funding of public education, necessitating a deep understanding of these state-specific statutes, which vary widely. In New York, for example, the state education law establishes standards for teacher certification, ensuring only qualified professionals are employed in teaching positions, and mandates that all public schools provide access to a curriculum that aligns with the New York State Learning Standards. Compliance with this state law requires that schools employ certified educators and that the curriculum development and instructional methods align with the established state guidelines. Conversely, in California, the state's education laws focus more significantly on school finance and student support services, requiring that districts adhere to funding allocations and address the needs of diverse student populations through targeted programs and services. The impact of these legal variations underscores the necessity for educational leaders to be aware of and adhere to the specific laws of their state while also recognizing the broader mandates of federal laws.

In addition to these statutory requirements, professional standards offer an ethical framework that educational leaders must embrace, acting as guides that supplement legal obligations. The Professional Standards for Educational Leaders (PSEL), developed by the National Policy Board for Educational Administration, outline the key competencies that all educational leaders should possess, such as creating a vision for the school, developing effective instructional practices, and fostering a school culture that supports all students and staff. The PSEL standards also emphasize the need for ethical leadership that prioritizes the well-being of students and community engagement. State-specific leadership standards, which often align with the PSEL framework, provide the specific benchmarks by which educational leaders in each state are evaluated, including those related to ethical conduct, instructional leadership, and management of resources. For example, in Texas, the state leadership standards require that principals foster a school culture based on ethical principles, equity, and shared decision making. Furthermore, many school districts adopt ethical guidelines that dictate the expected behavior of educational leaders, supplementing both the federal laws and professional standards. These guidelines often focus on conflicts of interest, confidentiality, and the responsible use of resources, further shaping the framework for ethical decision making in schools. Practical applications demonstrate the critical intersection of legal and ethical requirements in daily school operations. For instance, consider a scenario where a school receives a complaint that a student is being bullied based on their sexual orientation. Legally, this implicates Title IX, which requires the school to thoroughly investigate the complaint and take action to protect the student from discrimination or harassment. Ethically, the principal needs to consider how to create a safe, inclusive environment for all students, which may require further interventions such as training for staff, implementing anti-bullying programs, and initiating restorative justice practices to repair the harm and rebuild the school community. A different scenario involves a case where a student with a learning disability is not making sufficient progress under their current IEP. Legally, this invokes IDEA, which mandates that the school must review and revise the IEP to ensure the student's access to a free appropriate public education. Ethically, the school leaders need to also ensure that the student's current special education program is well-planned, supported by all teachers and staff, and is tailored to the student's specific educational needs. They must communicate openly with the student and family and give them a voice in the changes to their program.

To properly evaluate situations that involve both legal and ethical considerations, school leaders can use a structured framework that integrates both perspectives. The first step of this approach involves identifying the legal aspects of the situation by gathering all facts to determine if there are any federal and/or state laws that may apply to the case. The second step involves analyzing the ethical dimensions, and the relevant ethical standards in the PSEL and state and district guidelines should be reviewed and analyzed. Following that step, a comprehensive evaluation and decision should be made by combining both the legal and ethical frameworks and creating a decision that takes into account all aspects. The consequences of violating either legal or ethical standards can be severe for educational leaders and for the school community. Legally, noncompliance can lead to lawsuits, fines, loss of funding, and legal action against the school and individual employees, which can damage the school's reputation and drain resources. Ethically, breaches can result in loss of trust, compromised relationships with staff and families, decreased teacher morale, and a toxic school climate, undermining the foundation of a positive and nurturing school. A case in point is a scenario where a principal knowingly misuses allocated funds for unapproved purposes, which would constitute a violation of both legal and ethical guidelines. If this were discovered, the leader could face legal penalties and lose their position, in addition to eroding the trust in the school leadership.

Therefore, it is critical for educational leaders to maintain a commitment to continuous learning and ethical development. This involves staying current on the latest changes in federal and state education laws, regularly reviewing school policies to ensure they remain compliant and up to date, and engaging in ongoing professional development to learn ethical principles and best practices. Staying abreast of changing legal standards and ethical expectations can be facilitated through workshops, professional development conferences, and partnerships with educational law experts, school boards, and professional associations. Engaging in proactive education helps leaders create a school environment where ethical conduct and compliance are priorities, establishing a solid foundation for student and staff well-being.

Decision-Making Frameworks

Ethical decision-making in educational leadership requires a robust framework that extends beyond simple adherence to legal statutes, encompassing a deep consideration of moral values, stakeholder interests, and the potential consequences of actions. Educational leaders are often confronted with complex ethical dilemmas that necessitate a structured approach to ensure decisions are just, fair, and promote the well-being of all members of the school community. Three prominent ethical decision-making frameworks—the ethics of justice, the ethics of care, and the ethics of critique—offer distinct but complementary lenses through which leaders can navigate these challenges.

The ethics of justice framework, rooted in principles of fairness and equality, emphasizes the importance of adhering to rules, laws, and established protocols.

This approach is based on the premise that ethical decisions should be made impartially, ensuring that all individuals are treated equally and that their rights are protected. In the context of educational leadership, the ethics of justice framework often involves the application of legal statutes such as the Individuals with Disabilities Education Act (IDEA), Title IX, and the Family Educational Rights and Privacy Act (FERPA), each of which outlines specific rights and responsibilities for students and educators. For example, when addressing a disciplinary issue, a leader applying the ethics of justice framework would ensure that due process is followed, that all students involved are treated fairly, and that disciplinary actions are consistent with school policies. This framework operates on the premise that clear rules, consistently applied, promote equity and maintain order in the school environment. However, it's imperative to recognize that a strict focus on rules without regard for individual circumstances can sometimes lead to outcomes that are not truly equitable, thereby underlining the importance of balancing this framework with others. Decision-making within this justice-oriented framework involves several steps. First, there's a thorough identification of the ethical issue and the relevant stakeholders. Subsequently, applicable rules, laws, and policies are examined. A rigorous analysis of how these rules should be applied in the specific situation follows, always ensuring that all stakeholders are treated fairly. The leader should verify that all procedures and policies are followed, before making a final decision. A clear decision-making protocol based on this framework begins with identifying the specific ethical dilemma, followed by a review of relevant policies and laws. Then, the leader should analyze the situation against these rules, ensuring that any course of action aligns with principles of equality and fairness. Finally, the decision and its rationale should be communicated transparently to all stakeholders. Practical applications of this framework can be seen in scenarios such as determining eligibility for special education services, managing student discipline cases, and allocating school resources, each requiring the impartial application of existing policies and procedures. A rights-based approach, a cornerstone of the justice framework, guarantees that all stakeholders receive the rights and protections that are legally due to them. This approach makes sure that individuals have their fundamental rights upheld when a decision is made.

In contrast to the rule-based focus of the ethics of justice, the ethics of care framework prioritizes relationships, context, and consequences when making ethical decisions. This approach emphasizes the importance of empathy, compassion, and responsiveness to individual needs, rather than simply applying universal principles. The central premise of the ethics of care is that ethical decisions should be guided by a concern for the well-being of all members of the school community, especially those who are most vulnerable. Leaders operating within this framework seek to understand the unique circumstances and perspectives of each individual, considering how their decisions will affect the lives of others, often by listening to the narratives of affected people. For example, when addressing a conflict between students, a leader using the ethics of care framework would focus on understanding the root causes of the conflict, fostering empathy among the students involved, and promoting restorative justice practices that aim to repair relationships rather than simply punish wrongdoers. The framework is less about following strict procedures and more about understanding the impact that a decision can have on individuals and their relationships. Key to this framework is the act of listening to the voices of all parties involved to gain a deeper appreciation for the issue before making a decision. The framework stresses that decisions must be based on the individual and the situation rather than on the universal application of rules or the consideration of rights. This approach to ethical decision-making involves a series of steps. The first step entails fully understanding the context of a given issue by gathering detailed information about the individuals involved and their unique circumstances. Following that, the impact of potential solutions on the individuals and community is analyzed, giving special attention to the consequences a decision could have on the most vulnerable people. The decision that is made must be rooted in empathy and compassion for all affected parties. This leads to solutions that take care of the needs of everyone involved, seeking to build positive relations. The decision-making protocol begins by identifying the specific ethical dilemma. Next, the leader should gather information about the affected parties and their perspectives and seek out the underlying causes of the situation, paying particular attention to their needs. Then, potential solutions should be assessed by considering the consequences for the individuals and the school. Lastly, a decision should be made with empathy and compassion, prioritizing the well-being of all stakeholders. Practical examples of this framework can be observed in creating individualized education programs (IEPs) for students with disabilities, supporting students experiencing trauma or hardship, and mediating conflicts between students or staff, each of which requires an understanding of individual needs and a commitment to building positive relationships. In this framework, consequences are not just considered as outcomes but also as the impact on relationships and community bonds. This approach underscores the need for leaders to cultivate a caring and supportive school culture where individual needs are valued and relationships are prioritized.

The ethics of critique framework offers a third perspective by emphasizing the analysis of power dynamics, equity considerations, and the potential systemic impact of decisions. This framework is rooted in the notion that ethical decision-making must involve a critical examination of the social, political, and historical forces that shape our understanding of right and wrong. Leaders using this framework recognize that ethical dilemmas are not simply individual issues but also reflect broader structural inequalities and power imbalances within the school system and the larger society. For example, when examining disparities in academic achievement among different student groups, a leader applying the ethics of critique framework would not only consider individual factors but also analyze how systemic barriers such as biased curricula, inequitable resource allocation, and discriminatory school policies contribute to these disparities. The framework challenges the status quo and calls for a proactive approach to addressing systemic injustice, requiring leaders to critically examine their own beliefs and biases, question the dominant narratives, and advocate for change that promotes equity and social justice. The framework makes leaders consider the influence of power in a system in all decision-making, advocating for the dismantling of any structures that uphold oppression and injustice. This ethical decision-making process typically starts with a full analysis of power dynamics at play, involving a critical review of the systemic influences. Once this evaluation is done, it's necessary to understand how the situation impacts the lives of underserved individuals. A decision will then be made that is rooted in social justice and will strive to correct any injustice found within the system. The decision-making protocol begins with identifying the specific ethical dilemma. The leader should then identify and examine the power dynamics at play. An assessment of the systemic impact on marginalized groups should follow. Leaders should advocate for equity and justice by challenging policies that create inequalities. Practical applications of the ethics of critique framework can be observed in initiatives aimed at reducing achievement gaps among diverse student populations, developing culturally responsive curricula, and creating inclusive school environments that affirm the identities of all students, which often entails challenging traditional assumptions about teaching and learning, and actively working to dismantle barriers to equal access and opportunity. Furthermore, the ethics of critique requires leaders to reflect on their own positionality and the influence that their backgrounds have on their thinking and actions. This ongoing self-assessment is essential for promoting a more inclusive and equitable school system.

To effectively address complex ethical dilemmas, educational leaders must be capable of integrating these three frameworks, recognizing that each offers valuable insights. Rather than choosing one approach over another, they should seek a balanced perspective that incorporates elements of justice, care, and critique. The use of multiple frameworks in the decision-making process helps in a more comprehensive analysis of the ethical complexities and promotes a decision that is both just and fair for all members of the community, addressing potential shortcomings and biases that may emerge if one framework is used on its own. A decision-making process that uses multiple frameworks might start by using the ethics of justice approach to evaluate whether legal rights are protected, then follow up with the ethics of care approach to assess the human impact on all involved and finally use the ethics of critique approach to ensure that systemic inequalities are being addressed.

In practical terms, educational leaders can utilize decision-making worksheets and templates that guide them through the steps outlined by each framework. A template might include sections for identifying the ethical issue, analyzing relevant rules and policies, considering the perspectives of all stakeholders, assessing the potential consequences of different actions, and evaluating the power dynamics at play, creating a step-by-step approach to address ethical issues. Common ethical dilemmas, such as conflicts of interest, confidentiality breaches, or instances of discrimination, can be analyzed using multiple frameworks to develop solutions that are both legally sound and morally just. For example, in a situation involving a teacher accused of misconduct, a leader might first apply the ethics of justice to ensure a fair investigation and due process, then utilize the ethics of care to support both the teacher and the students involved, and finally employ the ethics of critique to examine any systemic issues that might have contributed to the situation. The use of these frameworks is not intended to make decision-making a mechanistic process. Instead, they provide a structure for thoughtful and reflective analysis, empowering educational leaders to make decisions that align with their values and promote the best interests of their school community.

Selecting and adapting ethical frameworks must be done on a case-by-case basis, recognizing that the most appropriate approach will depend on the specific context and nature of the ethical dilemma. A situation that presents a clear violation of legal rights will often benefit from a justice framework, whereas a situation involving conflict between individuals will require the empathy and compassion of the care framework. When the concern is about inequitable treatment, the critique framework can identify social injustices and work to overcome them. The most crucial aspect of ethical decision-making in educational leadership is not simply the outcome, but the process, which should be transparent, inclusive, and grounded in a deep commitment to the principles of fairness, justice, and care. Continuous reflection, critical assessment, and willingness to learn from experience are vital to continuous ethical growth.

Professional Conduct

Professional conduct for educational leaders necessitates a rigorous commitment to maintaining the highest ethical standards across all facets of school administration. This commitment extends beyond legal compliance to encompass a deeply rooted sense of moral responsibility and a dedication to fostering a positive and equitable educational environment. Maintaining such high ethical standards is crucial for building trust, ensuring the integrity of educational processes, and promoting the well-being of all members of the school community.

Professional boundaries are paramount in educational leadership, delineating the appropriate interactions between leaders and staff, students, parents, and the broader community. These boundaries are essential for safeguarding both the leader's integrity and the welfare of those they serve. In staff relationships, leaders must avoid favoritism, personal relationships that could compromise professional judgment, and any actions that create a hostile or uncomfortable work environment. Respect, fairness, and objectivity should govern all interactions. Clear and consistent communication is essential, ensuring that all staff members are treated with dignity and are evaluated based on objective criteria rather than personal preferences. Establishing well-defined reporting structures and clear expectations can further contribute to maintaining professional boundaries in the workplace.

Interactions with students also require careful consideration of professional boundaries. Educational leaders must serve as positive role models, demonstrating respect, empathy, and fairness in all their dealings with students. They must avoid any behavior that could be interpreted as exploitative, inappropriate, or biased. Leaders should maintain a professional distance, refraining from developing close personal relationships with students, whether physical, digital or emotional. Moreover, they are responsible for ensuring the safety and well-being of all students, protecting them from harm, and promoting a learning environment free from harassment, bullying, and discrimination. Clear policies regarding interactions with students, training for staff, and accessible reporting mechanisms are essential to uphold these boundaries.

Engaging effectively with parents and the community is a critical aspect of an educational leader's role. Maintaining professional boundaries in these interactions means communicating openly and transparently, respecting confidentiality, and acting in the best interest of students. Educational leaders must be approachable and willing to listen to the concerns of parents and community members, while maintaining impartiality and objectivity. Leaders should avoid becoming personally entangled in community disputes or family matters and, rather, should focus on their professional responsibilities. They should aim to build trust through ethical, consistent, and responsive interactions.

The digital age has introduced new challenges to maintaining professional boundaries, particularly with the use of social media. Educational leaders must exercise extreme caution in their digital communications, mindful that their online presence reflects their professional role. They must avoid posting anything that could be considered inappropriate, offensive, or disrespectful, ensuring that their online activities do not compromise their position or undermine the trust placed in them by the school community. Maintaining separate personal and professional accounts can help to minimize the risk of blurring boundaries. Furthermore, leaders should adopt clear communication policies regarding the use of social media by staff and students, ensuring that all members of the school community understand the importance of maintaining respectful online behavior.

Accountability measures are a cornerstone of professional conduct in educational leadership, ensuring that leaders are responsible for their actions and decisions. Transparency in decision-making is crucial for building trust and promoting a culture of integrity. Leaders should make sure that the rationales behind their decisions are well-documented and accessible to stakeholders. Open communication, involving the school community in the decision-making process, promotes both accountability and trust. Decisions must be made objectively, without favoritism, bias, or personal gain. A culture that encourages constructive feedback is crucial for leaders to remain accountable.

Financial integrity is a non-negotiable aspect of ethical leadership. Educational leaders are entrusted with public funds and must be exemplary stewards, adhering to strict accounting principles and regulations. Financial records must be meticulously maintained, transparent, and subject to regular audits. Leaders must avoid conflicts of interest, ensuring that their personal financial dealings do not interfere with their professional responsibilities. Financial decisions should be made with the best interests of the school and its students at heart, using resources efficiently and effectively. Developing robust internal controls and compliance procedures can ensure financial accountability.

Ethical resource allocation is another critical dimension of accountability. Educational leaders must ensure that resources are allocated fairly and equitably, based on student needs and educational priorities. Decisions about resource allocation should be transparent, data-driven, and aligned with the school's mission and strategic goals. Leaders must avoid using resources for personal gain, or allowing favoritism to influence the allocation of funds, personnel, or other resources. The use of objective criteria to guide decisions about resource allocation can enhance transparency and ethical conduct.

Documentation and reporting are essential elements of accountability, ensuring that all school activities are properly recorded and communicated. Leaders must maintain accurate and detailed records of student progress, staff performance, financial transactions, and any other relevant data. They must comply with all legal and regulatory reporting requirements, submitting required documentation in a timely and accurate manner. Transparency and accessibility of documentation are crucial, allowing stakeholders to review school operations and verify accountability. The use of secure and reliable systems for data management is essential for maintaining confidentiality and ensuring data integrity.

Ethical leadership behaviors are characterized by integrity, trustworthiness, and a deep commitment to serving the best interests of the school community. Role modeling is a powerful tool for promoting ethical conduct; leaders must embody the values and principles they seek to instill in others. Consistency in behavior and decision-making builds trust among stakeholders, creating a positive environment where ethical standards are upheld and valued. Leaders must act with integrity in all their interactions, keeping their promises, and being transparent in their dealings.

Building trust is essential for effective leadership, requiring leaders to act with fairness, transparency, and consistency. Trust is earned over time through consistent ethical behavior, open communication, and a willingness to listen to the concerns of stakeholders. Leaders must actively promote a culture of trust within the school community, valuing collaboration, and respecting the views of others. Actions that damage trust must be avoided, and any breaches must be addressed promptly and transparently to rebuild confidence.

Maintaining confidentiality is a critical responsibility for educational leaders, ensuring that sensitive information is protected from unauthorized access and disclosure. Leaders often have access to confidential student records, staff evaluations, and other sensitive data that must be handled with the utmost discretion. They should strictly follow confidentiality policies, sharing information only when necessary and in accordance with legal and ethical guidelines. Confidentiality fosters trust and ensures that stakeholders feel safe sharing sensitive information with school leaders.

Managing conflicts of interest is essential for maintaining ethical standards in educational leadership. Leaders must recognize situations where their personal interests may conflict with their professional responsibilities, disclosing any potential conflicts and recusing themselves from decisions where their impartiality may be compromised. Leaders must also avoid using their position for personal gain, whether financial or otherwise. Implementing clear conflict-of-interest policies and providing training to staff on how to manage such situations is necessary to uphold ethical integrity.

Developing and implementing professional conduct policies is essential for establishing clear expectations and providing guidance to all members of the school community. These policies should cover all aspects of professional conduct, including boundaries, accountability, and ethical behavior. They must be developed collaboratively, involving input from staff, students, parents, and community members. Policies should be clearly communicated, consistently enforced, and regularly reviewed to ensure they remain relevant and effective.

Addressing misconduct and ethical violations promptly and transparently is vital for maintaining accountability and restoring trust. Procedures for reporting and investigating allegations of misconduct must be established, ensuring fairness and impartiality throughout the process. Consequences for misconduct must be consistent and proportionate to the severity of the violation. Corrective actions should be taken to address the underlying causes of the misconduct and prevent future occurrences. A culture that encourages reporting ethical violations, without fear of retaliation, is essential.

Creating a culture of ethical behavior requires a comprehensive approach involving leadership, communication, and ongoing training. Leaders must actively promote ethical standards, modeling integrity, and holding others accountable for their actions. Ethical dilemmas should be discussed openly, providing staff with opportunities to learn and develop their ethical decision-making skills. A shared sense of responsibility for ethical conduct must be instilled throughout the school community.

Maintaining professional integrity under pressure is a critical challenge for educational leaders. The demands of the job, coupled with the pressure to improve student outcomes and satisfy stakeholders, can create difficult situations where leaders face pressure to compromise their ethical standards. It is important that leaders maintain their integrity, upholding their values and resisting the temptation to take shortcuts. They should seek advice and support from mentors, colleagues, and professional organizations when faced with ethical dilemmas, reinforcing that maintaining integrity is essential for their long-term success as a leader.

Continuous professional growth and ethical development are essential for educational leaders, requiring a commitment to ongoing learning and reflection. Staying abreast of changes in laws, policies, and ethical guidelines, through participation in workshops, conferences, and continuing education opportunities, is essential for maintaining competence. Leaders should also engage in self-reflection, assessing their own ethical practices and seeking feedback from others. Mentoring programs, peer coaching, and professional learning communities can all support the ongoing growth of ethical leaders.

In summary, professional conduct for educational leaders is not merely about adherence to rules and regulations, but about embodying a deep commitment to ethical values, demonstrating integrity in all aspects of their work, and fostering a culture of trust and accountability within the school community. Maintaining high ethical standards is not just a professional obligation, but a moral imperative.

Student Rights and Privacy

Student rights and privacy form the bedrock of a just and equitable educational environment, demanding that school leaders possess a comprehensive understanding of their legal and ethical obligations to safeguard student interests. This responsibility encompasses a wide array of considerations, from adhering to constitutional rights and ensuring academic freedom to implementing robust privacy protocols and managing sensitive information with utmost care.

The constitutional rights of students in schools are not absolute, yet they remain fundamental. The First Amendment protects students' rights to free speech, albeit with limitations to prevent disruption of the learning environment. Landmark cases like Tinker v. Des Moines Independent Community School District underscore the principle that students do not shed their constitutional rights at the schoolhouse gate, while also allowing schools to regulate speech that causes significant disturbance. Academic freedom, while not expressly protected under the First Amendment for K-12 students, also bears consideration; the goal should be the promotion of open inquiry and critical thinking. In cases of student expression, school leaders must navigate a delicate balance between protecting student rights and maintaining an orderly and safe learning atmosphere. This requires clear, consistently applied policies that are transparent to both students and parents.

Due process, guaranteed by the Fourteenth Amendment, is a critical protection for students facing disciplinary actions, particularly suspension or expulsion. Procedural due process requires schools to provide students with notice of the charges, an opportunity to be heard, and a fair hearing where they can present their side of the story. Substantive due process ensures that disciplinary actions are not arbitrary or capricious, but are grounded in a clear violation of school rules. School leaders must ensure that all disciplinary actions adhere to these due process requirements, particularly for marginalized student groups disproportionately affected by disciplinary policies. This requires training for all staff involved in disciplinary actions, emphasizing the importance of fairness, consistency, and impartiality.

Religious and cultural rights represent another facet of student rights that school leaders must respect. The First Amendment prohibits the establishment of religion while also protecting students' rights to exercise their religion freely. Schools must provide reasonable accommodations for religious practices, such as prayer or dress codes, provided these do not disrupt the educational environment. In terms of cultural rights, schools must be sensitive to the diversity of their student population, ensuring that curriculum and policies are inclusive and respectful of all cultures and backgrounds. Failure to accommodate diverse religious and cultural practices can lead to exclusion and discrimination, undermining the school's efforts to foster a positive and inclusive culture. School leaders need to develop protocols for addressing potential conflicts and ensuring that the school environment is welcoming for all students, regardless of their religious or cultural background.

The rights of students with disabilities are protected by laws such as the Individuals with Disabilities Education Act (IDEA), mandating that schools provide a free and appropriate public education (FAPE) to all students with disabilities. This involves developing Individualized Education Programs (IEPs) tailored to each student's unique needs, ensuring access to necessary accommodations and supports, and providing appropriate specialized instruction. School leaders must be deeply knowledgeable about IDEA requirements, ensuring compliance with all legal mandates and fostering an inclusive environment where students with disabilities can fully participate in the school community. This involves providing resources and training for staff to effectively implement IEPs and accommodate the diverse needs of students with disabilities.

Privacy protections for students are paramount, requiring school leaders to navigate complex legal and ethical considerations. The Family Educational Rights and Privacy Act (FERPA) is a federal law that protects the privacy of student education records. FERPA grants parents certain rights, including the right to access their children's education records, the right to request amendments to those records, and the right to consent to the disclosure of personally identifiable information from those records, with exceptions made for school officials with legitimate educational interests. School leaders must ensure complete compliance with FERPA, developing policies and procedures to prevent unauthorized access to student records. This includes providing training to all staff members who handle student information, emphasizing the importance of confidentiality and adherence to FERPA guidelines.

Digital privacy considerations pose increasingly complex challenges for school leaders in an age where much student information is stored and shared electronically. Digital privacy protections must be rigorously implemented to prevent breaches and safeguard student data. This requires comprehensive policies about data collection, storage, and use by educational technology platforms, ensuring that student data is not shared or sold for commercial purposes without parental consent. School leaders should also consider the impact of data mining and algorithmic bias in educational tools, striving for equity and transparency in data practices. Implementing strong cybersecurity measures, such as encryption and access controls, is essential to protect student data from unauthorized access and cyber threats.

The protection of student health information is another critical area of concern. Under laws such as the Health Insurance Portability and Accountability Act (HIPAA), though it is generally more applicable to medical institutions, and state health privacy laws, schools must take precautions to keep student health records private. This includes storing records securely and limiting access to only those individuals who have a need to know the information. School leaders must develop clear protocols for handling medical information, ensuring that staff members who handle this data are trained on the relevant privacy laws. When sharing health information with other parties, schools must obtain the necessary consents and ensure that the data is transmitted securely. This practice requires a delicate balance between protecting student privacy and ensuring they receive the necessary support and care.

Social media policies are an essential component of any comprehensive strategy for protecting student privacy, given how pervasive social media is in modern society. School leaders must develop clear policies regarding the use of social media, addressing issues like cyberbullying, inappropriate content, and the disclosure of sensitive student information. These policies should provide guidance for both staff and students, outlining expected conduct and the consequences of violations. Additionally, school leaders should consider the impact of social media on students' mental health and well-being, promoting responsible social media habits and fostering a positive digital environment. This also includes training on the importance of digital citizenship and ethical social media use.

Effective record-keeping and access protocols are essential to safeguarding student information, requiring school leaders to implement a systematic approach to data management. This includes procedures for creating, storing, updating, and destroying student records. Access to student records should be limited to authorized personnel only, with clear protocols in place to track who accesses what data, and when. School leaders should regularly review their record-keeping procedures, ensuring that they comply with all applicable laws and regulations. Additionally, it is crucial that there is a well-defined process for students and their parents to access their records, ensuring transparency and accountability.

Case studies of student rights violations can illuminate the practical challenges faced by school leaders in balancing the need for a safe and orderly environment with the protection of student rights. For instance, cases involving free speech violations highlight the importance of clearly defining the boundaries of student expression and providing training for staff on the nuanced legal considerations. Similarly, cases involving due process violations underscore the need for transparent disciplinary policies and procedures, ensuring that all students receive fair treatment. Furthermore, case studies about privacy breaches, particularly in the digital environment, underscore the need for robust data protection measures and policies, coupled with rigorous training for all staff. Analyzing these cases helps school leaders to develop preventative strategies, promoting a more inclusive and rights-respecting school environment.

Implementing comprehensive protocols for handling sensitive student information is a critical responsibility for school leaders. These protocols should cover all forms of student data, including academic records, health information, disciplinary actions, and special education records. The protocols should detail procedures for data collection, storage, use, and disclosure, ensuring that data is handled securely and ethically. Additionally, protocols should provide guidance on how to respond to data breaches or unauthorized disclosures of student information. Regular audits of data practices and continuous training for staff can help to ensure that these protocols are consistently and effectively implemented.

Guidelines for electronic data protection are essential given the increasing reliance on digital systems in education. These guidelines should cover the use of passwords, encryption, and access controls, along with protocols for data backup and recovery. School leaders should work with their technology departments to implement robust cybersecurity measures, protecting student information from cyber threats. Additionally, they should ensure that data is only stored on secure servers and is accessible only to authorized personnel. Regularly updating security protocols, monitoring for potential vulnerabilities, and providing training on cybersecurity best practices are essential.

Procedures for managing student records should be aligned with FERPA requirements and other relevant laws and regulations. These procedures should detail the process for creating, updating, and storing records, as well as the protocols for accessing and sharing data. School leaders must clearly outline the rights of parents and students with respect to their records, ensuring that they have access to their data and the ability to correct any inaccuracies. Furthermore, schools should have procedures in place for securely destroying student records when they are no longer needed, following established retention schedules.

Balancing transparency with privacy represents a fundamental challenge for school leaders. While parents and other stakeholders have a legitimate need to know about school activities and student outcomes, there is also a need to protect the privacy of individual students. School leaders must develop policies that are clear about what information will be shared, who it will be shared with, and under what circumstances. The goal should be to provide as much transparency as possible, without compromising the privacy rights of individual students. This often requires creative solutions, such as aggregating data, sharing anonymized results, and using secure communication channels.

In conclusion, creating and maintaining a school environment that respects and protects student rights requires ongoing commitment from school leaders. This responsibility includes not just compliance with laws but also adherence to high ethical standards. School leaders must develop comprehensive policies, provide thorough training for all staff, and continuously evaluate their practices to ensure they align with best practices and remain vigilant about protecting the rights of their students. By prioritizing the rights and privacy of their students, school leaders can create a more just, equitable, and supportive learning environment for all.

Ethical Communication

Ethical communication in educational leadership necessitates a comprehensive approach that prioritizes clarity, honesty, and appropriateness in all interactions with stakeholders. Effective communication is not merely about transmitting information; it is about building trust, fostering understanding, and promoting a collaborative environment conducive to student success. This requires educational leaders to adhere to stringent ethical standards, particularly when navigating the complex dynamics of communicating with diverse groups such as parents, staff, students, and the broader community. The challenge lies in crafting messages that are not only informative but also culturally sensitive, respectful, and tailored to the specific needs of each audience. This necessitates the development and implementation of clear communication policies, protocols, and practices that underpin every aspect of school operations, from routine updates to critical emergency communications.

Stakeholder communication in education demands a nuanced approach that acknowledges the unique perspectives and communication preferences of different groups. Parent communication protocols must ensure that parents are kept informed about their children's academic progress, school activities, and any relevant policy changes. This requires schools to adopt a variety of communication channels, such as newsletters, emails, phone calls, and parent-teacher conferences, providing a multitude of opportunities for engagement. Furthermore, these protocols must be sensitive to cultural and linguistic differences, providing translations and other accommodations as necessary to ensure that all parents can fully participate in their children's education. The objective is to establish a two-way communication system where parents are not only recipients of information but also active partners in the educational process. Staff communication guidelines must ensure transparency and fairness in how information is shared within the school community. This involves establishing clear channels for distributing school-wide announcements, departmental updates, and performance feedback, promoting consistency and accountability in how educators are informed of relevant changes and initiatives. Staff communication should encourage open dialogue and feedback, fostering a culture where staff feel empowered to voice their concerns and contribute to decision-making processes. This approach not only strengthens morale but also harnesses the collective intelligence of the teaching community. Student communication boundaries must be carefully defined to ensure that students receive information that is appropriate for their age and developmental level. This necessitates the use of age-appropriate language and communication channels, and that teachers are sensitive to the diverse social and emotional needs of their students. Direct communication with students should focus on academic guidance, support services, and school policies, avoiding the dissemination of sensitive information that could be harmful or inappropriate for young learners. Community engagement strategies should be geared towards building positive relationships with the broader community. This involves creating opportunities for community members to interact with the school, participate in events, and provide input on school initiatives. These strategies may include town hall meetings, community outreach programs, and partnerships with local organizations, highlighting the vital role the school plays within its community. It is also essential for school leaders to be proactive in sharing information about school successes and addressing any concerns from the community, reinforcing the commitment to transparency and community partnership.

Crisis communication in educational settings demands meticulous planning and execution, particularly when dealing with emergencies or sensitive situations. Emergency response protocols must be clear, comprehensive, and regularly practiced to ensure that all stakeholders are prepared to respond effectively in times of crisis. These protocols should outline specific procedures for handling various types of emergencies, including medical incidents, natural disasters, and security threats. Training and simulations should be conducted regularly to familiarize staff and students with the protocols, reinforcing their readiness to respond calmly and effectively. Media relations requires a strategic approach that balances transparency with the need to protect student privacy and maintain the integrity of the school's reputation. School leaders should designate a spokesperson to handle media inquiries, ensuring that all communication with the media is consistent, accurate, and timely. Furthermore, leaders should establish protocols for sharing information with the media, while also protecting sensitive information related to students, staff, and ongoing investigations. Managing sensitive information during a crisis requires strict adherence to confidentiality protocols. This involves protecting personally identifiable information of students and staff, particularly in cases involving disciplinary matters, health issues, or legal investigations. Schools must follow all relevant legal requirements for data privacy and security. The dissemination of sensitive information should be limited to those with a legitimate need to know, ensuring that the information is used only for its intended purpose. Timing and transparency are crucial elements of effective crisis communication. Schools must prioritize the timely release of information to the community, while also ensuring that the information is accurate and complete. Transparent communication should include clear explanations of the situation, the steps taken by the school to address the issue, and the resources available to those who are impacted. Transparency builds trust and demonstrates the school's commitment to accountability during challenging times, reinforcing the idea that the leadership is handling the issue with care and thoroughness.

Digital communication ethics is an increasingly important aspect of educational leadership, given the proliferation of social media, email, and other digital platforms. Social media guidelines should provide clear expectations for how educators and students use social media both inside and outside of school settings. These guidelines should address issues such as cyberbullying, inappropriate content, and the disclosure of sensitive information, ensuring that all users engage in responsible and ethical digital practices. Furthermore, the guidelines must emphasize the importance of protecting the school's reputation, encouraging users to think critically about the messages and content they share online. Email communication protocols should outline best practices for email etiquette, addressing the use of appropriate language, tone, and formatting. Educators should use their school email accounts for all official communications with parents, staff, and students. Protocols should also address the management of email distribution lists, ensuring that only appropriate recipients receive emails. Furthermore, the handling of confidential information via email should be addressed, emphasizing the need to protect sensitive data and maintain professional boundaries. Digital platform usage should be governed by clear policies that outline the appropriate use of various online learning platforms, communication systems, and other digital resources. These policies should address data privacy, online safety, and responsible digital citizenship, promoting ethical online behavior for all members of the school community. Online presence management is an important aspect of maintaining a positive professional reputation for educational leaders. This includes ensuring that their online presence is consistent with the school's values and ethical standards. School leaders should be mindful of the content they post on social media, personal blogs, and other digital platforms, maintaining a professional and respectful tone in all online interactions. This focus on a clear and ethical online presence helps to reinforce the integrity of the school's leadership.

Developing clear communication policies is a fundamental step in establishing a foundation for ethical communication within an educational institution. These policies should outline the expectations for communication across all contexts, ensuring that there is a shared understanding of how messages should be conveyed. These policies should address all modes of communication, including face-to-face interactions, written documents, email, social media, and digital platforms. The policies should clearly articulate the school's commitment to transparency, accountability, and respect in all communication practices. Managing confidential information is a vital aspect of ethical communication in educational settings. All school personnel should be trained on how to handle confidential information, including student records, health information, and disciplinary matters. Confidential information should be shared only on a need-to-know basis, and should be kept secure in both physical and digital forms. The school should establish protocols for responding to data breaches and unauthorized disclosure of confidential information. Addressing communication challenges effectively requires a proactive and responsive approach. Schools should establish clear procedures for managing complaints and concerns related to communication practices. These procedures should ensure that all stakeholders have an opportunity to voice their concerns, and that concerns are addressed in a fair and timely manner. School leaders should also be willing to engage in dialogue with staff, parents, and students to identify and resolve communication challenges, reinforcing a culture of continuous improvement. Building trust through transparent communication is paramount for cultivating a positive and supportive school environment. Transparency involves the open sharing of information, as well as a willingness to acknowledge mistakes and address concerns openly. School leaders should strive to create a culture where all stakeholders feel valued and heard, and where they can trust that information is shared accurately and fairly. This sense of trust is essential for building strong relationships and fostering effective communication. Cultural sensitivity in communication requires an awareness of and respect for the diverse backgrounds, languages, and communication styles of all members of the school community. School leaders should provide training for staff on cultural sensitivity, ensuring that all staff members are equipped to communicate effectively with individuals from diverse backgrounds. Furthermore, the communication materials of the school should be developed in multiple languages, and should be respectful of the cultural norms and preferences of different communities.

Maintaining ethical communication standards requires continuous effort, training, and evaluation. Schools should conduct regular reviews of their communication policies and practices, ensuring that they are up-to-date and align with best practices. Professional development should be provided for staff, training on ethical communication, data privacy, and cultural sensitivity. The school should also establish mechanisms for feedback and evaluation, allowing stakeholders to provide input on communication practices. Effective management of the diverse communication needs of an educational institution requires a strategic and comprehensive approach. Schools should prioritize the development of clear communication plans, specifying the communication goals, target audiences, channels, and timelines. Furthermore, the effectiveness of these plans should be evaluated continuously, and adjustments made as needed. Schools must also invest in the necessary technologies, systems, and infrastructure to facilitate effective communication with diverse groups. By prioritizing ethical communication, educational leaders can build strong relationships, foster trust, and create a school environment that is supportive, inclusive, and conducive to student success. This comprehensive approach ensures that communication becomes a tool for promoting educational excellence and positive community engagement.

5

ORGANIZATIONAL LEADERSHIP

Human Resources Management

Human resources management in educational settings constitutes a foundational element of school effectiveness, impacting all facets of organizational function and significantly influencing the quality of educational outcomes. This area encompasses the strategic planning, implementation, and oversight of policies and procedures related to the school's most valuable asset: its personnel. Effective human resources management extends beyond the mere transactional tasks of hiring and firing; it embodies a comprehensive approach to attracting, developing, supporting, and retaining a skilled and dedicated workforce that is committed to the institution's mission and objectives. This multifaceted role directly affects the school's capacity to foster a positive learning environment, enhance teaching practices, and ultimately improve student achievement.

The recruitment and hiring processes within educational institutions must be meticulously designed to attract the highest caliber of educators and support staff. This process begins with the development of detailed and accurate job descriptions, which clearly articulate the required qualifications, responsibilities, and expected performance outcomes for each position. These job descriptions must go beyond generic statements, including specific skills and experience relevant to the context of the school and its specific student population. For instance, a job description for an inclusion specialist should incorporate specific knowledge of differentiated instruction, adaptive technologies, and collaboration with special education teams. Similarly, a school leader job description should specify experience in school improvement, change management, and instructional leadership. Posting requirements should then align with these job descriptions, targeting relevant professional networks, educational job boards, and professional organizations to ensure maximum visibility to the desired candidate pool. This strategic approach to recruitment is essential to ensure that the school attracts candidates who possess the knowledge, skills, and disposition necessary to succeed in the challenging environment of modern education.

The interview process should be similarly rigorous, structured to evaluate not only the candidates' qualifications but also their alignment with the school's values and culture. The utilization of structured interview questions, employing a combination of behavioral, situational, and technical inquiries, allows for a more objective evaluation of candidates. Behavioral questions assess past performance to predict future behavior, situational questions gauge problem-solving skills, and technical questions verify subject matter competency and pedagogical approach. Employing a rubric to evaluate responses is essential to minimize bias and ensure consistency across all interviews. Furthermore, diverse interview panels, incorporating various stakeholders including administrators, teachers, and sometimes even students or parents, provides a more comprehensive view of each candidate's potential fit within the school community. These interviews should be followed by a thorough background and reference checks, verifying the candidate's claims and ensuring the safety and security of all students and staff. Effective recruitment procedures are not only about selecting the best candidates, but also about creating a professional and positive experience that attracts a talented and diverse workforce.

Staff evaluation and performance management are crucial for promoting continuous improvement and enhancing the quality of instruction. A comprehensive teacher evaluation system encompasses a range of measures, including structured observations, student performance data, peer reviews, and self-reflection. Observations should be structured around clear and specific criteria aligned with teaching standards and school improvement goals. Pre- and post-observation conferences offer teachers the opportunity to reflect on their practice, receive targeted feedback, and discuss areas for professional growth. Multiple data sources, such as student assessment results, surveys, and parent feedback, should be considered to provide a holistic view of teacher performance. Evaluation should be ongoing and consistent, providing constructive feedback that is timely, specific, and actionable, rather than punitive. This ongoing feedback loop promotes a culture of continuous learning and facilitates ongoing professional growth.

Performance management extends beyond teacher evaluation to include all school staff, establishing clear performance expectations, conducting regular reviews, and setting goals for improvement. Performance reviews should be conducted at least annually, using clearly defined performance metrics, and include opportunities for two-way dialogue and feedback. These evaluations should identify strengths and areas for growth, leading to the development of personalized professional development plans tailored to each individual's needs and goals. Performance improvement plans, when needed, should be collaborative, specific, and measurable, outlining clear strategies and timelines for improvement. These plans should also include ongoing support and resources, ensuring that all staff have the opportunity to meet the school's performance expectations.

Professional development planning must be aligned with the school's strategic objectives and the identified needs of individual staff members. Effective professional development should incorporate research-based instructional strategies, address current educational trends, and promote the use of technology to enhance teaching practices. Professional development programs should also include opportunities for collaboration, peer observation, and coaching. Job-embedded professional learning activities, such as collaborative planning sessions, mentoring, and coaching, ensure that professional development translates into improved classroom practices. The professional development process should be both ongoing and iterative, incorporating feedback and evaluation to refine and improve programming. Individualized professional growth plans should be developed in consultation with each staff member, based on performance evaluations, individual interests, and school wide needs, linking directly to improved job performance and career advancement.

Employee relations and conflict resolution require a proactive approach that prioritizes clear communication, mutual respect, and transparent procedures. Establishing clear guidelines and expectations for staff behavior, coupled with accessible communication channels, allows for the early detection and resolution of potential issues. Conflict resolution strategies should be grounded in restorative justice principles, focusing on repairing harm and restoring relationships, rather than simply imposing punishment. Utilizing mediation and facilitation techniques to resolve disagreements can promote collaboration and maintain a positive work environment. Regular communication forums, including staff meetings, newsletters, and informal discussions, facilitate the exchange of information, encourage feedback, and help to build trust amongst staff. Effective employee relations management should cultivate an environment where staff members feel valued, respected, and supported in their roles, promoting a cohesive and collaborative work environment.

Legal compliance in human resources practices is a non-negotiable aspect of effective school administration, requiring a thorough understanding of federal, state, and local regulations pertaining to employment law, labor relations, and equal opportunity. Schools must ensure compliance with anti-discrimination laws, such as Title VII of the Civil Rights Act, the Americans with Disabilities Act (ADA), and the Age Discrimination in Employment Act (ADEA), to prevent discrimination based on race, color, religion, sex, national origin, disability, and age. Additionally, schools must adhere to federal and state laws related to wage and hour laws, child labor regulations, and employee leave policies. Maintaining accurate personnel records, and implementing fair and consistent HR practices ensures that the school is adhering to applicable legal standards. Thorough training for HR personnel and school administrators on these legal requirements is essential, promoting awareness of legal obligations and compliance procedures, and avoiding any liability.

Practical examples of effective HR tools include teacher evaluation forms that are aligned with teaching standards and designed to collect diverse evidence of teacher performance. These forms should be detailed enough to provide specific feedback but user-friendly to ensure efficient documentation. A sample evaluation form might include sections for lesson planning, instructional delivery, classroom management, student assessment, professional collaboration, and growth. Performance improvement protocols should include clearly outlined steps for addressing performance deficiencies, including timelines, resources, and support mechanisms. Professional development plans should incorporate SMART (Specific, Measurable, Achievable, Relevant, Time-bound) goals, reflecting both individual growth and the needs of the school. Staff handbooks should offer clear and concise guidance on school policies, procedures, and expectations. These handbooks should be reviewed regularly to ensure they are up-to-date with current legal and ethical standards, and accessible to all staff members. Additionally, templates for performance reviews, job descriptions, interview protocols, and staff development plans can enhance the consistency and effectiveness of HR practices.

Ultimately, effective human resources management is foundational to creating a positive and collaborative school culture. It involves more than just administrative tasks; it requires a strategic approach that values and supports all staff members. By prioritizing effective recruitment, providing ongoing professional development, conducting fair evaluations, promoting positive employee relations, and ensuring legal compliance, school leaders can build a high-performing and dedicated workforce that is committed to fostering the success of all students. This commitment to human resources management is not just an operational necessity but a moral imperative, ensuring that every staff member is supported and empowered to contribute their best efforts to the educational mission. Through this, schools can develop a culture of respect, collaboration, and continuous improvement that significantly impacts educational outcomes and contributes to the long-term success of the entire school community.

Budget and Finance

Effective school budget and finance management constitutes a critical operational function within educational institutions, influencing not only the allocation of resources but also the overall capacity of schools to achieve their educational missions. This complex area requires a deep understanding of the fundamental principles of educational finance, combined with practical skills in budget development, resource allocation, expenditure monitoring, and ensuring fiscal compliance. A comprehensive approach to school budget and finance integrates strategic planning, data-driven decision-making, and a commitment to transparency and accountability, creating a foundation for sustainable educational improvements.

The budgeting process within schools is not merely a mechanical exercise of accounting; it is a strategic undertaking that aligns financial resources with the institution's educational objectives. The development of an annual budget begins with a comprehensive assessment of the school's needs, incorporating input from various stakeholders, including administrators, teachers, staff, and, where applicable, community members. This needs assessment involves the examination of various data points, including student enrollment projections, academic performance metrics, facility requirements, and staff development goals. The school's strategic plan provides a foundational framework for translating these needs into measurable financial objectives, ensuring that all budget allocations support the long-term educational vision of the institution. The planning process should be inclusive, participatory, and transparent, promoting a shared understanding of priorities and fostering a culture of financial responsibility.

Budget development typically progresses through several phases, starting with the formulation of budget assumptions, which are projections about expected revenues and expenditures. These assumptions are based on historical data, current market trends, and anticipated changes in demographics or policy. Revenue forecasting, a critical aspect of this phase, involves estimating the anticipated income from local, state, and federal sources, as well as any other revenue generating activities. These estimations, which should be based on accurate data and a conservative approach, form the basis for formulating the expenditure budget. Detailed expenditure plans outline the specific resource requirements for various programs, departments, and services. The categorization of expenditures into areas such as salaries, benefits, instructional materials, facility maintenance, and technology facilitates a clearer understanding of resource allocation patterns and provides a basis for informed decision-making.

After the budget proposal is developed, it undergoes a review process that includes administrative approval and potentially review by the school board or other governing bodies. This review phase involves careful scrutiny of the proposed budget, assessing its alignment with strategic goals, and evaluating the reasonableness of the resource allocations. Budget adjustments might be necessary based on the feedback received from these reviews, ensuring that the final budget proposal is both fiscally responsible and educationally sound. The final adopted budget serves as the financial roadmap for the school, guiding its financial operations for the entire fiscal year.

Understanding revenue sources and implementing effective allocation strategies is central to the financial sustainability of any educational institution. Schools typically rely on a combination of local, state, and federal funding to support their operations. Local revenues come primarily from property taxes and other local levies, which vary widely across different jurisdictions. State funding is typically distributed to schools based on a formula that considers factors such as student enrollment, poverty rates, and special needs. Federal funding often provides supplemental support for specific programs and initiatives. This combination of revenue streams, which is influenced by demographic and policy changes, adds complexity to the financial planning of the school.

Effective revenue allocation is not merely about distributing funds; it is about ensuring equity and alignment with the institution's educational priorities. Resource allocation strategies should be data-driven, using student performance data, needs assessments, and strategic objectives to inform funding decisions. In practice, this can involve weighted funding models that provide additional resources to schools serving high-needs students, or the implementation of performance-based budgeting where funding is linked to outcomes or achievement levels. Equitable allocation of resources ensures that all schools have adequate financial support to meet the diverse needs of their student populations, promotes transparency, and minimizes the likelihood of resources being disproportionately allocated.

Expenditure monitoring and control are critical ongoing processes that involve regular tracking of actual expenditures against budget allocations, and taking corrective measures to address any deviations. This active monitoring requires the use of financial management systems that allow school leaders to access real-time data on budget balances, encumbrances, and expenditure patterns. Effective expenditure controls include implementing purchasing policies, requiring pre-approval for significant expenditures, and ensuring that all expenditures are properly documented. Regular review of financial statements, performance reports, and budget variance reports are important for identifying potential issues and taking proactive steps to rectify them. This process involves not only checking financial accounts, but also aligning purchases and financial decisions to the educational objectives of the school.

Financial reporting represents an essential mechanism for ensuring fiscal transparency and accountability in educational settings. Schools are required to produce regular financial reports that detail revenue sources, expenditure patterns, and budget balances. These reports are often required by regulatory agencies, such as the state Department of Education, and are also important for keeping stakeholders informed about the school's financial health. Financial reporting must comply with established accounting standards and regulatory guidelines. Accurate reporting, together with compliance, is crucial for maintaining public trust and ensures that public funds are used responsibly and in alignment with the school's purpose.

Grant management and fundraising represent critical components of a comprehensive financial strategy that supplements the school's core funding. Schools often seek grants from foundations, corporations, and government agencies to support specific programs and initiatives. This involves identifying potential funding opportunities, developing competitive grant proposals, and managing the awarded grants according to the requirements of the funding agencies. The grant application process should involve a clear understanding of the grant guidelines, the articulation of program goals, the development of a detailed budget, and the alignment of proposed activities with the school's strategic plan. Effective grant management also requires the accurate tracking of grant expenditures, as well as compliance with reporting requirements, which are crucial for maintaining positive relationships with funding agencies and securing future grants.

Fundraising activities can include a variety of approaches, from annual campaigns and special events to donor cultivation and planned giving. Fundraising should be viewed as an integral part of the school's overall financial strategy, requiring a coordinated effort that involves the school leadership, staff, parents, and community members. It also requires a clear understanding of the school's mission, a well-articulated case for support, and the development of strategies that resonate with different types of donors. Successful fundraising involves building relationships with donors, demonstrating the impact of their contributions, and maintaining a transparent and accountable process.

Effective financial management also includes practical exercises that enhance the skills of school leaders in various financial areas. Budget forecasting requires the use of data analysis to predict future revenue streams and expenditure patterns. Scenario planning exercises help leaders anticipate potential financial challenges and develop contingency plans, thus improving their adaptive capacity to financial fluctuations. Resource allocation exercises involve simulated scenarios where school leaders must prioritize funding for various programs and services, making decisions based on their understanding of educational priorities and financial constraints. Finally, financial decision-making scenarios provide school leaders with a practical framework for approaching various financial challenges and making informed decisions that are both fiscally sound and educationally beneficial.

Implementing robust internal financial controls is crucial for safeguarding school assets and ensuring adherence to financial regulations. These controls encompass a range of policies and procedures designed to prevent errors, fraud, and misappropriation of funds. Segregation of duties is essential, ensuring that no single individual has complete control over all aspects of a financial transaction. Reconciliation of bank statements, internal audits, and regular review of financial records help in identifying any discrepancies or irregularities, which allows for timely corrective action. Clear and consistent purchasing procedures ensure that all expenditures are appropriately approved and documented.

Payroll and benefits management require meticulous attention to detail and compliance with labor laws and contractual agreements. Schools must ensure accurate calculation and timely distribution of paychecks, and they must also manage a range of employee benefits, including health insurance, retirement plans, and leave policies. They also must maintain accurate records of employee compensation, deductions, and benefits. Payroll processing should incorporate automated systems, internal audits, and strong internal controls to prevent errors and ensure compliance with all applicable laws.

Cost-benefit analysis represents a valuable tool that supports strategic financial decision-making. This involves systematically comparing the cost of a particular activity with the expected benefits, which is particularly useful when evaluating different options for program implementation or resource allocation. It can help school leaders make informed decisions that optimize the use of resources, enhancing overall efficiency and maximizing the impact of educational expenditures.

Ensuring fiscal compliance and accountability is paramount for maintaining public trust and avoiding legal and financial penalties. School leaders must be thoroughly familiar with all applicable federal, state, and local regulations that govern school finance. Adherence to financial regulations requires diligent monitoring of financial transactions, thorough documentation, and regular internal and external audits. Transparency in financial reporting is critical, providing stakeholders with clear and accurate information about the school's financial status. This active commitment to transparency and accountability ensures the integrity of financial operations, builds public trust, and supports the long-term sustainability of the institution.

Maximizing resource efficiency constitutes a primary focus of effective financial management in education. This involves a comprehensive approach that includes not only optimizing resource allocation but also seeking out cost savings, exploring alternative funding sources, and promoting the use of technology for enhancing productivity. It can also involve shared service agreements, collaborative purchasing, and the implementation of energy conservation programs.

Continuous evaluation of financial practices and a proactive approach to identifying opportunities for improvement ensures that resources are used in the most efficient and effective manner. A commitment to financial transparency ensures that financial decisions are made with the active involvement of various stakeholders, fostering a culture of shared responsibility for fiscal management.

Facilities Management

Effective educational facilities management is crucial for creating safe, efficient, and conducive learning environments that support the academic mission of a school. This comprehensive function extends beyond mere upkeep of buildings to encompass strategic planning, meticulous execution, and a commitment to continuous improvement that directly influences the learning experiences of students and the working conditions of educators. The holistic nature of facilities management demands a nuanced understanding of various interconnected areas, including building maintenance and operations, safety and security protocols, space utilization and planning, environmental sustainability, and emergency preparedness. This interconnectedness necessitates an integrated approach that aligns physical infrastructure with educational objectives, ensuring that every aspect of the school environment contributes positively to the learning process.

Building maintenance and operations form the bedrock of effective facilities management, encompassing a broad array of tasks designed to ensure that school facilities are in optimal working condition. This encompasses routine maintenance activities such as cleaning, repairs, and preventative measures that prevent minor issues from escalating into costly problems. Developing structured maintenance schedules and protocols is essential, typically involving regular inspections, planned maintenance of key systems (like HVAC, plumbing, electrical), and timely repairs. These structured procedures help to avoid disruptions to school operations, prolong the lifespan of the building and its assets, and create a clean and welcoming environment for students and staff. In this respect, a proactive rather than reactive approach to maintenance is key, requiring a systematic approach to addressing potential issues and maintaining facility standards.

Effective maintenance management must be grounded in clear protocols and standards that define the required level of cleanliness and functionality. It involves the creation of work orders, the effective tracking of maintenance activities, and the regular assessment of the effectiveness of maintenance operations. Utilizing a computerized maintenance management system (CMMS) can enhance efficiency, improve the monitoring of maintenance tasks, and provide data for informed decision making. The data gathered in CMMS can assist in identifying persistent issues, informing resource allocations, and ultimately enhancing the effectiveness of maintenance operations, while also ensuring a safe and secure environment, and supporting the effective functioning of the school's educational programs.

Safety and security protocols constitute a critical component of facilities management, with an emphasis on the protection of students, staff, and visitors from potential threats. Implementing robust safety measures involves the development and consistent application of safety inspection procedures, the installation of security systems, and the development of emergency response plans. Safety inspections should be conducted regularly to identify and address hazards, while security systems may include controlled access points, surveillance cameras, and alarm systems. In addition, emergency preparedness requires coordinated action, involving both procedural readiness and a culture of safety. This involves conducting risk assessments to identify potential security threats and developing comprehensive plans to manage those threats effectively, while ensuring compliance with local and national building and safety codes, which provide the legal frameworks for safety and security measures.

Creating a comprehensive safety program also involves proactive measures, such as staff training on safety procedures, awareness programs for students, and regular emergency drills that build capacity to respond to a variety of incidents. School administrators need to promote a security-conscious mindset that focuses on vigilance and reporting of security concerns, fostering a culture of shared responsibility. They also need to be responsive to emerging security challenges, and should seek out resources and information to enhance the security measures in place. Regular safety and security audits are needed to ensure continuous improvement and compliance.

Space utilization and planning is an essential consideration in facilities management, requiring strategic alignment of physical spaces with the needs of students, staff, and the educational programs. This involves analyzing space utilization data, such as class sizes, program requirements, and common areas, to make informed decisions about space allocation. Effective space planning involves optimizing room configurations, providing for adaptable learning spaces, and aligning the layout of facilities with student movement patterns, which can enhance learning outcomes and improve the overall functionality of the school. Long-term space planning is an ongoing process of review and adjustments, requiring a balance of current needs and future requirements, with the use of space mapping tools to visualize utilization patterns.

Effective space planning also involves careful consideration of the types of spaces needed to support different educational activities, including classrooms, labs, libraries, and recreational spaces. Thoughtful design and proper space management can promote student engagement, encourage collaboration, and support varied instructional methods, which are key components of effective education. In addition to academic spaces, common areas such as cafeterias, hallways, and outdoor areas also need careful consideration, designed to support student safety, movement, and interaction. This strategic approach to space utilization can enhance student learning and the operational efficiency of the school.

Environmental sustainability is an increasingly important aspect of facilities management, reflecting a commitment to reducing the ecological footprint of the school and promoting environmental stewardship. The implementation of sustainable practices involves energy and water conservation measures, waste reduction, and the use of environmentally friendly products and materials. Energy conservation efforts may include implementing energy-efficient lighting and HVAC systems, while water conservation can involve low-flow fixtures and landscaping practices that minimize water usage. A comprehensive approach to sustainability will involve integrating sustainable principles into all aspects of the school's operations, and should be an ongoing process that requires regular monitoring and review.

Incorporating sustainability in facilities management involves broader educational goals, creating a school environment that fosters ecological awareness among students and the wider school community. Integrating sustainability into the curriculum, and promoting student engagement in environmental initiatives, can contribute to a culture of sustainability and build capacity for future action. School leaders also need to adopt sustainability as a core institutional value, promoting sustainable practices throughout all of the school's operations and decision-making processes. Ultimately, incorporating sustainability in educational facilities management should reduce environmental impact and create healthier learning environments.

Emergency preparedness is a crucial aspect of facilities management that requires meticulous planning, preparation, and regular practice. It involves developing comprehensive emergency response plans, establishing clear communication protocols, and conducting regular drills. Emergency response plans should cover a wide range of potential emergencies including fire, natural disasters, medical emergencies, and security threats. These plans must be aligned with local, state, and federal guidelines, ensuring that staff are aware of their roles and responsibilities during an emergency. In addition to developing the plans, implementing training for all school personnel is vital to ensure preparedness to respond effectively during emergencies.

Effective emergency management requires a coordinated effort involving school leaders, staff, students, and community stakeholders, as well as regular review and revision of emergency plans, based on feedback from drills and incident analysis. Communication protocols need to be clearly defined, and should include alternative methods of communication to ensure effective information sharing during an emergency. Regular drills are also important to assess the effectiveness of emergency response plans and to identify areas for improvement, and they also serve to reinforce safety procedures, reduce panic, and promote orderly evacuation.

Practical guidance in facilities management involves the use of various tools and processes that facilitate effective operations, beginning with the regular conduct of facility audits, which provide a systematic method for evaluating the conditions of the physical plant. Audits identify needed repairs and areas for improvement, and they support long-term planning. Vendor relationships are another essential element requiring a comprehensive approach to procurement and contract management, ensuring that vendor agreements comply with legal and financial regulations, with the vendor selection based on a transparent and competitive bidding process. Sustainable practices, which are essential for both environmental and economic reasons, require the implementation of sustainable purchasing practices, the use of energy-efficient systems, and the promotion of recycling programs. Long-term facilities plans should align the school's physical infrastructure with its strategic goals, and should include timelines for renovations, expansions, and major maintenance projects. These long-term facility plans should be created with input from stakeholders, and be reviewed regularly to ensure the plans remain relevant.

Integrating facilities management with educational goals and student needs requires a shift away from viewing it as a peripheral activity and instead as a core component of the overall educational mission. This integration requires a holistic understanding of how physical learning environments impact student learning and well-being, thus ensuring facilities align with the school's strategic plan and learning outcomes. A collaborative approach with educational leadership is needed to make certain that facilities management decisions prioritize the needs of students and teachers, and are integrated with educational program objectives. Ultimately, this active alignment promotes a learning environment that supports educational goals and contributes to student success.

Policy Development

Effective educational policy development is a multifaceted endeavor, essential for establishing governance frameworks that support student learning and school operations. The creation of educational policies involves a systematic process that encompasses identifying needs, drafting clear guidelines, ensuring legal compliance, and implementing and evaluating outcomes. The policy creation process often commences with a thorough needs assessment, identifying gaps or areas requiring policy intervention. This initial phase might involve the examination of student performance data, analysis of school climate surveys, and review of existing policies to pinpoint areas where new or revised guidelines are necessary. Data analysis provides a crucial foundation for evidence-based policy development, ensuring that policy initiatives are responsive to the actual needs of the school community. Once policy gaps are identified, the process moves towards drafting the policy, which demands a clear and concise articulation of the policy's purpose, scope, and specific procedures. Effective policies are unambiguous, easily understood by all stakeholders, and provide practical guidance for implementation.

Stakeholder involvement constitutes a critical component of policy development, ensuring that policies are inclusive and reflective of the diverse perspectives within the school community. Including teachers, administrators, parents, students, and community members in the policy development process fosters a sense of ownership and promotes greater adherence to the new guidelines. Stakeholder engagement can take various forms, including open forums, surveys, focus groups, and committee participation. The information gleaned from these diverse sources is invaluable for understanding the potential impacts of proposed policies and making informed adjustments. By providing multiple avenues for stakeholder feedback, educational leaders can build consensus and create policies that are more relevant, equitable, and effective. Collaboration and communication during this phase are essential, ensuring that all stakeholders feel heard and valued, thus promoting a collaborative approach to school governance.

Legal compliance requirements are paramount in the development of educational policies, as policies must adhere to a complex framework of federal, state, and local laws. This entails a thorough understanding of statutes such as the Family Educational Rights and Privacy Act (FERPA), Individuals with Disabilities Education Act (IDEA), Title IX, and Section 504, which protect student privacy, ensure access to education for students with disabilities, prohibit discrimination, and guarantee reasonable accommodations. Furthermore, it is necessary to incorporate state and local educational codes and regulations into policy development, which vary across jurisdictions. A careful review of relevant legislation should be undertaken during policy creation to avoid conflicts and ensure legal soundness. Policies that do not align with legal requirements can expose the school to potential liabilities and legal challenges. In order to ensure compliance, school leaders should engage legal counsel or utilize expertise to guarantee that every policy reflects current legal standards. This step is essential to mitigate risks and uphold the rights of all students and staff.

Effective implementation strategies are vital for translating policy goals into practical action. Implementation involves more than simply disseminating the policy; it requires careful planning, resource allocation, and professional development for those involved in carrying out the policy. A detailed implementation plan should specify timelines, responsibilities, and communication strategies, ensuring that all stakeholders are aware of their roles and the procedures they need to follow. Professional development is an essential aspect of implementation, ensuring that teachers and staff have the necessary knowledge and skills to apply the policy consistently and effectively. Ongoing monitoring during implementation is also needed to identify challenges and make necessary adjustments. Communication should be ongoing, transparent, and proactive, using various mediums to reach all stakeholders. This proactive approach not only mitigates potential resistance but also fosters a culture of continuous improvement and accountability.

Policy evaluation and revision form the final stage of the policy development process, ensuring that policies remain relevant and effective in supporting school goals. The evaluation process should include both quantitative and qualitative data, focusing on assessing the impact of the policy on student outcomes, staff practices, and school climate. Quantitative data might include student achievement data, attendance rates, and disciplinary incidents, while qualitative data could be collected through surveys, interviews, and focus groups. The evaluation should also involve feedback from stakeholders, giving opportunities to share their experience and provide insights for future policy refinement. Based on this data analysis, policies should be revised or refined to address any shortcomings or emerging issues. Policy revision is not a one-time event but an ongoing process of continuous improvement. This cyclical approach to policy development, implementation, and evaluation promotes adaptability and effectiveness, ensuring that school policies remain aligned with the evolving needs of the school community.

Effective policy development demands that educational leaders possess the capacity to recognize policy needs, and the process begins with a thorough needs assessment that involves examining existing data, analyzing stakeholder feedback, and observing the school environment for inconsistencies or gaps. This process requires a deep understanding of the school's strategic goals and a commitment to using data to inform decision-making. For instance, if there is a notable achievement gap among certain student groups, this indicates that a policy focused on equity and inclusion is warranted. This identification of gaps lays the groundwork for creating policies that are directly relevant and impactful.

Drafting clear and effective policies involves using unambiguous language, specifying procedures, and defining roles and responsibilities for implementation. Policies should be structured logically, making use of clear headings, bullet points, and numbered lists to ensure that the content is easy to comprehend. Avoid using technical jargon or ambiguous terms. In order to ensure clarity, define key terms when first introduced. Effective policies should also specify the consequences for non-compliance, ensuring that they are consistently applied across the school community. Additionally, it is important that policies are consistent with legal requirements, school district regulations, and the overall school mission. In developing the policy, make use of templates and resources that are available from educational organizations and legal experts. This meticulous approach contributes to the creation of policies that are not only clear but also actionable.

Ensuring alignment with legal requirements is a critical aspect of policy development, and requires a proactive approach that includes regular monitoring of legal updates and revisions of policies as needed. Compliance involves more than just the initial drafting phase; it entails continuous monitoring to ensure that policies remain in accordance with current laws and regulations. Educational leaders should seek legal expertise and participate in professional development programs that focus on legal issues in education. Staying informed of legal changes and integrating these into policy updates mitigates the risk of legal challenges and promotes a culture of compliance within the school community. This process is an ongoing commitment to legal and ethical standards.

Implementing new policies effectively necessitates careful planning and a systematic approach that prioritizes communication, training, and support. Implementation plans should outline specific steps, timelines, and roles for each stakeholder involved. Providing training to teachers and staff who are required to implement the policy is an essential step, ensuring they understand the new requirements, their roles, and the goals. Support mechanisms, such as mentorship or coaching, should also be made available to guide staff through the implementation process and address challenges. Additionally, it is important to proactively address potential resistance by encouraging open dialogue, soliciting feedback, and emphasizing the rationale behind the new policy. This multifaceted approach ensures that policy implementation is both effective and embraced by the school community.

Monitoring policy effectiveness should be a systematic and ongoing process, employing a range of data collection methods to assess impact and make informed adjustments. Regular monitoring provides opportunities to review policy implementation and to measure progress toward the policy goals. Data should be collected from multiple sources such as student assessments, behavior data, survey results, and feedback from staff and parents. Analyzing data can assist in assessing the extent to which the policy is achieving its stated outcomes and identify areas for improvement. Based on this data analysis, policies should be revised or refined as needed. The evaluation process must be transparent, involving stakeholders in discussions about the collected data and necessary modifications. This transparent approach fosters a culture of accountability and continuous improvement.

Practical exercises play a key role in building capacity for policy development within school leadership teams. A policy writing and revision exercise should focus on crafting a new policy based on a specific need identified by the school, and in this exercise, participants will learn to draft policies using clear language and logical structure. They will develop skills in structuring policies, writing effective procedures, and incorporating legal requirements. Additionally, policy revision exercises are essential, allowing participants to take an existing policy and revise it in light of new information, feedback, and legal requirements. Stakeholder communication exercises should emphasize the importance of effectively conveying policy information to diverse audiences. Participants will learn to design communication plans that use various methods, ensuring that all stakeholders have a clear understanding of the policy and their roles in its implementation.

Implementation planning exercises should teach educational leaders to design comprehensive strategies for policy implementation, with emphasis on timelines, resource allocation, and role assignments. They should learn to develop detailed plans that outline each phase of implementation and address potential challenges. Additionally, they will explore techniques for training staff and engaging the school community. Policy evaluation methods exercises focus on building skills in data collection and analysis, teaching participants how to design evaluation plans, gather relevant data, and interpret the results to measure policy effectiveness. Through these exercises, participants can gain the necessary knowledge for evaluating the policy impact and make informed revisions, thereby promoting an ongoing process of improvement.

Maintaining current and relevant policies that support school improvement goals requires consistent attention and a proactive approach. Policy management should involve regular reviews to ensure that policies remain effective, relevant, and aligned with the school's goals, as well as changes in legal, community, and educational best practices. These reviews should utilize data and feedback to assess the impact of current policies, and to identify areas where revision or new policy creation is required. Regular monitoring of policy effectiveness, coupled with consistent stakeholder engagement, ensures that school policies are not static but instead adapt to the school's changing needs. This ongoing approach to policy management is essential for supporting continuous improvement, and ensuring that the school's governance structures are aligned with its educational mission.

Organizational Systems

Organizational systems in educational leadership are foundational to creating efficient and effective school operations, requiring a comprehensive approach that integrates various components to ensure a cohesive and productive environment. Systems thinking, a crucial framework in this context, necessitates that educational leaders view their institutions not as isolated parts but as interconnected entities, where changes in one area inevitably affect others. This holistic approach requires that leaders understand the complex interactions within a school system and how each component contributes to the overall performance. Implementing systems thinking involves mapping the different parts of the school organization, identifying their interactions, and assessing the impact of changes across the entire system. Leaders must, therefore, move beyond linear cause-and-effect thinking to embrace a more dynamic and systemic view of their organizations. This perspective is especially critical when implementing new policies, initiating strategic changes, or addressing systemic issues, as it enables leaders to anticipate potential impacts and optimize their interventions.

The design of organizational structures in schools is critical for establishing clear lines of authority, defining responsibilities, and facilitating smooth operations. An effectively designed structure promotes coordination, accountability, and communication, and its configuration is not universal but should be tailored to the unique context and needs of each school. A hierarchical structure, for example, is characterized by a clear chain of command, which ensures that all staff members are aware of their reporting relationships and responsibilities. In such systems, decision-making is typically centralized, which can facilitate efficient responses to operational issues. In contrast, a flatter structure promotes greater collaboration, decentralizing decision-making and empowering staff at all levels. This approach may encourage innovation and adaptability, but it also requires well-defined communication protocols and a collaborative organizational culture. Matrix structures, a third alternative, are often used when a school needs to combine functional and project-based operations, thus creating cross-functional teams that address specific initiatives. Regardless of the structure chosen, clarity in roles and responsibilities is paramount. This clarity minimizes confusion, avoids duplication of effort, and ensures that all staff members understand how their work contributes to the school's overall goals.

Effective communication systems are the lifeblood of a functional educational organization. They ensure that information is transmitted accurately, promptly, and consistently across all levels of the school community. A robust communication system should include both formal channels, like staff meetings and written memos, and informal channels, such as casual conversations and online communication platforms. Formal channels are essential for disseminating official policies, procedures, and updates, and their effectiveness relies on clarity, timeliness, and appropriate media selection, which might include email, newsletters, or dedicated communication portals. Informal channels, on the other hand, are important for fostering a sense of community, building trust, and promoting open dialogue. These channels can include informal meetings, online forums, or social events, and should be used to facilitate a collaborative environment. Effective leaders are adept at both creating and maintaining effective communication systems, using multiple channels to reach all stakeholders and ensure that information flows freely and transparently within the school organization. They also actively seek feedback to improve communication practices and address any barriers that may exist.

Decision-making processes within educational institutions must be both efficient and inclusive, balancing the need for timely action with the importance of stakeholder input. A well-defined decision-making framework provides clear guidelines on who is involved in the decision-making process, what criteria are used to evaluate options, and how decisions are communicated to stakeholders. Centralized decision-making models typically place authority at the top of the organizational hierarchy, which allows for consistent and rapid decision-making. Decentralized approaches, by contrast, involve teachers, staff, and parents, which fosters a collaborative environment. A participatory decision-making approach actively engages stakeholders in the process, considering diverse perspectives and promoting ownership of the decisions made. Whatever the chosen approach, the decision-making process should be transparent, ensuring that the rationale behind decisions is clearly communicated to all affected parties. This transparency builds trust, reduces resistance to change, and promotes a sense of shared responsibility within the school community.

Change management strategies are essential for navigating the complexities of organizational transformation within educational settings, particularly as these institutions adapt to evolving societal needs and pedagogical advances. These strategies must consider the potential for disruption, resistance, and the necessity for collaborative effort, and therefore effective implementation requires careful planning, clear communication, and continuous evaluation. The process typically involves diagnosing the need for change, developing a clear vision, building stakeholder support, implementing the change gradually, and monitoring its impact. Effective leaders recognize that change is a continuous process, not a singular event, and therefore they adopt a systemic approach, adjusting their strategies as needed to ensure that change is sustainable and impactful. Overcoming resistance to change, which is a common challenge, requires strategies like involving stakeholders in the process, creating open communication channels, and addressing concerns proactively. Tools like change management plans, communication protocols, and evaluation templates can significantly enhance the effectiveness of change initiatives, ensuring that the changes are not only implemented but also integrated into the long-term practices of the school.

Master scheduling, a core operational component, is instrumental in optimizing resource allocation and facilitating the smooth delivery of curriculum within educational settings. Master schedules should be created by taking into consideration student needs, instructional priorities, staff availability, and facility constraints. Effective master schedules minimize conflicts, maximize instructional time, and support equitable access to educational resources for all students. The development process involves a meticulous analysis of data on student enrollment, course requests, and teacher qualifications, followed by strategic allocation of time and resources. Technology tools can be invaluable in this process, providing the capacity for modeling different scheduling scenarios and optimizing the schedule to meet school-specific needs. A well-designed master schedule reflects the school's educational priorities and promotes efficiency in the use of time and resources, fostering a structured and predictable environment that supports effective teaching and learning.

Information flow management within a school organization involves ensuring that critical information is communicated effectively to the right people at the right time. This requires creating clear communication pathways, utilizing appropriate technology, and establishing protocols for information dissemination. Effective information flow prevents miscommunication, reduces errors, and ensures that all stakeholders have the information they need to perform their roles efficiently. Information management systems may include a variety of tools and strategies, such as using digital communication platforms, developing standard reporting templates, and implementing regular communication meetings. Leaders should monitor these systems continuously to identify any bottlenecks and to optimize the flow of information within the organization. A well-managed information system enhances transparency, promotes collaboration, and ultimately improves the overall efficiency of the school operations.

Process improvement, a critical aspect of organizational leadership, entails systematically reviewing and optimizing operational processes to enhance efficiency, effectiveness, and outcomes. This process begins with an analysis of current practices, followed by the identification of areas for improvement and the implementation of changes designed to achieve higher performance. The improvement of processes often involves the use of tools and methodologies such as Lean, Six Sigma, and process mapping, all of which offer structured approaches to problem-solving and process optimization. For example, process mapping can visually represent the steps involved in a particular process, allowing leaders to identify inefficiencies and potential bottlenecks. The implementation of improvement initiatives is typically followed by data collection to measure the impact of changes. Continuous monitoring and evaluation are essential to ensure that improvements are sustainable and contribute to the overall goals of the school. Leaders who are dedicated to continuous process improvement foster a culture of efficiency and effectiveness within their organizations.

System evaluation and adjustment are essential for ensuring that organizational systems remain relevant and effective in supporting the school's mission. Evaluation involves gathering and analyzing data on system performance, assessing the impact of systems on student outcomes, and identifying areas that require adjustments or improvements. The evaluation process should be both formative, which involves ongoing assessment and feedback, and summative, which provides a comprehensive analysis of the system's performance at specific intervals. Formative evaluations assist in making continuous improvements to the system, while summative evaluations provide insight into the overall effectiveness of the system and guide future policy and system revisions. The evaluation process should be data-driven and should involve stakeholders at all levels of the school community. Based on the evaluation findings, adjustments should be made to the systems to ensure that they continue to meet the needs of the school. This continuous loop of evaluation and adjustment ensures that school organizational systems are dynamic, adaptable, and supportive of continuous improvement.

The integration of all organizational leadership components, from strategic planning to operational systems, is essential for creating a cohesive and effective school environment. These components are not isolated entities, but rather interconnected parts of a larger whole, each contributing to the school's overall effectiveness. Strategic leadership provides direction, while instructional leadership focuses on teaching and learning. Climate and cultural leadership create a positive environment, while ethical leadership establishes the values and principles that guide the school. Organizational leadership then provides the structure and systems needed to translate these goals into concrete action. When these components work together in harmony, a school can maximize its efficiency, optimize its resources, and ultimately provide the best possible educational experience for its students. This requires a leadership approach that is both strategic and holistic, emphasizing collaboration, communication, and continuous improvement.

6

COMMUNITY ENGAGEMENT LEADERSHIP

Stakeholder Engagement

Stakeholder engagement, a cornerstone of effective community leadership, necessitates a clear understanding of who the stakeholders are within the educational ecosystem, encompassing a wide array of individuals and groups that are invested in the success of a school or district. These stakeholders include, but are not limited to, students, parents, teachers, administrators, support staff, local businesses, community organizations, alumni, and governmental entities. Each stakeholder group brings a unique set of perspectives, needs, and resources to the educational setting; therefore, a nuanced understanding of their roles is essential for school leaders seeking to foster collaborative and supportive environments. The engagement of these varied groups is crucial, as it directly influences student outcomes, school climate, and the overall effectiveness of the educational system.

To initiate the process of effective engagement, a comprehensive stakeholder analysis is essential, which typically begins with the identification and mapping of the individuals and groups that have a vested interest in the school's performance and operations. This mapping exercise categorizes stakeholders based on their level of influence and interest, allowing school leaders to prioritize engagement efforts. Stakeholder analysis methodologies often involve creating a matrix or diagram that visually represents stakeholders, which helps in understanding the relationships between various stakeholders and their potential impact on school initiatives. Mapping also entails the examination of different power dynamics, acknowledging that some groups may have more influence than others, and that all stakeholders must be engaged, even those who have less influence, to ensure a comprehensive understanding of community needs. Prioritization of stakeholder engagement is crucial, as resources and time are not unlimited. Therefore, leaders must decide which stakeholders are most critical to the success of a particular project or initiative.

Identifying and prioritizing the needs of diverse stakeholders requires multiple methods of data gathering. Surveys are a common method used to collect broad feedback about stakeholder satisfaction and concerns. Focus groups with smaller, targeted groups of stakeholders provide a platform for more in-depth discussions and exploration of complex issues. One-on-one interviews allow for personalized understanding of individual perspectives and experiences. These qualitative and quantitative methods provide varied insights, allowing leaders to identify common themes and specific needs. Analysis of these varied perspectives often reveals nuanced differences within stakeholder groups; for example, parents of elementary students may have distinct needs from those of secondary students, or teachers of special education may have needs different from general education teachers. Prioritizing stakeholder needs is not a simple process; it involves balancing the needs of various stakeholders and making decisions that serve the overall mission of the school. This involves considering the potential impact of various decisions on different groups, while aiming to foster equity and inclusion.

Effective engagement strategies must be tailored to the unique characteristics and preferences of each stakeholder group. For instance, parents may prefer face-to-face meetings, while teachers may value online collaboration tools, and students might be most responsive to peer-led initiatives. Teachers and administrators often benefit from structured professional development sessions or workshops that address specific needs, while students require active learning approaches to foster genuine engagement. Local businesses and community organizations can be engaged through partnerships, joint projects, or volunteer opportunities, promoting a shared sense of responsibility and contribution to the school's mission. Building effective partnerships involves establishing clear communication channels, outlining shared goals, and creating opportunities for collaborative work. It is also essential to be mindful of cultural differences and communication styles that may affect stakeholders' ability to engage, ensuring inclusivity and respect across diverse groups.

To ensure that the engagement efforts are effective and yielding positive outcomes, tools for measuring and evaluating stakeholder engagement are essential. Regular feedback mechanisms such as surveys, feedback forms, and suggestion boxes provide ongoing information about the level of engagement and satisfaction among stakeholders. Analyzing participation rates in various activities and events is also a practical measure of engagement levels, showing which efforts are working and which need adjustment. Data analysis of student performance, school climate, and other key indicators can also provide evidence of the impact of stakeholder engagement on educational outcomes. Evaluation methods should be both quantitative, using metrics such as survey scores and participation rates, and qualitative, gathering narrative data about the experiences of stakeholders. The analysis should focus on the alignment of school activities with stakeholder needs, indicating where improvements are necessary.

Successful stakeholder engagement programs often share common characteristics. For example, the implementation of a parent leadership program can involve parents in school decision-making processes, resulting in increased parent involvement, improved school-family relationships, and a more positive school climate. Schools that have created a student advisory council that meets regularly with school leaders and provides input on school policies and initiatives have proven to improve student engagement and promote a more responsive school environment. The establishment of business partnerships that involve mentoring, internships, or financial support often results in mutually beneficial outcomes, providing resources for the school and opportunities for local businesses to connect with their communities. These examples highlight the importance of strategic planning, clear communication, shared responsibility, and a collaborative spirit as key components for effective stakeholder engagement. The analysis of these programs often reveals that building trust and demonstrating respect for all stakeholders is foundational to their success.

Despite the benefits of stakeholder engagement, challenges often emerge that can hinder effective partnership building. Resistance from stakeholders, particularly when facing change, can be a significant barrier, requiring proactive measures to engage stakeholders in the change process. Overcoming this resistance involves clear communication about the reasons for change, engaging stakeholders in discussions, and addressing their concerns with sensitivity. Time constraints, limited resources, and logistical challenges can make engagement more difficult, requiring creative and flexible strategies to reach all stakeholders. Effective resource management strategies, such as using technology to facilitate communication and collaboration, can be used to overcome these challenges. The implementation of culturally sensitive engagement strategies that accommodate differences in language, cultural background, and communication styles is also important. Addressing these challenges requires a systematic approach, a willingness to adapt, and the commitment of all involved parties to the common goal of improving education.

Maintaining long-term stakeholder relationships requires a continuous effort of communication, collaboration, and mutual respect. It is important that school leaders build strong personal relationships with stakeholders through regular interaction and communication. Open communication channels should be established to facilitate ongoing dialogue, providing opportunities for feedback and addressing concerns as they arise. Formal communication, including emails and newsletters, is essential, but also opportunities for informal conversations should be provided. Regular feedback mechanisms, such as periodic surveys and focus groups, enable schools to monitor the effectiveness of stakeholder engagement efforts and make necessary adjustments. Inclusive engagement, in particular, is essential for ensuring that all stakeholders feel valued, respected, and empowered. Cultivating a culture of collaboration, shared responsibility, and transparent communication is important, ensuring that the school community is working together towards a common goal of educational excellence.

Best practices for maintaining long-term stakeholder relationships often include the creation of a shared vision that is collaboratively developed with all stakeholders and is widely communicated, ensuring all stakeholders understand the goals of the school. Regularly recognizing the contributions of stakeholders fosters a sense of belonging and reinforces the value of their engagement. Regular communication updates should focus on the progress the school is making, helping stakeholders understand the effectiveness of their contribution to the school's mission. Continuous evaluation and adaptation, in particular, are essential components of a successful engagement plan, allowing schools to identify areas for improvement, adjust strategies to meet evolving needs, and ensure inclusivity. Ultimately, successful stakeholder engagement is an ongoing process that requires commitment, communication, and collaboration, building strong and supportive relationships that benefit the entire school community.

Communication Strategies

Effective communication strategies in educational leadership are essential for fostering transparency, building trust, and ensuring the smooth operation of educational institutions. These strategies encompass various components, from selecting appropriate communication channels to crafting clear and consistent messages, and they must also be sensitive to diverse cultural contexts. The strategic deployment of diverse communication channels, including newsletters, social media, and direct communications, requires thoughtful planning to ensure that the message reaches its intended audience effectively.

Different communication channels serve distinct purposes and necessitate careful selection based on the specific context and objectives of the communication. For instance, email remains a cornerstone of formal communication in educational settings, allowing for detailed messages, attachments, and record-keeping. It is particularly suitable for conveying important updates to staff, parents, and community members, such as policy changes, meeting notices, or academic progress reports. In contrast, school newsletters, whether print or digital, provide a more comprehensive platform for sharing school news, celebrating student achievements, and highlighting upcoming events. These are typically distributed periodically, serving as a valuable resource for keeping the community informed about school activities and initiatives. Social media platforms, such as Twitter, Facebook, and Instagram, offer opportunities for real-time engagement with a broader audience. These channels are ideal for sharing quick updates, promoting school events, and showcasing positive aspects of the school community. However, they must be managed carefully to ensure accurate information and positive representation of the school. Direct communications, such as phone calls and in-person meetings, facilitate immediate feedback and personal interaction. Phone calls may be utilized to address specific concerns or to provide urgent updates, while face-to-face meetings allow for more in-depth discussions and relationship building. The use of multiple channels ensures that information is accessible to stakeholders with diverse preferences and needs, promoting comprehensive communication.

Creating clear and consistent messaging across diverse communication platforms requires a cohesive communication strategy. This involves crafting messages that are not only clear and concise but also aligned with the school's overall mission and values. Consistent branding, including the school's logo and visual elements, reinforces the school's identity and facilitates easy recognition across various platforms. Consistent messaging ensures that all stakeholders receive the same information regardless of the communication channel used. A well-defined communication calendar helps to plan and schedule communication activities in advance, ensuring a steady stream of information and preventing information overload. Centralizing communication responsibilities with a dedicated team or individual ensures that messages are consistent, accurate, and disseminated in a timely manner. Utilizing message templates that are adaptable to various contexts and channels can ensure consistency and efficiency. For example, standardized templates can be used for parent notifications, emergency alerts, and general school announcements, streamlining communication processes. This unified approach helps stakeholders to easily access and process information, contributing to a clearer understanding and a stronger sense of community engagement.

Developing robust crisis communication protocols is a vital component of effective educational leadership. These protocols should outline procedures for responding to various types of emergencies, such as natural disasters, security threats, or public health crises. A crisis communication plan includes a clear chain of command, identifying who is responsible for what during an emergency. This structure ensures that communication is coordinated and that information is delivered accurately. Pre-defined communication channels, such as dedicated emergency notification systems, ensure that stakeholders receive timely alerts and instructions during critical situations. These systems may include text messages, email notifications, and website updates. Clear and concise messages should be pre-drafted, if possible, and adapted as needed for each situation to avoid confusion and misinformation. Training for staff members on crisis communication protocols is critical, including regular drills and simulations to prepare them for responding to different types of emergencies effectively. This preparation ensures that stakeholders receive clear, accurate, and timely information in the event of a crisis. A designated spokesperson, who is trained in crisis communication techniques, acts as the primary point of contact for all media inquiries to control the flow of information and to prevent misinformation. Post-crisis evaluations and debriefings provide opportunities to learn from past events and make adjustments to the crisis communication protocols, ensuring continuous improvement and a more robust system.

Cultural sensitivity is an indispensable consideration in all communication strategies in the educational system. Schools are often composed of diverse communities, including different cultural backgrounds, languages, and communication styles. Culturally sensitive communication involves awareness and respect for these differences. Translation and interpretation services are crucial for ensuring that all stakeholders, including parents and guardians who may not speak the dominant language, have access to important information. Using inclusive language and avoiding idioms or slang that may not be universally understood helps to create accessible and equitable communication. Providing communications in various formats, such as written, audio, or visual, helps to accommodate different learning styles and preferences. Seeking input from diverse groups ensures that communication strategies are culturally relevant and inclusive. Creating communication materials that are representative of the diversity of the school community helps to build trust and strengthen relationships. Cultural competency training for staff and leaders fosters a deeper understanding of cultural differences and promotes more effective communication practices. Such training can include exploring cultural nuances, addressing biases, and practicing communication techniques that foster inclusivity and understanding. Utilizing a variety of channels to communicate with families, such as face-to-face meetings, phone calls, and virtual platforms, allows flexibility to meet families' specific needs.

Practical examples of communication templates are essential for facilitating clear and efficient communication within an educational context. A well-designed newsletter, whether print or electronic, is a useful way to disseminate information about school activities and achievements. It includes a consistent header that displays the school name and logo, and a table of contents for easy navigation. The content of the newsletter should be organized into sections, including updates from the principal, student and staff spotlights, upcoming events, and reminders. Using high-quality photos or graphics can enhance visual appeal and engagement, while short, engaging paragraphs ensure readability. Newsletters should also include contact information for school staff or other key contacts.

Social media guidelines are also important for schools using these platforms. These guidelines should establish clear expectations for staff and student use of social media, emphasizing responsible communication and the importance of maintaining privacy. Policies should address what content is acceptable for posting, ensuring that all content is aligned with the school's mission and values. Schools need to specify that social media accounts must be managed by designated staff members and that monitoring and evaluation are performed regularly. Guidelines should also address the potential risks of using social media, including cyberbullying and sharing private information. It is also important to establish appropriate procedures for handling online conflicts and for protecting students' online safety.

Parent communication protocols are another key aspect of a sound communication strategy. These protocols should outline the methods for communicating with parents about their children's academic progress, behavioral issues, and other important matters. Regular communication should occur at various levels of the organization, from teachers to administration. Regular communication channels include progress reports, parent-teacher conferences, emails, and phone calls. Protocols should also specify procedures for communicating sensitive information, ensuring student privacy and maintaining confidentiality. It is also important to use a variety of communication channels to meet diverse needs, ensuring that all parents have access to critical information. Protocols should address parental concerns promptly and respectfully, encouraging two-way communication to foster open and collaborative relationships.

Emergency notification systems should also be well-defined and reliable. These systems should include multiple channels for disseminating emergency alerts, such as text messages, email notifications, website updates, and public address announcements, to ensure timely communication during critical situations. They should also be accessible for all stakeholders, including those with disabilities or those who do not speak the dominant language. Emergency notification systems should include regular testing, drills, and training to ensure their reliability and efficacy. Protocols for activating and managing the system should be clear, and those responsible for managing the emergency communication should receive regular training. These systems should be user-friendly and allow designated staff members to send alerts swiftly and efficiently.

Case studies provide valuable insights into the effectiveness of various communication strategies in educational leadership. One example of a successful communication scenario could be a school implementing a new curriculum using a multi-faceted communication approach. The school began with a series of informational meetings for parents and teachers, detailing the reasons for the change and addressing concerns. Regular updates were provided through the school website, newsletters, and social media channels. Teachers received ongoing professional development and support, which ensured the success of the implementation. This resulted in widespread understanding and support of the curriculum changes, which led to better implementation of the curriculum, and positive student outcomes. This case highlights the importance of transparent, multi-channel communication, as well as stakeholder engagement.

In contrast, a problematic communication scenario might involve a school that experienced a sudden crisis with the school building and did not communicate effectively. In this case, the initial communication was limited, and details were scarce, resulting in widespread confusion and anxiety among parents and staff. The lack of clear information allowed for rumors and misinformation to spread quickly, which further exacerbated the situation. This lack of effective communication resulted in mistrust and a negative perception of the school's leadership. This case study highlights the critical need for well-defined crisis communication protocols, emphasizing the importance of prompt, clear, and accurate information dissemination during emergencies. These cases indicate the importance of two-way communication and feedback mechanisms, which allow stakeholders to share their input, concerns, and suggestions.

Partnership Development

The establishment and cultivation of meaningful partnerships between schools and community organizations represent a critical facet of effective educational leadership, providing access to diverse resources and fostering a supportive environment for student development. This process, which encompasses the identification of potential partners, the development of compelling proposals, the creation of mutually beneficial agreements, the maintenance of sustainable collaborations, and the rigorous evaluation of partnership effectiveness, requires strategic planning and ongoing commitment. Effective engagement with external stakeholders can significantly enhance the educational experience, creating a synergy between the academic environment and the broader community.

The initial step in developing such partnerships involves identifying potential community organizations that align with the school's goals and objectives. This requires a comprehensive needs assessment, which analyzes the school's resources, identifies gaps, and determines areas where external support could be beneficial. This analysis considers various aspects of school operations, such as academic enrichment, extracurricular activities, student support services, and community outreach initiatives. Potential partners may include local businesses, universities, non-profit organizations, government agencies, and other community groups. This identification process should be informed by data on student demographics, academic performance, and community needs. The selection of partners should be based on their ability to provide resources, expertise, or opportunities that directly benefit the school and its students. For instance, if the school seeks to enhance STEM education, partnering with a local tech company or university engineering department could provide access to cutting-edge resources and expert mentorship. Similarly, collaborations with non-profit organizations specializing in youth development or social services could offer crucial support for at-risk students or underserved populations. The process should not only focus on immediate needs but also on fostering long-term relationships that can evolve and adapt to the changing needs of the school. Schools can utilize a variety of methods, including community surveys, stakeholder meetings, and online databases, to identify organizations that share similar goals. This proactive approach helps in creating a pool of potential partners who are genuinely interested in supporting the school's mission.

Following the identification of potential partners, the next critical step involves developing partnership proposals that clearly articulate the intended benefits for all parties involved. A well-structured proposal outlines the goals of the partnership, the specific activities that will be undertaken, the roles and responsibilities of each partner, the resources that will be contributed, the anticipated outcomes, and the timelines for implementation. The proposal should be tailored to the specific interests and capabilities of the potential partner, demonstrating a clear understanding of their mission and priorities. This customized approach ensures that the proposal is perceived as a valuable opportunity rather than a generic request for assistance. It should also include an explanation of the alignment between the partnership activities and the school's strategic plan. This alignment demonstrates a strategic approach to partnership development and helps ensure that collaborations contribute to the school's overarching educational goals. The proposal should also highlight the potential impact on students, teachers, and the broader community. This focus on positive impact helps to create a shared vision and motivates potential partners to invest their time and resources. The development of proposals involves a collaborative effort that includes teachers, administrators, and sometimes community stakeholders, ensuring a comprehensive representation of the school's needs and perspectives. Furthermore, proposals should be clear and concise, avoiding jargon or technical terms that may be unfamiliar to potential partners. This enhances readability and makes it easier for partners to understand the scope and objectives of the proposed collaboration. The proposal should also incorporate a budget outlining the financial resources required and a detailed timeline showing the phasing of project activities.

The establishment of mutual benefit agreements is essential to creating sustainable partnerships based on shared values and clear expectations. These agreements, which are often formalized through written contracts or memoranda of understanding (MOUs), stipulate the terms of the partnership, outlining the specific obligations, commitments, and responsibilities of each partner. A well-crafted mutual benefit agreement delineates the scope of the collaboration, ensuring that all parties understand the parameters of the partnership. It specifies the type of services or resources that will be provided by each partner, as well as any required timelines or performance metrics. A clearly defined legal framework protects both parties and prevents misunderstandings. The agreement should include clauses relating to intellectual property, confidentiality, and liability, addressing any potential legal issues that may arise. Moreover, it should incorporate a dispute resolution process to facilitate the smooth resolution of any conflicts that may emerge during the course of the partnership. It should articulate the expected outcomes and specify how the success of the partnership will be measured. This aspect ensures that partners are held accountable for their contributions and that progress is tracked effectively. The agreements should also include a clause for regular review and revision, allowing the partnership to evolve and adapt to the changing needs and priorities of both the school and the community organization. The MOU should not only include legal elements but also should reflect the shared values, goals, and objectives, which builds trust and ensures that all parties are working towards a common purpose. Including specific examples of anticipated activities within the agreement makes the expectations transparent and reduces confusion. The agreement should also specify the point person from each organization who will be responsible for the partnership's implementation, facilitating clear lines of communication and accountability.

Maintaining sustainable partnerships requires continuous effort and open communication, which also involves regular meetings between school and community partners, allowing for updates on progress, addressing challenges, and identifying new opportunities. This collaborative approach ensures that the partnership remains relevant and responsive to the evolving needs of the school and the community. A proactive communication plan should be developed that outlines the channels and frequency of communication. This plan should include various methods, such as email updates, scheduled meetings, and collaborative online platforms, to ensure that all partners are kept informed and engaged. Active engagement by school leadership, teachers, and support staff is crucial to the partnership's success. This involvement ensures that there is a broad understanding and support for the partnership's goals and activities across the school community. Regular feedback should be solicited from both the school and the community partners to identify areas for improvement, to enhance collaboration, and to address any concerns. This feedback mechanism should be formalized through surveys, focus groups, or informal meetings. Recognition of contributions by partners is an important strategy for maintaining strong relationships. This recognition could take various forms, such as public acknowledgments, awards, or participation in school events. Demonstrating appreciation helps to foster goodwill and reinforces the importance of the partnership. Another component of maintaining long-term partnerships is flexibility. The collaboration should be adaptable to changing circumstances, ensuring that the partnership remains relevant and valuable over time. This flexibility requires open-mindedness and a willingness to adjust plans and strategies as needed. This flexibility can also involve developing new initiatives within the framework of the agreement to meet emerging needs or capitalize on new opportunities.

The evaluation of partnership effectiveness is essential for ensuring that collaborations are achieving their intended goals and providing valuable outcomes for all parties involved. This evaluation process should involve regular assessments of the partnership activities and their impact on students, teachers, and the school community. Data collection methods should include surveys, interviews, observations, and analysis of student performance data. The evaluation should examine both quantitative and qualitative outcomes, including measurable improvements in student achievement, as well as less tangible but equally important aspects such as increased student engagement, improved school climate, and strengthened community relationships. The evaluation should be conducted in a collaborative manner, involving all partners, to promote transparency, mutual understanding, and accountability. Feedback from the evaluation should be used to inform the ongoing development of the partnership, allowing for adjustments to be made as needed to maximize its effectiveness. Evaluation findings should also be shared with relevant stakeholders, including school staff, parents, and community members, to promote broader awareness and support for the collaboration. The evaluation should not only focus on immediate outcomes but also on the long-term sustainability of the partnership. This includes assessing the partnership's financial viability, the commitment of partners, and the alignment with the school's strategic goals. Regular reviews of the partnership agreements should be conducted to ensure that the terms and conditions continue to meet the needs of all parties. The evaluation should also consider external factors that may impact the partnership's effectiveness, such as changes in the community environment or shifts in educational priorities. This holistic approach ensures that the evaluation process is comprehensive and that the partnership is effectively serving its intended purpose. Evaluation data should also be used to demonstrate the value of the partnership to external stakeholders, which helps to secure future funding and support.

Specific examples of successful school-community partnerships highlight the diverse forms that these collaborations can take. Business partnerships that create internship programs provide students with valuable real-world experiences, preparing them for future careers. These partnerships allow students to apply what they have learned in the classroom to real-world settings and to develop essential skills for the workforce. University collaborations involve partnerships with higher education institutions that provide access to research facilities, expertise, and opportunities for dual enrollment. These partnerships enrich the curriculum and provide students with a pathway to higher education. Partnerships with non-profit organizations can address specific needs, such as social-emotional learning, mental health support, or enrichment activities for at-risk students. These partnerships are essential for providing crucial support services that the school may not be able to offer on its own. Relationships with government agencies may provide funding, resources, or access to specialized programs. These relationships are important for leveraging community assets and for maximizing support for students and families. These examples demonstrate the varied ways that schools can engage with their communities to support student success.

The implementation of templates for partnership agreements and evaluation tools is important for streamlining the partnership development process and ensuring consistency. A standardized partnership agreement template should include sections for outlining the parties involved, the purpose of the partnership, the specific roles and responsibilities, the resource commitments, the timelines, and the legal provisions. Evaluation templates should include metrics for assessing partnership outcomes, such as surveys, checklists, and rubric. These templates should be customizable to meet the unique needs of each partnership.

Scaling successful partnerships involves replicating effective models in other settings or expanding the scope of existing collaborations. This process requires careful planning, documentation of best practices, and training of staff and stakeholders. Common challenges in partnership development include resistance to change, resource limitations, communication breakdowns, and conflicting priorities among partners. These challenges can be addressed through open communication, collaboration, and the creation of clear expectations. Leadership support, adequate resources, and a focus on mutual benefit are essential for overcoming these challenges and creating sustainable partnerships that enhance the educational experience for all students.

Community Resources

The process of identifying, accessing, and leveraging community resources represents a critical aspect of effective educational leadership, directly influencing a school's capacity to provide comprehensive support and enrichment opportunities for its students. This endeavor necessitates a systematic approach, encompassing the mapping of community assets, the development of resource databases, the creation of sustainable sharing networks, and the maximization of resource utilization. Each of these components requires a strategic focus, guided by a clear understanding of community dynamics and a commitment to data-driven decision-making. By effectively integrating community resources into the educational ecosystem, schools can enhance academic programs, bolster student support services, and foster a more vibrant and inclusive learning environment.

The initial step in this strategic approach is the meticulous mapping of community assets and resources. This process requires a detailed understanding of the diverse entities that operate within the school's vicinity, including non-profit organizations, local businesses, government agencies, cultural institutions, and volunteer groups. Conducting a comprehensive community resource assessment is essential to accurately identify these assets, which are categorized by their function and capacity to support educational goals. Various data-gathering methods are employed in the assessment process, such as surveys distributed to local organizations and businesses, interviews with community leaders, focus groups with parents and other stakeholders, and detailed reviews of publicly available information, such as online directories and agency reports. The surveys, for example, are designed to collect specific information about each organization, such as its mission, services provided, target population, geographic reach, and contact information. These detailed surveys enable the collection of relevant information that can be used to identify alignment between the needs of the school and the capacity of potential partners. Interviews with community leaders and representatives of these organizations provide additional insight into the nuances of the community's resources, identifying both the strengths and the challenges, as well as the organizations' willingness to engage in partnerships with educational institutions. This qualitative approach is valuable for understanding the broader social context and fostering relationships with key community stakeholders. Focus groups involving parents, teachers, and students allow educators to gain an understanding of the community from multiple perspectives and to identify specific unmet needs within the student population. By combining quantitative data from surveys with qualitative insights, a comprehensive picture of the available community resources is constructed and then analyzed for its relevance to the educational context. The data is then organized into a format that facilitates the quick identification of opportunities, gaps, and priorities, informing subsequent steps in resource development.

Following the asset mapping, the development of a resource database is essential for effective access and management of identified resources. A resource database serves as a centralized repository of information, providing school personnel with a comprehensive overview of the available community support. It typically includes detailed profiles of each organization or entity, encompassing information gathered during the community resource assessment, including the organization's name, contact information, mission statement, services provided, target population, service area, program schedules, eligibility criteria, and the process for accessing their services. A well-structured resource database includes a robust search functionality, allowing school staff to quickly locate appropriate resources based on specific criteria, such as the type of service, target population, or geographical proximity. This functionality is critical for facilitating prompt response to urgent needs or to find specialized support services for students with unique requirements. The database is designed to be user-friendly, with an intuitive interface, ensuring accessibility for all school staff members. Additionally, regular updates and maintenance are required to maintain the accuracy and currency of the resource database. This involves routinely verifying the contact information, service details, and operating hours of each listed organization. This ensures that the database remains a reliable and credible tool for school administrators, teachers, and counselors. The resource database also includes a feature for reporting usage and feedback. This enables the school to track which community resources are being utilized, to identify gaps in services, and to make informed decisions about resource allocation and partnership development. This data-driven approach to resource management ensures that the database is continuously improved and adapted to meet the evolving needs of the school community. Furthermore, ethical considerations are integral to the database design, particularly in terms of data privacy and confidentiality. Ensuring the database adheres to relevant privacy regulations, particularly regarding student and family information, is crucial.

The next crucial phase is the establishment of sustainable resource-sharing networks that foster collaborative relationships among schools and community organizations. These networks are predicated on the principle of mutual benefit, ensuring that partnerships are equitable and sustainable over time. The development of resource-sharing agreements is critical, defining the specific terms of engagement, delineating the responsibilities of each partner, outlining the duration of the agreement, and articulating the expected outcomes. These formal agreements help to avoid misunderstandings and to promote transparency in collaborative endeavors. The agreements clearly specify the types of resources that will be shared, how those resources will be accessed, and how any challenges or conflicts will be resolved. These agreements can vary in scope, from short-term project-based collaborations to long-term partnerships with strategic objectives. Formal agreements not only define the terms of the partnership but also provide a legal framework that protects the interests of all parties. This legal framework reduces risks and ensures that partners are held accountable for their commitments. The agreements should include a process for regular review and revision, allowing the partnership to adapt and evolve in response to changing needs and priorities. The establishment of these networks also involves cultivating personal relationships with key community representatives. Regular communication, in the form of scheduled meetings, progress updates, and open communication channels, is important to maintain the partnerships. The schools should be proactive in promoting the work of their community partners and in publicly acknowledging their contributions. This recognition is a vital strategy for fostering good will and reinforcing the importance of the collaboration. Resource-sharing networks also involve exploring opportunities for the joint development of programs and services. By combining the expertise and resources of schools and community organizations, it is possible to create innovative and impactful programs that address complex challenges. This collaborative approach fosters a sense of shared ownership and enhances the sustainability of the partnership.

Maximizing resource utilization is essential to ensure that community resources are effectively integrated into educational programs and services. This requires a strategic approach to resource allocation, ensuring that resources are channeled to areas of greatest need and that their impact is rigorously evaluated. Effective resource utilization involves several steps. Initially, a clear understanding of student and school needs is crucial. This requires a continuous cycle of data analysis to identify areas where community resources can be most effective. The data may include academic performance data, student attendance data, and student and parent feedback, used to identify the specific areas where community resources are most needed. Schools need to align resource utilization with their overall educational goals and objectives. This strategic alignment involves using resources in a manner that directly supports the school's mission and vision, ensuring that community engagement is not an isolated activity but an integral part of the school's strategic plan. School leaders need to actively promote and encourage the use of community resources. This may involve organizing workshops and training sessions to familiarize staff with the available resources, creating a culture of collaboration, and promoting shared responsibility for community engagement. The school should also integrate community resources into the curriculum, providing opportunities for students to engage with community members in a manner that supports classroom-based learning. This integration of resources into the curriculum also increases student engagement and enhances their connection to the community. The school should adopt an intentional approach to data-driven decision making related to resource utilization, and it should analyze the impact of community resources on student success. This requires the use of multiple data points to assess program effectiveness and to identify areas for improvement.

To illustrate these principles in action, several case studies highlight how schools have successfully leveraged community resources to enhance their educational programs. For instance, one case study might focus on a school that partnered with local businesses to create internship programs for its students, enabling students to apply academic knowledge in real-world settings and gain valuable work experience. Another case study might describe a school that formed a partnership with a local non-profit organization to provide social-emotional learning programs for students, addressing mental health needs and improving the school's climate. Yet another example might focus on a school that collaborated with a university to offer dual enrollment programs, providing students with access to higher education courses and opportunities for advanced learning. These case studies provide tangible examples of the potential impact of community engagement. Each case study would detail the specific strategies employed, the challenges encountered, and the measurable outcomes achieved, serving as a practical guide for other educational leaders. These examples showcase the diversity of partnerships that schools can develop and the varied ways in which community resources can be integrated into educational settings.

Maintaining and expanding resource networks requires continuous effort and a commitment to building long-term, collaborative relationships. Schools should ensure that their resource databases and sharing agreements are continuously reviewed and updated. Regularly assessing the needs of the school community, engaging with key stakeholders, and adjusting strategies based on assessment and feedback will also help maintain partnerships. Leaders must champion community engagement, ensuring that it remains a strategic priority, and they should empower staff to develop meaningful partnerships with community organizations. To expand the networks, school leaders should be proactive in seeking new partnerships, reaching out to underrepresented community groups, and building relationships with new stakeholders. This includes organizing community events to connect potential partners with school leaders, teachers, and parents. They should also be transparent with their communication, building trust, and fostering a sense of shared ownership in the success of the school.

In sum, accessing and leveraging community resources is essential for creating a comprehensive, supportive educational environment. By conducting thorough community resource assessments, developing detailed databases, establishing formal agreements, and continually evaluating impact, school leaders can strategically leverage the diverse assets of their communities. These efforts result in not just enhanced programs but also stronger community ties and greater success for all students.

Public Relations

Public relations within educational leadership constitutes a multifaceted discipline, requiring a strategic and proactive approach to cultivate positive relationships with various stakeholders. It is not merely about managing communications; it is about strategically shaping perceptions, building trust, and fostering a supportive environment for students, staff, and the broader community. Effective public relations in education involves a range of interconnected activities, including media relations, brand development, digital presence management, and crisis communication.

Media relations and press management in educational contexts require a nuanced approach to ensure accurate, positive, and timely communication with the public. The initial step involves developing a media contact list that includes local, regional, and, when relevant, national journalists and outlets, segmented by their respective areas of focus. This proactive approach ensures that the school or district has established relationships with reporters who are most likely to cover their news. Developing a clear media policy is also essential to ensure consistent communication practices and to protect the institution's interests. This policy should delineate who is authorized to speak to the media, what information can be shared, and the protocols for handling media inquiries. Training designated spokespeople is paramount to guarantee that all interactions with the media are handled professionally and effectively, emphasizing key talking points and messaging. Creating well-crafted press releases is a critical part of media management. Press releases should adhere to journalistic conventions, presenting key information concisely and compellingly. This involves using a structured format, including a clear headline, a summary of the key information, and contact details for follow-up inquiries. These releases must be disseminated through the appropriate channels, whether via email, press wires, or targeted outreach to key reporters. The strategic distribution ensures that the message reaches the right audience through appropriate platforms. Media relations further require the development of a comprehensive media relations calendar that includes anticipated announcements, events, and other newsworthy activities. The calendar not only aids in planning but also ensures a consistent and proactive approach to media engagement. Regular media monitoring is essential to track coverage, assess its accuracy, and identify potential issues. This process involves the use of media monitoring tools and may entail engaging a dedicated media analysis service to obtain insights into media representation and public sentiment. By establishing these protocols, educational institutions can proactively manage their media presence, ensuring that their message is conveyed accurately and strategically.

Brand development and maintenance within the educational context extends beyond simple marketing; it involves creating and sustaining a consistent identity and reputation that reflects the school's values, mission, and educational philosophy. Brand development is initiated through a comprehensive process that includes defining the school's mission and vision, identifying its target audience, and conducting a thorough analysis of the competitive landscape. This analysis involves evaluating the strengths, weaknesses, opportunities, and threats (SWOT) associated with the school's brand relative to that of other institutions. The results should inform the development of a unique value proposition that underscores what makes the school distinctive, and therefore, desirable. This involves crafting a compelling narrative that highlights the school's unique attributes and educational focus, which is then incorporated into all internal and external communications. Developing a visual identity that is consistent across all channels, including the school's website, social media profiles, and print materials, is paramount. This visual identity includes the school logo, color schemes, typography, and images. These visual elements contribute to building a recognizable brand identity. It is imperative that brand messaging be consistent, conveying core values and principles. This includes clear messaging that communicates the school's commitment to excellence, diversity, equity, and inclusion. Regular brand audits are essential for evaluating how well the brand is being represented and perceived. These audits involve collecting data from a variety of sources, including surveys, interviews, and social media analytics, to gauge perceptions of the school's brand among students, parents, staff, and the community. The data is used to adjust branding strategies to ensure brand consistency and to maintain a positive image. A crucial aspect of maintaining a school brand is ensuring that all internal stakeholders, including faculty, staff, students, and volunteers, understand the brand identity and how they contribute to it. This is accomplished through workshops, training sessions, and ongoing communication, ensuring that all internal stakeholders are brand ambassadors. The goal is to ensure that every member of the school community embraces the brand values and represents the school positively.

Digital presence and social media management in educational leadership are now critical components of effective public relations. A comprehensive digital strategy should align with the school's overall communications plan. This begins with selecting appropriate platforms that target the specific audiences that the school wishes to reach. A robust website serves as a foundational element, providing comprehensive information, resources, and updates for students, parents, and the community. The website must be user-friendly, accessible, and regularly updated with relevant content, such as academic programs, school events, faculty profiles, and admissions information. Social media management involves several steps, beginning with the development of a content strategy. This strategy should define what types of content will be posted, on which platforms, and at what frequency. Content should be diverse, combining academic achievements, community activities, school events, student and staff spotlights, and other topics that enhance engagement. The school should adopt a clear and consistent social media policy that defines acceptable usage and behavior, including guidelines for posts, interactions, and responses to comments or messages. This policy protects the institution's image and promotes responsible online behavior among all members of the school community. Schools should create separate accounts for different audiences. For example, different social media accounts may be used to target prospective students and their families, alumni, community partners, and current staff members. Each account should be managed according to its unique audience and messaging needs. Active monitoring of social media is essential to engage with followers, respond to queries, and address negative comments or feedback. Prompt and constructive responses can effectively defuse potential issues and demonstrate a commitment to transparency and community engagement. Social media analytics should be used to assess the performance of social media efforts, track engagement levels, and optimize strategies for greater impact. Analysis of social media data will help identify what content resonates most effectively, the optimal posting times, and the platforms that are most successful for reaching the target audience.

Crisis management and reputation protection are integral components of public relations within education. A comprehensive crisis communication plan must be established before any incident occurs. This plan should outline specific protocols for responding to various types of crises, such as accidents, security breaches, natural disasters, or negative media coverage. The crisis communication plan should identify key stakeholders, including administrators, public relations officers, legal counsel, and designated spokespersons. Each role should have clearly defined responsibilities for managing different aspects of the crisis. The plan must establish communication channels for use during a crisis, including internal and external channels. This may involve the use of email, text messaging, the school website, social media platforms, and a dedicated phone line. Effective crisis communication requires prompt, transparent, and consistent messaging. All communications must be accurate and avoid speculation. The school's messages should be empathetic, reflecting an understanding of the concerns of the stakeholders. The crisis plan should include a process for media management, which includes designated spokespersons, protocols for media inquiries, and a strategy for managing the narrative. The school should proactively reach out to media contacts to provide updates. Post-crisis evaluation is essential for identifying lessons learned and improving the school's crisis communication protocols. The school should assess the response, identify areas of strength and weakness, and make revisions to the crisis management plan. This iterative approach ensures that the school is prepared for any future crises. A core element of reputation management involves engaging proactively with the community, and a well-managed crisis can be an opportunity to strengthen relationships, build trust, and demonstrate the institution's resilience.

The practical aspects of educational public relations involve a range of activities. Writing effective press releases is a skill that involves understanding journalistic conventions, focusing on newsworthiness, and crafting clear messages. Managing social media accounts requires a strategic approach that integrates regular content updates with active engagement. Handling media interviews requires training and preparation, emphasizing concise messages, and staying on point. Developing effective PR campaigns involves thorough planning, targeting specific objectives, and managing diverse platforms. Managing crisis communication involves clear protocols, timely information, and empathetic messaging. Several case studies showcase successful school PR campaigns, such as initiatives to highlight academic achievements, promote student engagement programs, or celebrate milestones in the school's history. Conversely, the study of case studies involving crisis scenarios will highlight the significance of a well-developed and practiced crisis management plan.

In maintaining positive public relations, best practices include proactively communicating with stakeholders, building trust, being transparent, and consistently reinforcing the school's core values and educational philosophy. This proactive engagement involves maintaining open channels of communication, engaging with the community, and being responsive to inquiries. These practices foster a sense of trust and confidence in the school. Measuring PR effectiveness requires defining specific objectives, collecting data, and tracking engagement across various platforms. Measuring PR outcomes involves evaluating changes in public perception, media representation, and community engagement levels. By strategically implementing these practices, educational institutions can effectively manage their public relations, enhance their reputation, and foster a positive learning environment.

7.1 Full-Length Practice Test 1

Section 1: Strategic Leadership

1. A principal is working with staff to align the school's mission statement with its goals and values. Which of the following is the most effective way to ensure stakeholder buy-in?
A) Require all staff to sign a copy of the mission statement.
B) Allow stakeholders to provide input during the development process.
C) Post the mission statement in all classrooms and common areas.
D) Focus on communicating the mission to students only.

2. A school leader analyzes data to improve instructional programs. Which type of data is most useful for identifying gaps in student achievement?
A) School-wide attendance records
B) Formative assessment results
C) Teacher performance evaluations
D) Extracurricular participation rates

3. Which of the following is a characteristic of a strategic leadership plan focused on continuous improvement?
A) One-time professional development workshops
B) Fixed goals that remain unchanged for years
C) Regular monitoring and adjustment of goals
D) Exclusive reliance on teacher evaluations

4. When evaluating school improvement initiatives, what is the primary benefit of using a SWOT analysis (Strengths, Weaknesses, Opportunities, Threats)?
A) It eliminates the need for stakeholder input.
B) It focuses exclusively on weaknesses to address.
C) It provides a balanced perspective on internal and external factors.
D) It relies on anecdotal evidence for decision-making.

Section 2: Instructional Leadership

5. A principal wants to ensure alignment between curriculum standards and classroom instruction. What is the first step they should take?
A) Conduct classroom walkthroughs to observe teaching strategies.
B) Review state and district curriculum standards with teachers.
C) Purchase new instructional materials for teachers.
D) Require teachers to submit lesson plans weekly.

6. Which of the following strategies best promotes differentiated instruction in a diverse classroom?
A) Using identical assessments for all students
B) Assigning the same reading material to the entire class
C) Providing multiple options for demonstrating understanding
D) Relying solely on textbook resources for lessons

7. What is the primary role of formative assessments in improving student learning?
A) To assign grades at the end of a unit
B) To provide ongoing feedback to students and teachers
C) To evaluate teacher performance
D) To replace standardized testing

8. A school leader is introducing a professional learning community (PLC) to improve teacher collaboration. What is the key focus of a successful PLC?

A) Socializing and networking among staff

B) Sharing strategies to improve student learning

C) Planning extracurricular activities

D) Reducing teacher workload

Section 3: Climate and Cultural Leadership

9. A principal observes that certain student groups feel excluded in school activities. Which of the following is the best approach to address this issue?

A) Create separate activities for each student group.

B) Implement inclusive practices and encourage diverse representation.

C) Ask teachers to monitor and address any exclusion.

D) Focus on academic issues only, as activities are secondary.

10. What is the primary purpose of implementing restorative practices in a school setting?

A) To eliminate punitive discipline measures entirely

B) To address student behavior while maintaining relationships

C) To avoid reporting incidents to parents

D) To focus exclusively on teacher authority

11. A school leader wants to promote equity in educational outcomes. What is the most effective first step?

A) Provide identical resources to all classrooms.

B) Analyze achievement data to identify disparities.

C) Focus on standardized testing results only.

D) Create policies that discourage parent involvement.

12. What is the most significant benefit of creating a culturally responsive classroom environment?

A) It reduces the need for individualized instruction.

B) It ensures all students feel respected and valued.

C) It focuses solely on multicultural celebrations.

D) It eliminates the need for professional development.

Section 4: Ethical Leadership

13. A teacher shares confidential student information with a colleague who does not teach that student. Which principle of ethical leadership is violated in this scenario?

A) Fairness and equity

B) Confidentiality

C) Transparency

D) Professional development

14. What is the best way for a school leader to model ethical decision-making?

A) Always seek approval from district officials before taking any action.

B) Align decisions with the school's mission and ethical standards.

C) Avoid involving staff or stakeholders in sensitive issues.

D) Focus solely on academic results when making decisions.

15. Which of the following best exemplifies an ethical dilemma in a school setting?

A) Deciding whether to allocate funds for new technology or sports equipment

B) Choosing a vendor for a new cafeteria service

C) Addressing a situation where a teacher favors certain students

D) Scheduling a staff meeting during non-contract hours

16. How can school leaders encourage an ethical school culture?

A) By creating a clear code of conduct and consistently enforcing it

B) By allowing teachers to determine their own ethical practices

C) By addressing ethical concerns only when complaints arise

D) By focusing solely on compliance with district policies

Section 5: Organizational Leadership

17. A principal notices inefficiencies in the use of school resources. What is the first step in addressing this issue?
A) Replace the staff responsible for managing resources.
B) Conduct a resource audit to identify gaps and redundancies.
C) Increase the school's budget to cover inefficiencies.
D) Focus on reducing staff to save costs.

18. Which of the following is a key characteristic of effective delegation in school leadership?
A) Assigning critical tasks to multiple staff members
B) Monitoring progress and providing support as needed
C) Delegating only routine or low-priority tasks
D) Avoiding follow-ups to encourage independence

19. A school leader wants to improve emergency preparedness. What is the most critical action to take?
A) Ensure staff reviews the emergency plan annually.
B) Conduct regular emergency drills with students and staff.
C) Share the emergency plan with parents only.
D) Focus on preventing emergencies instead of planning for them.

20. What is the most significant advantage of aligning the budget with the school improvement plan?
A) It ensures compliance with district mandates.
B) It reduces unnecessary spending on staff salaries.
C) It prioritizes funding for initiatives that directly support school goals.
D) It allows for flexible spending throughout the school year.

Section 6: Community Engagement Leadership

21. A principal is seeking ways to strengthen family and community partnerships. Which strategy is most effective?
A) Hosting events that highlight student achievements and invite community members
B) Requiring families to volunteer for school activities
C) Limiting community involvement to fundraising efforts
D) Providing minimal updates to families via newsletters

22. Which of the following best exemplifies community collaboration in addressing student needs?
A) Partnering with local businesses to provide internships for students
B) Relying solely on school resources for career preparation
C) Reducing interactions between students and community members
D) Prioritizing standardized test preparation over community engagement

23. A school leader is organizing a meeting with community stakeholders. What is the primary purpose of such meetings?
A) To delegate school responsibilities to community members
B) To build trust, gather feedback, and align efforts with community needs
C) To promote the school's achievements exclusively
D) To focus solely on fundraising opportunities

24. What is a critical component of successful communication with families from diverse cultural backgrounds?
A) Using a one-size-fits-all approach to communication
B) Providing translation and interpretation services when needed
C) Limiting communication to school policies only
D) Assuming all families have the same communication preferences

Section 1: Strategic Leadership

25. A principal is tasked with creating a long-term strategic plan for improving academic achievement. What is the first step in the planning process?

A) Conducting a needs assessment to identify current gaps
B) Writing the mission and vision statement
C) Setting academic improvement goals
D) Developing a professional development schedule for teachers

26. Which leadership strategy is most effective in gaining staff commitment to a new school initiative?

A) Mandating participation without consulting staff
B) Providing professional development on the initiative's benefits
C) Announcing the initiative without an implementation plan
D) Focusing only on staff members who are already supportive

27. How can a school leader ensure alignment between strategic goals and classroom practices?

A) By monitoring classroom practices monthly
B) By communicating the goals at the start of the school year
C) By involving teachers in the goal-setting process
D) By reviewing the goals only during end-of-year evaluations

28. Which of the following reflects a visionary leadership approach?

A) Establishing rigid policies for all situations
B) Encouraging innovation and adaptability
C) Relying on past practices for future decision-making
D) Avoiding stakeholder input during planning

Section 2: Instructional Leadership

29. A school leader observes that student performance in math is declining. Which of the following steps should be taken first?

A) Replace the math curriculum entirely.

B) Review assessment data to identify specific areas of weakness.

C) Assign additional homework to all students.

D) Focus resources on improving performance in other subjects.

30. How can a school leader best support teachers in implementing evidence-based instructional practices?

A) Conducting annual teacher evaluations only

B) Providing ongoing professional development opportunities

C) Focusing on standardized test results as the sole measure of success

D) Leaving instructional practices entirely to teacher discretion

31. Which of the following is a key characteristic of effective instructional feedback for teachers?

A) Feedback is vague and general to avoid criticism.

B) Feedback is detailed, actionable, and specific to observed behaviors.

C) Feedback is delayed until the end of the school year.

D) Feedback focuses only on negative aspects of performance.

32. A school leader notices that teachers are inconsistent in their use of formative assessments. What is the most effective step to address this issue?

A) Replace formative assessments with standardized tests.

B) Provide professional development on effective assessment strategies.

C) Require teachers to use identical assessments for all classes.

D) Eliminate formative assessments from classroom instruction.

Section 3: Climate and Cultural Leadership

33. A principal wants to address bullying in the school. What is the most effective approach?

A) Punish students involved in bullying without explanation.

B) Implement a school-wide anti-bullying program that promotes positive behaviors.

C) Address bullying only when parents report it.

D) Focus solely on academic performance and ignore behavior issues.

34. How can a school leader promote equity in discipline policies?

A) By enforcing identical punishments for all infractions.

B) By analyzing discipline data to identify disparities and address root causes.

C) By avoiding discussions of race, gender, or socioeconomic factors.

D) By leaving discipline decisions solely to individual teachers.

35. Which of the following strategies best fosters a culturally responsive school environment?

A) Standardizing teaching methods across all classrooms

B) Encouraging teachers to incorporate students' cultural backgrounds into lessons

C) Avoiding conversations about diversity to prevent conflict

D) Focusing solely on test preparation

36. A principal wants to improve teacher-student relationships. Which initiative is most effective?

A) Hosting weekly teacher-led discussions with students on topics of interest

B) Increasing administrative presence in classrooms

C) Limiting teacher-student interactions to instructional time

D) Reducing extracurricular opportunities to focus on academics

Section 4: Ethical Leadership

37. A teacher receives a gift from a student's family that exceeds the school's policy limits. What is the most ethical response?

A) Accept the gift and avoid reporting it.

B) Politely decline the gift and explain the school policy.

C) Accept the gift and donate it to the school.

D) Report the family to administration for violating policy.

38. What is the best way for a school leader to address an ethical concern raised by staff?
A) Ignore the concern if it involves a minor issue.
B) Investigate the concern thoroughly and address it transparently.
C) Address the concern only if it affects academic outcomes.
D) Dismiss the concern if it conflicts with the leader's goals.

39. Which of the following reflects ethical leadership in decision-making?
A) Prioritizing personal interests over school needs
B) Considering the impact of decisions on all stakeholders
C) Ignoring input from teachers and parents
D) Focusing solely on short-term benefits

40. A school leader is facing pressure to adjust grades for a high-profile student. What is the ethical course of action?
A) Adjust the grades to avoid conflict.
B) Refuse to alter grades and uphold academic integrity.
C) Consult with the parent to find a compromise.
D) Ignore the request without addressing it.

Section 5: Organizational Leadership

41. A principal wants to optimize the school's master schedule. What is the most important consideration?
A) Ensuring minimal disruptions to the school day
B) Maximizing instructional time for core subjects
C) Reducing the number of elective courses offered
D) Prioritizing teacher preferences over student needs

42. What is the primary purpose of using technology in managing school operations?
A) To reduce the workload of teachers entirely

B) To streamline communication and improve efficiency

C) To eliminate the need for administrative staff

D) To monitor student behavior exclusively

43. Which of the following best supports effective resource allocation?

A) Conducting regular reviews of budget expenditures

B) Allocating resources based on tradition rather than need

C) Avoiding stakeholder input during the budgeting process

D) Prioritizing administrative expenses over student needs

44. How can a principal ensure the safety of all students and staff?

A) By enforcing strict policies with minimal communication

B) By implementing and regularly updating emergency preparedness plans

C) By limiting safety drills to once a year

D) By focusing solely on high-risk scenarios

Section 6: Community Engagement Leadership

45. A principal wants to improve communication with families. Which strategy is most effective?

A) Sending out monthly newsletters with school updates

B) Limiting communication to parent-teacher conferences

C) Avoiding discussions about student challenges

D) Relying solely on email for communication

46. Which of the following best demonstrates successful collaboration with community organizations?

A) Partnering with local health services to offer free wellness checks

B) Focusing only on school-led initiatives

C) Limiting collaborations to fundraising events

D) Avoiding external partnerships to maintain autonomy

47. How can school leaders encourage active parental involvement?

A) Hosting events that accommodate diverse family schedules

B) Limiting participation to traditional volunteer roles

C) Focusing solely on academic discussions

D) Requiring mandatory attendance at school meetings

48. A school leader is working to build trust with the local community. What is the most effective approach?

A) Engaging in consistent, transparent communication

B) Avoiding sensitive topics in community discussions

C) Focusing on internal school matters only

D) Relying on formal presentations without dialogue

Section 1: Strategic Leadership

49. A school leader is developing a mission statement for a new initiative. What is the most critical element to include?

A) A detailed description of staff roles

B) Specific strategies for implementing the initiative

C) A clear vision of the desired outcome

D) A timeline for achieving goals

50. A principal wants to involve the community in the school's strategic planning process. What is the most effective way to do this?

A) Organize a series of focus groups to gather community input

B) Ask the school board to represent the community's interests

C) Limit participation to parent-teacher association (PTA) members

D) Develop the plan internally and present it for approval

51. Which of the following is a characteristic of an effective vision statement?

A) It is broad and open to multiple interpretations.

B) It is specific, measurable, and time-bound.

C) It focuses solely on academic achievement.

D) It addresses every detail of school operations.

52. What is the primary purpose of conducting a gap analysis in strategic planning?

A) To identify surplus resources

B) To compare current performance with desired outcomes

C) To allocate funding for extracurricular activities

D) To establish a new curriculum framework

Section 2: Instructional Leadership

53. A school leader observes that some teachers struggle to integrate technology into their lessons. What is the best initial step to address this issue?

A) Provide mandatory training on technology use in education

B) Replace outdated technology with newer tools

C) Evaluate the teachers' performance based on technology use

D) Limit technology use in classrooms

54. A principal wants to improve student learning by fostering teacher collaboration. Which of the following is the most effective strategy?

A) Scheduling weekly meetings for teachers to share best practices

B) Requiring teachers to observe each other's classes regularly

C) Assigning teachers to work in isolation on instructional plans

D) Evaluating teachers based solely on test scores

55. What is the most critical aspect of aligning assessments with curriculum standards?

A) Ensuring assessments cover a broad range of topics

B) Matching assessments to instructional pacing

C) Including questions from previous standardized tests

D) Developing assessments that accurately measure learning objectives

56. A school leader wants to implement peer coaching among teachers. What is the primary goal of peer coaching?

A) To provide constructive feedback for professional growth

B) To reduce the need for administrative observations

C) To standardize teaching practices across all classrooms

D) To identify underperforming teachers

Section 3: Climate and Cultural Leadership

57. A principal notices a decline in staff morale. What is the most effective initial step to address this issue?

A) Conduct anonymous surveys to gather feedback from staff

B) Increase teacher workload to improve productivity

C) Hold individual meetings to discuss performance concerns

D) Focus exclusively on student achievement data

58. Which of the following best promotes a positive school climate?

A) Enforcing strict disciplinary policies without explanation

B) Encouraging collaboration among staff, students, and families

C) Focusing solely on academic performance metrics

D) Limiting communication to top-performing staff members

59. How can a school leader address implicit bias within the school community?

A) Provide training on cultural awareness and inclusivity

B) Avoid discussing sensitive topics to prevent conflict

C) Encourage teachers to apply identical expectations to all students

D) Limit interactions between students and diverse community members

60. A principal wants to create a culture of respect among students. What is the most effective strategy?

A) Introduce peer mediation programs to resolve conflicts

B) Focus solely on academic achievement incentives

C) Limit communication between students during class

D) Implement strict rules without student input

Section 4: Ethical Leadership

61. A teacher uses social media to share concerns about a colleague's performance. What is the most ethical response for the school leader?

A) Ignore the post to avoid conflict

B) Address the teacher privately about professional conduct

C) Publicly respond to defend the colleague

D) Take no action unless complaints are received

62. Which of the following best demonstrates ethical decision-making in budgeting?

A) Prioritizing resources for the most vocal stakeholder groups

B) Allocating funds based on data and student needs

C) Focusing solely on technology upgrades

D) Avoiding budget changes once set

63. How can school leaders model transparency in decision-making?

A) By explaining the rationale behind decisions to stakeholders

B) By keeping decisions confidential to maintain control

C) By avoiding discussions about unpopular decisions

D) By relying solely on administrative staff for input

64. A principal discovers a conflict of interest in a vendor contract. What is the most ethical course of action?

A) Ignore the issue to avoid disrupting the contract

B) Disclose the conflict and seek a resolution

C) Continue with the contract but limit its use

D) Keep the conflict confidential to maintain relationships

Section 5: Organizational Leadership

65. A school leader wants to streamline the hiring process for new staff. What is the first step?

A) Review current job descriptions and update them as needed
B) Hire a consultant to manage the process
C) Focus on filling positions quickly regardless of qualifications
D) Limit input from staff in hiring decisions

66. Which of the following is a critical component of effective resource management?

A) Allocating resources based on tradition
B) Monitoring and evaluating resource usage regularly
C) Reducing spending on professional development
D) Avoiding input from stakeholders during planning

67. What is the primary benefit of using a performance management system for staff?

A) It eliminates the need for professional development
B) It provides clear expectations and tracks progress
C) It focuses solely on identifying underperforming staff
D) It replaces the need for teacher evaluations

68. A principal needs to address safety concerns during school renovations. What is the most effective strategy?

A) Develop a safety plan in collaboration with stakeholders
B) Delay renovations until safety issues are resolved
C) Limit access to information about the renovations
D) Focus only on short-term fixes to minimize costs

Section 6: Community Engagement Leadership

69. A school leader wants to increase parental involvement in student learning. Which strategy is most effective?
A) Host regular workshops to educate parents on supporting learning at home
B) Limit parental involvement to parent-teacher conferences
C) Require parents to volunteer in classrooms
D) Focus on communicating only academic progress

70. What is the primary goal of collaborating with local businesses?
A) To secure additional funding for school activities
B) To provide students with real-world learning opportunities
C) To reduce reliance on state and federal funding
D) To promote the school's image in the community

71. A principal wants to build trust with diverse community members. What is the most effective approach?
A) Hold regular meetings to discuss concerns and gather input
B) Limit community interactions to major school events
C) Focus solely on academic achievements during discussions
D) Avoid addressing controversial topics to prevent conflict

72. How can school leaders effectively communicate with families who have limited access to technology?
A) Rely solely on digital communication platforms
B) Use multiple communication methods, including paper notices
C) Focus on one primary communication method
D) Avoid sharing non-critical information

Section 1: Strategic Leadership

73. A principal wants to ensure that all staff members understand the school's strategic goals. What is the most effective method to achieve this?
A) Presenting the goals in an annual meeting

B) Incorporating the goals into regular staff discussions

C) Posting the goals in the teacher's lounge

D) Emailing the goals to all staff members

74. A school leader evaluates progress on strategic goals midway through the academic year. What is the primary benefit of this approach?

A) It reduces the workload at the end of the year.

B) It allows for adjustments to improve outcomes.

C) It minimizes the need for staff meetings.

D) It ensures all goals are met before the year ends.

75. Which of the following is an essential component of a data-driven strategic leadership process?

A) Using only state test results to evaluate progress

B) Collecting and analyzing multiple data sources

C) Ignoring qualitative data in decision-making

D) Prioritizing goals based on anecdotal evidence

76. What is the role of stakeholder feedback in the strategic planning process?

A) To validate decisions already made by leadership

B) To identify priorities and build consensus

C) To limit participation to a select group of stakeholders

D) To avoid conflicts during the planning process

Section 2: Instructional Leadership

77. A principal observes that some students struggle with reading comprehension. Which of the following interventions is most effective?

A) Assigning additional homework in all subjects

B) Implementing targeted small-group instruction

C) Focusing only on test preparation

D) Replacing the reading curriculum entirely

78. How can a principal promote the use of formative assessments in classrooms?
A) Requiring teachers to submit weekly reports on assessment use
B) Providing professional development on designing and using formative assessments
C) Mandating a single assessment format for all teachers
D) Eliminating summative assessments in favor of formative assessments

79. A school leader wants to improve instructional quality. Which strategy is most effective?
A) Observing classrooms and providing constructive feedback
B) Requiring teachers to follow identical lesson plans
C) Evaluating teachers solely based on student test scores
D) Focusing only on curriculum alignment

80. A principal wants to address gaps in math achievement. What is the first step?
A) Analyze performance data to identify specific areas of need
B) Replace the current math curriculum with a new program
C) Provide math enrichment opportunities only for advanced students
D) Assign additional homework for all students

Section 3: Climate and Cultural Leadership

81. A principal wants to promote a culture of collaboration among staff. Which action is most effective?
A) Scheduling regular team-building activities
B) Assigning tasks to individual staff members without input
C) Avoiding collaboration to minimize conflicts
D) Limiting communication to formal meetings

82. How can a school leader address cultural insensitivity among staff?
A) Implementing mandatory diversity and inclusion training
B) Avoiding discussions about cultural differences

C) Limiting opportunities for staff to interact with diverse groups

D) Allowing staff to handle issues individually

83. What is the most effective way to support students experiencing bullying?

A) Punishing the bully without addressing the victim's needs

B) Establishing a peer support system and counseling resources

C) Ignoring minor incidents to avoid escalation

D) Limiting communication between students involved

84. A school leader wants to increase student engagement in decision-making. What is the most effective strategy?

A) Establishing a student advisory council to provide input

B) Limiting student participation to academic matters

C) Avoiding student involvement to streamline decisions

D) Focusing on parent input exclusively

Section 4: Ethical Leadership

85. A teacher reports a suspected case of child abuse. What is the school leader's ethical responsibility?

A) Investigate the case independently

B) Report the suspicion to the appropriate authorities

C) Address the issue only if confirmed by a parent

D) Avoid involvement to protect the school's reputation

86. What is the most ethical way to handle conflicts of interest in decision-making?

A) Disclose the conflict and recuse oneself if necessary

B) Proceed without disclosure to avoid disruptions

C) Delegate the decision to another staff member

D) Ignore the conflict if it benefits the school

87. How can a school leader promote ethical behavior among staff?

A) Establishing and enforcing a clear code of conduct

B) Allowing staff to determine their own ethical standards

C) Avoiding discussions of ethics to prevent disagreements

D) Focusing only on compliance with policies

88. A school leader faces pressure to adjust grades for a high-profile student. What is the most ethical response?

A) Refuse to alter grades and uphold academic integrity

B) Adjust the grades to maintain community support

C) Consult with the parent to find a compromise

D) Avoid addressing the issue directly

Section 5: Organizational Leadership

89. A school leader wants to optimize resource allocation. What is the first step?

A) Conducting a comprehensive needs assessment

B) Reducing spending across all programs

C) Allocating resources based on past budgets

D) Focusing on short-term cost savings

90. How can a principal ensure compliance with safety regulations?

A) Conducting regular safety audits and drills

B) Limiting safety procedures to emergency situations

C) Delegating safety responsibilities entirely to staff

D) Avoiding updates to safety protocols

91. A school leader wants to improve operational efficiency. Which strategy is most effective?

A) Streamlining communication systems and processes

B) Reducing staff to minimize costs

C) Limiting technology use to reduce expenses

D) Focusing on academic outcomes exclusively

92. What is the role of a school improvement plan in resource allocation?

A) To align resources with identified goals and priorities

B) To reduce funding for low-performing programs

C) To focus solely on technology upgrades

D) To eliminate the need for stakeholder input

Section 6: Community Engagement Leadership

93. A principal wants to strengthen partnerships with local businesses. What is the most effective approach?

A) Identifying mutual goals and establishing collaborative programs

B) Asking businesses for donations without offering involvement

C) Limiting partnerships to financial support

D) Focusing on in-school initiatives exclusively

94. How can a school leader increase family involvement in school activities?

A) Offering flexible scheduling for events and meetings

B) Limiting participation to traditional parent groups

C) Avoiding outreach to families with busy schedules

D) Focusing solely on academic-related activities

95. A principal wants to improve communication with non-English-speaking families. What is the best strategy?

A) Providing translation services for key communications

B) Relying on students to interpret for their families

C) Avoiding complex communications to reduce misunderstandings

D) Limiting communication to written notices

96. Which of the following best demonstrates active community involvement in school decisions?

A) Holding regular town hall meetings to gather input

B) Limiting community participation to financial matters

C) Avoiding controversial topics in discussions

D) Focusing on internal staff decisions exclusively

Section 1: Strategic Leadership

97. A school leader is tasked with implementing a new reading program to improve literacy rates. What is the most effective way to begin this process?

A) Select the program independently without staff input

B) Review data on current literacy rates to identify needs

C) Focus on purchasing materials before training staff

D) Assign the task to a committee without setting goals

98. What is the primary purpose of involving staff in the strategic decision-making process?

A) To reduce the workload of school leaders

B) To ensure decisions reflect diverse perspectives and gain buy-in

C) To avoid accountability for outcomes

D) To limit disagreements by delegating responsibility

99. A principal develops a five-year strategic plan for the school. What is the best way to ensure the plan remains relevant over time?

A) Review and update the plan annually based on progress and emerging needs

B) Avoid changes to maintain consistency throughout the five years

C) Focus on achieving short-term goals exclusively

D) Limit feedback to administrative staff

100. Which of the following best supports a school leader's ability to align school operations with the strategic plan?

A) Clearly defining roles and responsibilities for all staff
B) Reducing the number of initiatives to a single focus
C) Delegating operational oversight entirely to department heads
D) Avoiding operational changes during the academic year

7.2 ANSWER SHEET - PRACTICE TEST 1

1. Answer: B) Allow stakeholders to provide input during the development process.
Explanation: Stakeholder engagement fosters a sense of ownership and commitment to the mission. Collaborative development is key to ensuring that the mission aligns with the values and goals of all involved parties.

2. Answer: B) Formative assessment results
Explanation: Formative assessments provide insights into students' strengths and weaknesses, helping leaders pinpoint achievement gaps and address them effectively.

3. Answer: C) Regular monitoring and adjustment of goals
Explanation: Continuous improvement involves regularly evaluating and updating goals to address emerging challenges and ensure sustained progress.

4. Answer: C) It provides a balanced perspective on internal and external factors.
Explanation: A SWOT analysis enables leaders to evaluate strengths and weaknesses within the organization and identify external opportunities and threats, creating a comprehensive improvement strategy.

5. Answer: B) Review state and district curriculum standards with teachers.
Explanation: Reviewing standards ensures that teachers understand the expectations and can align their instruction accordingly.

6. Answer: C) Providing multiple options for demonstrating understanding
Explanation: Differentiation involves tailoring instruction to meet diverse student needs, including offering varied ways for students to show mastery of the content.

7. Answer: B) To provide ongoing feedback to students and teachers
Explanation: Formative assessments are designed to monitor student progress and inform instructional adjustments to enhance learning outcomes.

8. Answer: B) Sharing strategies to improve student learning
Explanation: PLCs are centered on collaborative efforts to enhance teaching practices and address student learning needs effectively.

9. Answer: B) Implement inclusive practices and encourage diverse representation.
Explanation: Promoting inclusivity and representation ensures all students feel valued and fosters a sense of belonging within the school community.

10. Answer: B) To address student behavior while maintaining relationships
Explanation: Restorative practices aim to resolve conflicts, repair harm, and maintain positive relationships within the school community.

11. Answer: B) Analyze achievement data to identify disparities.
Explanation: Identifying disparities through data analysis allows leaders to allocate resources and implement strategies to address inequities effectively.

12. Answer: B) It ensures all students feel respected and valued.
Explanation: A culturally responsive environment acknowledges and incorporates students' diverse backgrounds, fostering a supportive and inclusive atmosphere.

13. Answer: B) Confidentiality

Explanation: Ethical leaders must safeguard sensitive student information and share it only with those directly involved in the student's education.

14. Answer: B) Align decisions with the school's mission and ethical standards.

Explanation: Ethical decision-making requires leaders to base their actions on established values and principles, ensuring transparency and integrity.

15. Answer: C) Addressing a situation where a teacher favors certain students

Explanation: Ethical dilemmas often involve decisions that could impact fairness, equity, or the well-being of stakeholders.

16. Answer: A) By creating a clear code of conduct and consistently enforcing it

Explanation: A well-defined code of conduct sets expectations for behavior and fosters a culture of accountability and integrity.

17. Answer: B) Conduct a resource audit to identify gaps and redundancies.

Explanation: A resource audit helps identify inefficiencies and guides data-driven decisions for optimal resource allocation.

18. Answer: B) Monitoring progress and providing support as needed

Explanation: Effective delegation involves assigning tasks with clear expectations and ensuring proper guidance and feedback throughout the process.

19. Answer: B) Conduct regular emergency drills with students and staff.

Explanation: Drills familiarize everyone with emergency procedures, ensuring a swift and effective response in critical situations.

20. Answer: C) It prioritizes funding for initiatives that directly support school goals.

Explanation: Aligning the budget with the improvement plan ensures resources are allocated to initiatives that enhance teaching, learning, and student outcomes.

21. Answer: A) Hosting events that highlight student achievements and invite community members
Explanation: Celebrating student success with the community fosters a positive relationship and encourages active participation in school initiatives.

22. Answer: A) Partnering with local businesses to provide internships for students
Explanation: Collaborating with local businesses creates valuable opportunities for students to gain real-world experience and build essential skills.

23. Answer: B) To build trust, gather feedback, and align efforts with community needs
Explanation: Regular stakeholder meetings enhance communication, foster trust, and ensure school initiatives address community priorities effectively.

24. Answer: B) Providing translation and interpretation services when needed
Explanation: Offering translation services ensures families from diverse backgrounds can fully engage and participate in their child's education.

25. Answer: A) Conducting a needs assessment to identify current gaps
Explanation: A needs assessment provides essential data to determine current strengths and weaknesses, forming the foundation for strategic planning.

26. Answer: B) Providing professional development on the initiative's benefits
Explanation: Professional development ensures staff understand the initiative's purpose, relevance, and benefits, increasing their commitment.

27. Answer: C) By involving teachers in the goal-setting process
Explanation: Involving teachers fosters ownership and ensures classroom practices are intentionally aligned with strategic objectives.

28. Answer: B) Encouraging innovation and adaptability

Explanation: Visionary leaders inspire innovation and adaptability, focusing on long-term goals while being open to new ideas and solutions.

29. Answer: B) Review assessment data to identify specific areas of weakness.

Explanation: Data analysis helps pinpoint the exact areas needing intervention, allowing targeted improvements to be implemented effectively.

30. Answer: B) Providing ongoing professional development opportunities

Explanation: Continuous professional development equips teachers with current, evidence-based practices to enhance their instructional effectiveness.

31. Answer: B) Feedback is detailed, actionable, and specific to observed behaviors.

Explanation: Constructive feedback provides clear guidance on what is being done well and areas for improvement, promoting professional growth.

32. Answer: B) Provide professional development on effective assessment strategies.

Explanation: Professional development ensures teachers understand how to design and use formative assessments effectively to monitor and enhance student learning.

33. Answer: B) Implement a school-wide anti-bullying program that promotes positive behaviors.

Explanation: A proactive, school-wide program fosters a positive school climate and addresses bullying comprehensively.

34. Answer: B) By analyzing discipline data to identify disparities and address root causes.

Explanation: Data analysis highlights patterns of inequity, enabling leaders to make informed adjustments to promote fairness.

35. Answer: B) Encouraging teachers to incorporate students' cultural backgrounds into lessons
Explanation: Culturally responsive teaching connects students' lived experiences with learning, enhancing engagement and inclusivity.

36. Answer: A) Hosting weekly teacher-led discussions with students on topics of interest
Explanation: Structured interactions beyond academics strengthen relationships and build trust between teachers and students.

37. Answer: B) Politely decline the gift and explain the school policy.
Explanation: Declining the gift while explaining the policy maintains ethical boundaries and transparency.

38. Answer: B) Investigate the concern thoroughly and address it transparently.
Explanation: Ethical leadership involves addressing concerns promptly and openly to maintain trust and integrity.

39. Answer: B) Considering the impact of decisions on all stakeholders
Explanation: Ethical leaders prioritize fairness and inclusivity, ensuring decisions benefit the entire school community.

40. Answer: B) Refuse to alter grades and uphold academic integrity.
Explanation: Maintaining academic integrity ensures fairness and reinforces the value of honesty in education.

41. Answer: B) Maximizing instructional time for core subjects
Explanation: Effective scheduling ensures sufficient time is allocated for critical subjects while balancing other priorities.

42. Answer: B) To streamline communication and improve efficiency
Explanation: Technology enhances operational efficiency and supports effective communication among stakeholders.

43. Answer: A) Conducting regular reviews of budget expenditures

Explanation: Reviewing expenditures ensures resources are used effectively and aligned with school goals.

44. Answer: B) By implementing and regularly updating emergency preparedness plans

Explanation: Comprehensive and current safety plans are essential for maintaining a secure school environment.

45. Answer: A) Sending out monthly newsletters with school updates

Explanation: Regular newsletters keep families informed and engaged in school activities and initiatives.

46. Answer: A) Partnering with local health services to offer free wellness checks

Explanation: Community partnerships enhance student well-being and address broader needs effectively.

47. Answer: A) Hosting events that accommodate diverse family schedules

Explanation: Flexible scheduling encourages greater participation by addressing families' varying needs.

48. Answer: A) Engaging in consistent, transparent communication

Explanation: Open and honest communication fosters trust and strengthens relationships between the school and the community.

49. Answer: C) A clear vision of the desired outcome

Explanation: A mission statement must articulate the initiative's purpose and vision, providing direction and focus for stakeholders.

50. Answer: A) Organize a series of focus groups to gather community input

Explanation: Focus groups provide a platform for diverse stakeholders to share perspectives, ensuring the plan reflects community needs.

51. Answer: B) It is specific, measurable, and time-bound.
Explanation: An effective vision statement clearly defines the organization's goals, providing measurable targets and a timeline for achievement.

52. Answer: B) To compare current performance with desired outcomes
Explanation: A gap analysis highlights the differences between current and desired states, guiding targeted strategies for improvement.

53. Answer: A) Provide mandatory training on technology use in education
Explanation: Training equips teachers with the necessary skills and confidence to effectively integrate technology into their instruction.

54. Answer: A) Scheduling weekly meetings for teachers to share best practices
Explanation: Collaborative meetings enable teachers to exchange ideas and strategies, enhancing instructional quality and student learning outcomes.

55. Answer: D) Developing assessments that accurately measure learning objectives
Explanation: Alignment ensures assessments evaluate the skills and knowledge outlined in curriculum standards, supporting meaningful measurement of progress.

56. Answer: A) To provide constructive feedback for professional growth
Explanation: Peer coaching promotes professional development through collaborative feedback and shared instructional strategies.

57. Answer: A) Conduct anonymous surveys to gather feedback from staff
Explanation: Anonymous surveys allow staff to voice concerns openly, providing valuable insights for improving morale and workplace culture.

58. Answer: B) Encouraging collaboration among staff, students, and families
Explanation: Collaboration fosters a supportive environment where all stakeholders feel valued and engaged in the school community.

59. Answer: A) Provide training on cultural awareness and inclusivity
Explanation: Training helps staff recognize and address implicit biases, promoting equity and inclusivity in the school environment.

60. Answer: A) Introduce peer mediation programs to resolve conflicts
Explanation: Peer mediation encourages students to address conflicts constructively, fostering mutual respect and understanding.

61. Answer: B) Address the teacher privately about professional conduct
Explanation: Ethical leadership involves addressing inappropriate behavior privately to maintain professionalism and resolve conflicts constructively.

62. Answer: B) Allocating funds based on data and student needs
Explanation: Ethical budgeting ensures resources are allocated equitably to address the most critical needs of the school community.

63. Answer: A) By explaining the rationale behind decisions to stakeholders
Explanation: Transparency builds trust and ensures stakeholders understand the reasoning behind leadership decisions.

64. Answer: B) Disclose the conflict and seek a resolution
Explanation: Ethical leadership requires addressing conflicts of interest openly to maintain integrity and trust.

65. Answer: A) Review current job descriptions and update them as needed
Explanation: Clear and accurate job descriptions are essential for attracting qualified candidates and aligning hires with school needs.

66. Answer: B) Monitoring and evaluating resource usage regularly
Explanation: Regular evaluation ensures resources are used efficiently and aligned with school priorities.

67. Answer: B) It provides clear expectations and tracks progress
Explanation: Performance management systems enhance accountability and support continuous improvement among staff.

68. Answer: A) Develop a safety plan in collaboration with stakeholders
Explanation: Collaborative planning ensures all safety concerns are addressed comprehensively and inclusively.

69. Answer: A) Host regular workshops to educate parents on supporting learning at home
Explanation: Workshops equip parents with strategies to support their children's academic success, fostering stronger home-school connections.

70. Answer: B) To provide students with real-world learning opportunities
Explanation: Partnerships with businesses enrich student learning by offering practical experiences and career exposure.

71. Answer: A) Hold regular meetings to discuss concerns and gather input
Explanation: Regular engagement builds trust and ensures the school reflects the needs and values of its diverse community.

72. Answer: B) Use multiple communication methods, including paper notices
Explanation: Offering various communication methods ensures all families receive important information, regardless of technology access.

73. Answer: B) Incorporating the goals into regular staff discussions
Explanation: Regular discussions keep goals at the forefront, ensuring staff understand and work towards achieving them collaboratively.

74. Answer: B) It allows for adjustments to improve outcomes.
Explanation: Mid-year evaluations enable leaders to identify challenges and make necessary adjustments to meet strategic objectives.

75. Answer: B) Collecting and analyzing multiple data sources
Explanation: Using diverse data sources ensures a comprehensive understanding of progress and areas for improvement.

76. Answer: B) To identify priorities and build consensus
Explanation: Stakeholder feedback provides valuable insights, aligns priorities, and fosters a sense of shared ownership in the plan.

77. Answer: B) Implementing targeted small-group instruction
Explanation: Small-group instruction allows teachers to address specific student needs and improve comprehension effectively.

78. Answer: B) Providing professional development on designing and using formative assessments
Explanation: Training ensures teachers understand how to effectively implement formative assessments to enhance student learning.

79. Answer: A) Observing classrooms and providing constructive feedback
Explanation: Observations and feedback help teachers refine their practices and improve instructional quality.

80. Answer: A) Analyze performance data to identify specific areas of need
Explanation: Data analysis identifies areas of weakness, enabling targeted interventions to close achievement gaps.

81. Answer: A) Scheduling regular team-building activities
Explanation: Team-building activities foster trust and collaboration, creating a positive and cooperative work environment.

82. Answer: A) Implementing mandatory diversity and inclusion training
Explanation: Training equips staff with the knowledge and skills to foster an inclusive and respectful school culture.

83. Answer: B) Establishing a peer support system and counseling resources
Explanation: Support systems address the emotional and social needs of victims while promoting a safer school environment.

84. Answer: A) Establishing a student advisory council to provide input
Explanation: Advisory councils empower students to contribute to decisions, fostering a sense of ownership and engagement.

85. Answer: B) Report the suspicion to the appropriate authorities
Explanation: Reporting suspected abuse is a legal and ethical obligation to protect the child's welfare.

86. Answer: A) Disclose the conflict and recuse oneself if necessary
Explanation: Transparency and recusal ensure decisions are free from bias and maintain trust.

87. Answer: A) Establishing and enforcing a clear code of conduct
Explanation: A code of conduct sets expectations and provides a framework for ethical behavior.

88. Answer: A) Refuse to alter grades and uphold academic integrity
Explanation: Maintaining academic integrity ensures fairness and reinforces the school's values.

89. Answer: A) Conducting a comprehensive needs assessment
Explanation: A needs assessment identifies priorities, ensuring resources are allocated effectively and strategically.

90. Answer: A) Conducting regular safety audits and drills
Explanation: Regular audits and drills ensure compliance and preparedness for emergencies.

91. Answer: A) Streamlining communication systems and processes
Explanation: Efficient communication enhances productivity and ensures smooth operations.

92. Answer: A) To align resources with identified goals and priorities
Explanation: Improvement plans guide resource allocation to support key objectives and initiatives.

93. Answer: A) Identifying mutual goals and establishing collaborative programs
Explanation: Collaborative partnerships create mutually beneficial opportunities for businesses and schools.

94. Answer: A) Offering flexible scheduling for events and meetings
Explanation: Flexible scheduling accommodates diverse family needs, encouraging greater participation.

95. Answer: A) Providing translation services for key communications
Explanation: Translation services ensure all families receive and understand important information.

96. Answer: A) Holding regular town hall meetings to gather input
Explanation: Town hall meetings provide a platform for open dialogue and active engagement with the community.

97. Answer: B) Review data on current literacy rates to identify needs
Explanation: Analyzing data ensures the program addresses specific gaps and aligns with the school's literacy improvement goals.

98. Answer: B) To ensure decisions reflect diverse perspectives and gain buy-in
Explanation: Staff involvement fosters ownership, collaboration, and alignment with the school's strategic goals.

99. Answer: A) Review and update the plan annually based on progress and emerging needs
Explanation: Regular reviews keep the plan aligned with changing priorities and ensure sustained progress toward long-term goals.

100. Answer: A) Clearly defining roles and responsibilities for all staff
Explanation: Clear role definitions ensure that all stakeholders contribute effectively to implementing and achieving the strategic plan's objectives.

8.1 Full-Length Practice Test 2

Section 1: Strategic Leadership

101. A school leader is introducing a new science curriculum aligned with state standards. What is the most effective way to ensure successful implementation?
A) Provide professional development for teachers on the new curriculum
B) Mandate immediate use of the curriculum without teacher input
C) Focus on purchasing materials before discussing goals
D) Limit feedback to department heads only

102. What is the best strategy for aligning strategic goals with the school's mission and vision?
A) Assigning goals to individual staff members for completion
B) Developing goals collaboratively with stakeholders
C) Creating broad goals to cover all potential areas of improvement
D) Reviewing the mission and vision only during annual evaluations

103. A principal is conducting a SWOT analysis for the school. What does the "O" in SWOT represent?
A) Obligations
B) Objectives
C) Opportunities
D) Operations

104. Which of the following demonstrates effective use of strategic leadership during budget planning?
A) Allocating funds based on historical spending patterns
B) Prioritizing resources for initiatives aligned with strategic goals
C) Limiting spending to areas with immediate results
D) Focusing budget decisions solely on administrative input

Section 2: Instructional Leadership

105. A school leader observes that some students are consistently underperforming in standardized tests. What is the first step in addressing this issue?
A) Replace the teaching staff for the affected subjects
B) Analyze data to identify specific areas where students are struggling
C) Focus on test preparation exclusively for the affected students
D) Implement a school-wide standardized curriculum

106. Which of the following best supports differentiated instruction in the classroom?
A) Providing all students with the same assignments and assessments
B) Offering multiple pathways for students to demonstrate their understanding
C) Focusing instruction only on the highest-performing students
D) Using a single teaching strategy for all lessons

107. A principal wants to evaluate the effectiveness of professional development sessions. What is the most effective method?
A) Conducting surveys to gather feedback from participants
B) Evaluating teachers based solely on student test scores
C) Limiting evaluations to administrative observations
D) Reviewing attendance records from the sessions

108. A school leader wants to improve collaborative lesson planning among teachers. What is the most effective approach?

A) Provide designated planning time during the school day

B) Require all teachers to submit identical lesson plans

C) Limit collaborative planning to department chairs

D) Focus collaborative efforts on test preparation

Section 3: Climate and Cultural Leadership

109. A principal notices that students from diverse cultural backgrounds feel excluded during school events. What is the best initial step to address this?

A) Create an inclusion committee to gather input and propose solutions

B) Limit cultural references in school events to avoid conflicts

C) Focus solely on academic performance initiatives

D) Post guidelines for event inclusivity without further action

110. Which of the following is a key characteristic of a positive school climate?

A) High levels of student and staff engagement

B) Strict enforcement of rules with no flexibility

C) Focus on academic performance over well-being

D) Minimal interaction between staff and students

111. A school leader wants to reduce disciplinary incidents. What is the most effective strategy?

A) Implementing restorative practices to address behavior issues

B) Increasing punishments for minor infractions

C) Avoiding discussions about student behavior

D) Limiting student participation in extracurricular activities

112. How can a school leader ensure that all students feel valued in the classroom?

A) Encouraging teachers to integrate diverse perspectives into lessons

B) Requiring all students to follow identical learning plans

C) Focusing on standardized testing as the sole measure of success

D) Avoiding discussions about cultural differences

Section 4: Ethical Leadership

113. A teacher has been accused of favoritism by students. What is the ethical response for the school leader?
A) Investigate the concern while maintaining confidentiality
B) Ignore the accusation unless it becomes a widespread issue
C) Publicly address the teacher's behavior without investigation
D) Dismiss the concern as student misperception

114. How can a school leader model ethical behavior during difficult decisions?
A) Clearly explain the rationale behind the decision to stakeholders
B) Avoid stakeholder input to expedite the process
C) Prioritize personal preferences over school needs
D) Keep decision-making processes confidential

115. A parent offers a gift to a teacher to secure preferential treatment for their child. What is the most ethical course of action?
A) Accept the gift to maintain a positive relationship with the parent
B) Decline the gift and explain the school's policies on ethical behavior
C) Accept the gift but avoid providing preferential treatment
D) Report the parent to the school board

116. A principal discovers an error in the school's published achievement data. What is the ethical response?
A) Correct the error and notify stakeholders of the mistake
B) Ignore the error to maintain the school's reputation
C) Adjust the data privately without informing stakeholders
D) Delay addressing the error until the next report

Section 5: Organizational Leadership

117. A principal is redesigning the school's master schedule. What is the primary consideration?

A) Maximizing instructional time for core subjects

B) Prioritizing teacher preferences over student needs

C) Reducing time allocated for extracurricular activities

D) Limiting student access to advanced courses

118. Which of the following is a critical element of effective resource management?

A) Aligning resources with school improvement goals

B) Focusing solely on immediate budget needs

C) Reducing spending on all professional development

D) Allocating resources equally without consideration of need

119. A school leader wants to improve operational efficiency. What is the first step?

A) Conducting a review of current processes and identifying areas for improvement

B) Reducing administrative staff to save costs

C) Limiting technology upgrades to essential needs only

D) Delegating operational decisions entirely to department heads

120. How can a principal ensure effective communication of operational changes to staff?

A) Holding regular meetings to explain changes and gather feedback

B) Announcing changes through email without follow-up discussions

C) Limiting communication to department heads

D) Focusing on written notices instead of direct interaction

Section 6: Community Engagement Leadership

121. A principal wants to build stronger partnerships with families. What is the most effective strategy?

A) Hosting regular family engagement nights to share information and build relationships

B) Requiring families to participate in all school events

C) Limiting communication to progress reports

D) Focusing solely on academic matters during interactions

122. How can a school leader involve the community in supporting student achievement?

A) Partnering with local organizations to provide mentoring programs

B) Limiting community involvement to fundraising efforts

C) Avoiding external partnerships to maintain autonomy

D) Focusing solely on in-school initiatives

123. A principal wants to improve communication with families about school initiatives. What is the most effective method?

A) Using multiple communication platforms to reach all families

B) Focusing solely on email updates for convenience

C) Limiting communication to parent-teacher conferences

D) Relying on students to convey information to their families

124. What is the best way to address concerns raised by the community about school policies?

A) Organizing town hall meetings to discuss concerns openly

B) Ignoring concerns unless they escalate

C) Limiting discussions to administrative staff only

D) Implementing changes without consulting the community

Section 1: Strategic Leadership

125. A principal is developing a long-term improvement plan for the school. What is the most important factor to consider during this process?

A) Focusing solely on short-term outcomes

B) Aligning goals with the school's mission and vision

C) Avoiding feedback from stakeholders to streamline the process

D) Limiting resources for the improvement plan

126. Which of the following best demonstrates strategic leadership during a staff hiring process?

A) Hiring candidates based solely on administrative recommendations

B) Prioritizing candidates whose skills align with the school's strategic goals

C) Focusing on filling vacancies quickly, regardless of qualifications

D) Limiting input from department heads during interviews

127. How can a school leader ensure that strategic initiatives are effectively implemented?

A) By assigning all tasks to department heads without oversight

B) By regularly monitoring progress and providing feedback

C) By limiting discussions about initiatives to annual meetings

D) By focusing only on initiatives with immediate results

128. What is the role of benchmarks in strategic planning?

A) To track progress toward long-term goals

B) To eliminate the need for stakeholder involvement

C) To focus exclusively on financial outcomes

D) To prioritize short-term successes over sustainable growth

Section 2: Instructional Leadership

129. A principal notices inconsistent grading practices across classrooms. What is the best initial step to address this issue?

A) Implementing a school-wide grading policy

B) Conducting professional development on fair grading practices

C) Requiring teachers to align their grading practices without guidance

D) Ignoring the issue unless it becomes a widespread concern

130. Which of the following best supports the use of data to improve instruction?

A) Reviewing assessment data quarterly and sharing findings with teachers

B) Using data only for administrative decision-making

C) Avoiding discussions about data to prevent over-analysis

D) Focusing solely on state test results to measure progress

131. A principal wants to increase teacher collaboration on curriculum design. What is the most effective approach?

A) Scheduling collaborative planning sessions during professional development days

B) Assigning curriculum design tasks to individual teachers

C) Limiting curriculum discussions to department heads

D) Focusing only on standardized test preparation

132. A school leader observes that some students are not engaged in classroom activities. What is the most effective intervention?

A) Encouraging teachers to incorporate active learning strategies

B) Reducing the length of classroom activities

C) Focusing solely on high-performing students

D) Implementing a rigid curriculum without adjustments

Section 3: Climate and Cultural Leadership

133. A principal wants to promote inclusivity among students and staff. What is the most effective strategy?

A) Implementing school-wide cultural competence training

B) Focusing only on academic performance metrics

C) Limiting conversations about inclusivity to administrative meetings

D) Requiring teachers to address inclusivity independently

134. How can a school leader effectively address conflicts between staff members?

A) Facilitating open dialogue to identify solutions collaboratively

B) Ignoring conflicts to avoid escalating tensions

C) Taking sides to resolve the issue quickly

D) Avoiding discussions about conflicts during staff meetings

135. What is the primary goal of restorative justice practices in schools?

A) To repair relationships and promote accountability

B) To replace traditional disciplinary measures entirely

C) To minimize the involvement of school leaders in discipline

D) To focus on punitive measures for rule violations

136. A principal wants to build trust among students, staff, and families. What is the most effective strategy?

A) Consistently communicating and involving stakeholders in decision-making

B) Limiting communication to formal announcements

C) Focusing solely on student-related matters

D) Avoiding transparency to maintain control

Section 4: Ethical Leadership

137. A school leader discovers that a staff member has violated the code of conduct. What is the ethical response?

A) Investigating the violation and addressing it according to policy

B) Ignoring the issue to avoid staff dissatisfaction

C) Publicly addressing the staff member's behavior during a meeting

D) Limiting action to a verbal warning without documentation

138. How can a school leader model ethical behavior for students?

A) Demonstrating fairness and integrity in decision-making

B) Avoiding student involvement in ethical discussions

C) Focusing solely on academic results

D) Ignoring minor ethical concerns

139. What is the most ethical way to handle confidential student records?

A) Sharing records only with authorized individuals

B) Allowing staff to access all records for reference

C) Storing records in an unsecured location for convenience

D) Discussing records openly in staff meetings

140. A teacher expresses concerns about a colleague's behavior toward students. What is the ethical course of action for the school leader?

A) Investigate the concerns while maintaining confidentiality

B) Ignore the concerns unless they are formally reported

C) Address the issue publicly to deter similar behavior

D) Wait for additional complaints before taking action

Section 5: Organizational Leadership

141. A school leader wants to evaluate the effectiveness of the current resource allocation. What is the first step?

A) Conducting a needs assessment to identify gaps

B) Reducing funding for underperforming programs

C) Increasing funding for all areas equally

D) Avoiding changes to maintain consistency

142. How can a principal improve the efficiency of school operations?

A) Streamlining processes based on feedback from staff

B) Limiting communication about changes to reduce confusion

C) Reducing staff to cut costs

D) Focusing only on academic outcomes

143. Which of the following best supports effective school safety planning?

A) Regularly updating and practicing emergency procedures

B) Focusing only on high-risk scenarios

C) Limiting safety drills to once per year

D) Delegating safety responsibilities entirely to external agencies

144. A principal wants to implement a new student support program. What is the first step?

A) Reviewing data to identify student needs

B) Selecting a program without input from stakeholders

C) Limiting the program to high-performing students

D) Focusing on short-term goals exclusively

Section 6: Community Engagement Leadership

145. How can a principal strengthen family-school partnerships?

A) Hosting workshops on supporting student learning at home

B) Limiting interactions to parent-teacher conferences

C) Requiring mandatory attendance at school events

D) Avoiding discussions about family involvement

146. What is the primary goal of involving community organizations in school activities?

A) Enhancing student opportunities and resources

B) Reducing reliance on school funding

C) Focusing exclusively on fundraising efforts

D) Limiting collaboration to academic initiatives

147. How can a school leader address communication barriers with families?

A) Offering multilingual communication options and accessible platforms

B) Relying solely on email updates

C) Avoiding complex topics in communications

D) Limiting communication to written notices

148. A school leader wants to involve the community in improving student outcomes. What is the most effective approach?

A) Partnering with local organizations to provide mentoring and support

B) Limiting involvement to financial contributions

C) Focusing solely on internal school resources

D) Avoiding community input to maintain autonomy

Section 1: Strategic Leadership

149. A school leader wants to improve stakeholder alignment with the school's vision. Which strategy is most effective?

A) Communicating the vision through multiple channels and inviting feedback

B) Mandating compliance without allowing questions

C) Limiting discussions about the vision to annual meetings

D) Relying on the school board to explain the vision to stakeholders

150. Which of the following is a key element of a successful strategic planning process?

A) Using data to set measurable and achievable goals

B) Focusing on short-term solutions exclusively

C) Avoiding feedback to prevent disagreements

D) Developing plans without stakeholder involvement

151. A principal identifies a gap in students' technology skills. What is the first step in creating a strategic initiative to address this?

A) Conducting a needs assessment to understand specific skill gaps

B) Replacing current technology with the latest devices

C) Assigning technology training responsibilities to teachers

D) Focusing solely on advanced learners

152. How can a school leader evaluate the effectiveness of strategic initiatives?

A) Regularly reviewing progress against measurable objectives

B) Limiting evaluations to end-of-year reports

C) Focusing on anecdotal feedback from staff

D) Avoiding revisions to maintain consistency

Section 2: Instructional Leadership

153. A principal notices varying levels of student engagement across classrooms. What is the most effective way to address this issue?

A) Conducting classroom walkthroughs and providing feedback to teachers

B) Requiring teachers to use identical instructional strategies

C) Focusing on high-achieving classrooms exclusively

D) Reducing classroom activities to minimize disengagement

154. Which of the following demonstrates effective use of peer observation among teachers?

A) Encouraging teachers to observe and discuss strategies for improving instruction

B) Limiting observations to high-performing teachers

C) Using peer observations solely for performance evaluations

D) Requiring peer observations without follow-up discussions

155. A school leader wants to ensure instructional alignment across grade levels. What is the most effective strategy?

A) Developing a vertical alignment plan with input from teachers

B) Requiring teachers to standardize lesson plans

C) Focusing alignment efforts only on standardized test content

D) Avoiding discussions about alignment to reduce workload

156. How can a school leader support teachers in integrating technology into the classroom?

A) Providing training on instructional technology tools and their applications

B) Requiring immediate integration without guidance

C) Limiting technology use to administrative tasks

D) Avoiding discussions about technology challenges

Section 3: Climate and Cultural Leadership

157. A principal notices a lack of participation from certain student groups in extracurricular activities. What is the best way to address this issue?

A) Surveying students to understand barriers to participation

B) Reducing the number of extracurricular options

C) Focusing on promoting activities to high-performing students

D) Limiting discussions about participation to staff meetings

158. What is the primary benefit of promoting cultural celebrations in schools?

A) Increasing student understanding and appreciation of diversity

B) Reducing the focus on academic activities

C) Limiting interactions among students from different backgrounds

D) Standardizing cultural activities across classrooms

159. A school leader wants to address staff burnout. What is the most effective strategy?

A) Providing wellness resources and encouraging work-life balance

B) Increasing workload to improve productivity

C) Limiting discussions about burnout to administrative meetings

D) Avoiding the issue unless it affects student outcomes

160. How can a principal promote a sense of belonging among students?

A) Encouraging teachers to build strong relationships with students

B) Focusing exclusively on academic performance metrics

C) Limiting student input in school decisions

D) Avoiding discussions about social-emotional learning

Section 4: Ethical Leadership

161. A teacher expresses concerns about a policy that may negatively impact students. What is the most ethical response for the school leader?

A) Listening to the concerns and evaluating the policy's impact

B) Dismissing the concerns as unfounded

C) Limiting discussions about the policy to administrative staff

D) Avoiding action unless the policy is widely criticized

162. Which of the following best exemplifies ethical behavior in decision-making?

A) Prioritizing decisions based on fairness and transparency

B) Focusing solely on administrative convenience

C) Ignoring stakeholder input to expedite decisions

D) Relying on personal preferences over established policies

163. How can a school leader promote ethical practices among staff?

A) Modeling ethical behavior and providing clear guidelines

B) Limiting discussions about ethics to annual trainings

C) Requiring staff to determine their own ethical standards

D) Avoiding enforcement of ethical guidelines

164. A principal learns about a breach of confidentiality involving student records. What is the ethical course of action?

A) Investigating the breach and taking corrective action

B) Ignoring the issue to avoid conflict

C) Publicly addressing the breach during a staff meeting

D) Delaying action until further breaches occur

Section 5: Organizational Leadership

165. A principal wants to improve staff allocation to meet student needs. What is the first step?

A) Reviewing student data to identify areas requiring additional support

B) Reassigning staff based solely on seniority

C) Limiting staff changes to reduce disruptions

D) Avoiding adjustments unless requested by staff

166. Which of the following is a key principle of effective school budgeting?

A) Aligning expenditures with strategic goals and priorities

B) Limiting stakeholder involvement in budget decisions

C) Avoiding adjustments to maintain consistency

D) Allocating resources equally without regard to need

167. How can a school leader enhance operational efficiency?

A) Streamlining processes through staff feedback and collaboration

B) Reducing staff input to avoid disagreements

C) Focusing exclusively on short-term cost savings

D) Ignoring operational challenges unless they affect instruction

168. A school leader wants to improve the effectiveness of safety protocols. What is the best approach?

A) Conducting regular safety drills and revising protocols based on feedback

B) Focusing only on high-risk scenarios

C) Limiting safety training to administrative staff

D) Avoiding updates to minimize disruptions

Section 6: Community Engagement Leadership

169. How can a principal increase community involvement in school initiatives?

A) Hosting community forums to gather input and share plans

B) Limiting involvement to financial contributions

C) Avoiding outreach to minimize community interference

D) Focusing solely on internal school resources

170. What is the primary goal of family engagement in education?

A) Enhancing student success through collaborative efforts

B) Focusing only on academic-related activities

C) Limiting family involvement to parent-teacher conferences

D) Requiring mandatory participation in school events

171. How can a school leader address barriers to family participation in school activities?

A) Offering flexible scheduling and multiple communication methods

B) Limiting activities to traditional parent groups

C) Avoiding family outreach to reduce workload

D) Focusing only on high-performing families

172. A principal wants to build trust with diverse community groups. What is the most effective strategy?

A) Engaging in open dialogue and addressing concerns collaboratively

B) Limiting discussions about diversity to staff meetings

C) Focusing solely on academic metrics

D) Avoiding controversial topics in conversations

Section 1: Strategic Leadership

173. A school leader is developing a plan to improve student achievement in science. What is the most critical first step?

A) Reviewing current achievement data to identify specific gaps

B) Replacing existing instructional materials with new resources

C) Assigning improvement responsibilities to science teachers

D) Focusing exclusively on standardized test preparation

174. How can a principal ensure that strategic goals remain relevant throughout the school year?

A) Conducting regular progress reviews and making adjustments as needed

B) Focusing exclusively on end-of-year evaluations

C) Avoiding changes to maintain consistency

D) Delegating responsibility for strategic goals to department heads

175. A principal wants to promote innovation in achieving the school's strategic goals. Which strategy is most effective?

A) Encouraging staff to propose creative solutions and pilot new initiatives

B) Limiting staff input to avoid disagreements

C) Focusing only on traditional methods to ensure predictability

D) Prioritizing quick fixes over long-term solutions

176. What is the role of stakeholder feedback in refining a school's strategic plan?

A) Identifying strengths and areas for improvement

B) Validating decisions already made by leadership

C) Limiting feedback to high-level stakeholders

D) Avoiding stakeholder input to streamline the process

Section 2: Instructional Leadership

177. A principal notices inconsistent implementation of the school's reading intervention program. What is the most effective way to address this?

A) Conducting training sessions to ensure staff understand the program

B) Allowing teachers to modify the program as they see fit

C) Limiting the program to high-performing classrooms

D) Replacing the program entirely without review

178. How can a school leader effectively use formative assessment data?

A) To identify student needs and adjust instructional strategies accordingly

B) To evaluate teacher performance exclusively

C) To focus solely on preparing students for summative assessments

D) To replace all other forms of assessment

179. A school leader wants to support new teachers in developing effective classroom management skills. What is the most effective approach?

A) Pairing new teachers with mentors who model effective management strategies

B) Requiring new teachers to attend annual training sessions without follow-up

C) Allowing new teachers to develop their own methods without guidance

D) Limiting support to classroom observations

180. What is the primary purpose of providing feedback after classroom observations?

A) To support teachers' professional growth and improve instructional practices

B) To document performance for administrative purposes only

C) To compare teachers against one another

D) To identify underperforming teachers for remediation

Section 3: Climate and Cultural Leadership

181. A principal wants to address tension between staff members from different cultural backgrounds. What is the most effective strategy?

A) Facilitating cultural competence training and promoting open dialogue

B) Avoiding discussions about cultural differences to prevent conflict

C) Requiring staff to resolve conflicts independently

D) Focusing solely on academic performance metrics

182. How can a school leader promote a culture of respect among students?

A) Modeling respectful behavior and setting clear expectations for interactions

B) Limiting discussions about respect to disciplinary situations

C) Avoiding the topic unless issues arise

D) Requiring students to address conflicts without guidance

183. A school leader notices a lack of collaboration among staff. What is the best way to address this issue?

A) Establishing team-building activities and shared planning time

B) Requiring staff to work independently to avoid conflicts

C) Limiting collaboration to administrative meetings

D) Focusing solely on individual performance evaluations

184. What is the primary benefit of creating a student advisory council?

A) Empowering students to have a voice in school decisions

B) Limiting student input to extracurricular activities

C) Reducing the need for staff involvement in decision-making

D) Avoiding discussions about student concerns

Section 4: Ethical Leadership

185. A parent requests that their child's disciplinary record be altered. What is the ethical response for the school leader?

A) Refuse the request and explain the importance of accurate records

B) Agree to the request to maintain a positive relationship with the parent

C) Delay addressing the request to avoid conflict

D) Consult with other parents before making a decision

186. How can a school leader encourage staff to uphold ethical standards?

A) Establishing a clear code of ethics and providing regular training

B) Allowing staff to determine their own ethical practices

C) Focusing on ethics only during annual evaluations

D) Ignoring minor ethical concerns to avoid disruptions

187. A teacher shares confidential student information with unauthorized individuals. What is the ethical course of action for the school leader?
A) Address the issue privately with the teacher and reinforce confidentiality policies
B) Publicly reprimand the teacher to set an example
C) Ignore the incident unless complaints are received
D) Delay addressing the issue until further incidents occur

188. What is the most ethical way to handle a staff complaint about workplace discrimination?
A) Investigate the complaint thoroughly and confidentially
B) Dismiss the complaint if there is no immediate evidence
C) Publicly address the complaint to deter similar issues
D) Avoid taking action unless more complaints are received

Section 5: Organizational Leadership

189. A principal wants to improve the school's professional development program. What is the first step?
A) Assessing staff needs and aligning training with school goals
B) Scheduling sessions without input from staff
C) Focusing on generic training topics
D) Replacing the program without evaluating its current effectiveness

190. How can a school leader ensure effective communication of operational changes?
A) Using multiple communication channels to share updates and gather feedback
B) Limiting communication to written memos
C) Avoiding communication until changes are fully implemented
D) Requiring staff to adapt without explanation

191. What is the most effective way to improve the use of resources in a school?
A) Conducting a thorough audit to identify inefficiencies and areas for improvement
B) Reducing spending across all departments equally
C) Avoiding changes to maintain consistency
D) Delegating resource management entirely to department heads

192. A school leader wants to streamline daily operations. What is the most effective approach?
A) Involving staff in identifying inefficiencies and proposing solutions
B) Focusing solely on administrative processes
C) Avoiding operational changes during the school year
D) Requiring staff to adapt to new processes without input

Section 6: Community Engagement Leadership

193. How can a school leader foster stronger partnerships with local businesses?
A) Collaborating on projects that benefit both students and businesses
B) Limiting partnerships to financial contributions
C) Focusing solely on academic initiatives
D) Avoiding outreach to maintain school autonomy

194. What is the best way to address language barriers in family communication?
A) Providing translation services and multilingual materials
B) Limiting communication to written notices
C) Relying on students to interpret for their families
D) Avoiding complex topics in communications

195. How can a principal engage families in the school improvement process?
A) Hosting focus groups to gather input and discuss strategies
B) Limiting family involvement to academic matters

C) Requiring mandatory attendance at school meetings
D) Avoiding family outreach to streamline decision-making

196. What is the primary benefit of hosting regular town hall meetings for the school community?
A) Building trust through open dialogue and transparency
B) Limiting communication to essential updates
C) Avoiding discussions about contentious topics
D) Focusing solely on administrative announcements

Section 1: Strategic Leadership

197. A school leader is setting priorities for the upcoming academic year. What is the most critical factor to consider when establishing these priorities?
A) Aligning them with the school's strategic goals and mission
B) Focusing only on immediate concerns raised by stakeholders
C) Limiting priorities to what can be accomplished within six months
D) Avoiding input from staff to streamline the process

198. How can a principal ensure that a new strategic initiative gains support from all stakeholders?
A) Clearly communicating the initiative's purpose and involving stakeholders in the planning process
B) Mandating compliance without allowing for questions or feedback
C) Limiting communication about the initiative to staff meetings
D) Focusing on quick implementation without stakeholder involvement

199. A principal wants to evaluate the effectiveness of the school's current strategic goals. What is the most effective approach?
A) Using data to measure progress and identify areas for improvement
B) Waiting until the end of the school year to assess outcomes

C) Comparing current practices to those of neighboring schools

D) Focusing solely on anecdotal feedback from staff and students

200. What is the primary purpose of developing a vision statement for a school?

A) To provide a clear and inspiring direction for the school's future

B) To outline the specific tasks required to achieve academic success

C) To focus solely on the immediate goals of the administration

D) To create a document for compliance with district policies

8.2 ANSWER SHEET – PRACTICE TEST 2

101. Answer: A) Provide professional development for teachers on the new curriculum
Explanation: Professional development ensures teachers understand the curriculum and feel confident implementing it effectively.

102. Answer: B) Developing goals collaboratively with stakeholders
Explanation: Collaboration ensures goals align with the mission and vision and have stakeholder buy-in for successful implementation.

103. Answer: C) Opportunities
Explanation: Opportunities represent external factors or situations that can be leveraged to improve school outcomes.

104. Answer: B) Prioritizing resources for initiatives aligned with strategic goals
Explanation: Aligning resources with strategic goals ensures funding supports the school's priorities and long-term success.

105. Answer: B) Analyze data to identify specific areas where students are struggling
Explanation: Data analysis helps pinpoint the exact challenges students face, enabling targeted interventions to address their needs.

106. Answer: B) Offering multiple pathways for students to demonstrate their understanding

Explanation: Differentiation allows teachers to meet the diverse needs of students by providing varied approaches to learning and assessment.

107. Answer: A) Conducting surveys to gather feedback from participants
Explanation: Surveys provide insights into the relevance and impact of professional development, helping leaders refine future sessions.

108. Answer: A) Provide designated planning time during the school day
Explanation: Allocating time for collaboration ensures teachers can share ideas and develop cohesive lesson plans without additional workload outside school hours.

109. Answer: A) Create an inclusion committee to gather input and propose solutions
Explanation: Inclusion committees provide a platform for diverse voices, ensuring school events reflect and celebrate cultural diversity.

110. Answer: A) High levels of student and staff engagement
Explanation: Engagement fosters a sense of belonging and collaboration, contributing to a supportive and positive school environment.

111. Answer: A) Implementing restorative practices to address behavior issues
Explanation: Restorative practices focus on resolving conflicts and repairing relationships, reducing the likelihood of repeated incidents.

112. Answer: A) Encouraging teachers to integrate diverse perspectives into lessons
Explanation: Including diverse perspectives helps students see themselves represented in the curriculum, fostering a sense of belonging and respect.

113. Answer: A) Investigate the concern while maintaining confidentiality
Explanation: Ethical leadership requires addressing concerns fairly and confidentially to protect all parties involved.

114. Answer: A) Clearly explain the rationale behind the decision to stakeholders
Explanation: Transparency and communication build trust and demonstrate integrity in leadership.

115. Answer: B) Decline the gift and explain the school's policies on ethical behavior
Explanation: Declining gifts while explaining policies ensures fairness and upholds ethical standards.

116. Answer: A) Correct the error and notify stakeholders of the mistake
Explanation: Ethical leadership involves acknowledging and correcting mistakes transparently to maintain trust.

117. Answer: A) Maximizing instructional time for core subjects
Explanation: Effective scheduling prioritizes core instruction while balancing other important activities.

118. Answer: A) Aligning resources with school improvement goals
Explanation: Resource alignment ensures that funds and materials support the school's strategic priorities.

119. Answer: A) Conducting a review of current processes and identifying areas for improvement
Explanation: Reviewing current processes identifies inefficiencies and informs strategies for improvement.

120. Answer: A) Holding regular meetings to explain changes and gather feedback
Explanation: Regular meetings provide opportunities for clarification, feedback, and collaboration on operational changes.

121. Answer: A) Hosting regular family engagement nights to share information and build relationships
Explanation: Family engagement nights encourage collaboration and strengthen the school-family relationship.

122. Answer: A) Partnering with local organizations to provide mentoring programs
Explanation: Community partnerships enhance student support and provide additional resources for success.

123. Answer: A) Using multiple communication platforms to reach all families
Explanation: Diverse communication methods ensure all families are informed and can participate effectively.

124. Answer: A) Organizing town hall meetings to discuss concerns openly
Explanation: Town hall meetings foster transparency, collaboration, and trust by addressing concerns directly with stakeholders.

125. Answer: B) Aligning goals with the school's mission and vision
Explanation: Long-term plans must reflect the school's core values and purpose to ensure consistency and sustained progress.

126. Answer: B) Prioritizing candidates whose skills align with the school's strategic goals
Explanation: Strategic leadership involves hiring individuals who can contribute to achieving the school's objectives and long-term vision.

127. Answer: B) By regularly monitoring progress and providing feedback
Explanation: Regular monitoring ensures initiatives stay on track, and feedback helps address challenges and refine implementation strategies.

128. Answer: A) To track progress toward long-term goals
Explanation: Benchmarks provide measurable milestones that help leaders evaluate progress and make adjustments as needed.

129. Answer: B) Conducting professional development on fair grading practices
Explanation: Professional development ensures that teachers understand best practices and apply consistent grading standards.

130. Answer: A) Reviewing assessment data quarterly and sharing findings with teachers
Explanation: Regular data reviews help teachers identify trends and make informed instructional decisions to support student learning.

131. Answer: A) Scheduling collaborative planning sessions during professional development days
Explanation: Dedicated planning time encourages teamwork and ensures that curriculum design reflects diverse perspectives.

132. Answer: A) Encouraging teachers to incorporate active learning strategies
Explanation: Active learning strategies increase student engagement by promoting participation and interaction in lessons.

133. Answer: A) Implementing school-wide cultural competence training
Explanation: Cultural competence training equips staff and students to create a welcoming, inclusive environment for all.

134. Answer: A) Facilitating open dialogue to identify solutions collaboratively
Explanation: Open dialogue fosters mutual understanding and helps resolve conflicts constructively.

135. Answer: A) To repair relationships and promote accountability
Explanation: Restorative justice focuses on addressing harm, fostering understanding, and creating a supportive school climate.

136. Answer: A) Consistently communicating and involving stakeholders in decision-making
Explanation: Transparent communication and collaboration build trust and strengthen relationships within the school community.

137. Answer: A) Investigating the violation and addressing it according to policy
Explanation: Ethical leadership requires handling violations fairly, transparently, and in alignment with established policies.

138. Answer: A) Demonstrating fairness and integrity in decision-making
Explanation: Ethical leaders serve as role models by upholding fairness and integrity in their actions.

139. Answer: A) Sharing records only with authorized individuals
Explanation: Confidentiality is critical to protecting student privacy and maintaining trust.

140. Answer: A) Investigate the concerns while maintaining confidentiality
Explanation: Ethical leadership involves promptly addressing concerns while protecting the privacy of all parties involved.

141. Answer: A) Conducting a needs assessment to identify gaps
Explanation: Needs assessments provide data to ensure resources are allocated efficiently and strategically.

142. Answer: A) Streamlining processes based on feedback from staff
Explanation: Staff input ensures changes address practical challenges and improve operational efficiency.

143. Answer: A) Regularly updating and practicing emergency procedures
Explanation: Regular updates and drills ensure preparedness for a range of potential emergencies.

144. Answer: A) Reviewing data to identify student needs
Explanation: Data analysis ensures the program addresses specific gaps and supports all students effectively.

145. Answer: A) Hosting workshops on supporting student learning at home
Explanation: Workshops provide families with tools to support their children's education and foster collaboration.

146. Answer: A) Enhancing student opportunities and resources
Explanation: Community organizations provide valuable support, enriching the educational experience.

147. Answer: A) Offering multilingual communication options and accessible platforms
Explanation: Inclusive communication ensures all families can engage effectively with the school.

148. Answer: A) Partnering with local organizations to provide mentoring and support
Explanation: Community partnerships enhance student outcomes by providing additional resources and expertise.

149. Answer: A) Communicating the vision through multiple channels and inviting feedback
Explanation: Regular communication and stakeholder engagement foster alignment and shared ownership of the vision.

150. Answer: A) Using data to set measurable and achievable goals
Explanation: Data-driven planning ensures goals are realistic, targeted, and aligned with the school's priorities.

151. Answer: A) Conducting a needs assessment to understand specific skill gaps

Explanation: A needs assessment identifies the specific areas requiring improvement, ensuring targeted and effective solutions.

152. Answer: A) Regularly reviewing progress against measurable objectives
Explanation: Ongoing evaluations provide data to adjust strategies and ensure initiatives achieve their intended outcomes.

153. Answer: A) Conducting classroom walkthroughs and providing feedback to teachers
Explanation: Walkthroughs provide opportunities to observe instructional practices and offer actionable feedback to enhance engagement.

154. Answer: A) Encouraging teachers to observe and discuss strategies for improving instruction
Explanation: Peer observations promote collaboration and professional growth by facilitating the exchange of best practices.

155. Answer: A) Developing a vertical alignment plan with input from teachers
Explanation: Vertical alignment ensures consistency and continuity in instruction, supporting student learning as they progress through grade levels.

156. Answer: A) Providing training on instructional technology tools and their applications
Explanation: Training equips teachers with the skills and confidence to effectively use technology to enhance instruction.

157. Answer: A) Surveying students to understand barriers to participation
Explanation: Surveys provide insights into obstacles and help develop strategies to increase engagement among all student groups.

158. Answer: A) Increasing student understanding and appreciation of diversity
Explanation: Cultural celebrations foster respect and inclusivity, enriching the school climate and promoting unity.

159. Answer: A) Providing wellness resources and encouraging work-life balance
Explanation: Supporting staff well-being helps reduce burnout and fosters a positive work environment.

160. Answer: A) Encouraging teachers to build strong relationships with students
Explanation: Positive teacher-student relationships create a supportive environment where students feel valued and included.

161. Answer: A) Listening to the concerns and evaluating the policy's impact
Explanation: Ethical leadership involves addressing concerns thoughtfully and ensuring policies align with students' best interests.

162. Answer: A) Prioritizing decisions based on fairness and transparency
Explanation: Ethical leaders ensure their decisions are fair, transparent, and align with the organization's values.

163. Answer: A) Modeling ethical behavior and providing clear guidelines
Explanation: Leaders set the tone for ethical practices by demonstrating integrity and establishing clear expectations.

164. Answer: A) Investigating the breach and taking corrective action
Explanation: Addressing breaches promptly ensures accountability and reinforces the importance of confidentiality.

165. Answer: A) Reviewing student data to identify areas requiring additional support
Explanation: Data analysis ensures staff allocation aligns with students' academic and social-emotional needs.

166. Answer: A) Aligning expenditures with strategic goals and priorities

Explanation: Strategic alignment ensures resources support initiatives that advance the school's objectives.

167. Answer: A) Streamlining processes through staff feedback and collaboration

Explanation: Collaboration ensures solutions address practical challenges and improve overall efficiency.

168. Answer: A) Conducting regular safety drills and revising protocols based on feedback

Explanation: Regular drills and updates ensure the school is prepared for emergencies and that protocols remain relevant.

169. Answer: A) Hosting community forums to gather input and share plans

Explanation: Forums encourage collaboration and strengthen community ties by involving stakeholders in school initiatives.

170. Answer: A) Enhancing student success through collaborative efforts

Explanation: Family engagement supports student achievement by fostering a strong partnership between schools and families.

171. Answer: A) Offering flexible scheduling and multiple communication methods

Explanation: Flexibility and diverse communication strategies accommodate families' varied needs, increasing participation.

172. Answer: A) Engaging in open dialogue and addressing concerns collaboratively

Explanation: Open dialogue fosters mutual understanding and trust, strengthening relationships with diverse community groups.

173. Answer: A) Reviewing current achievement data to identify specific gaps

Explanation: Data analysis provides insight into areas needing improvement, ensuring targeted and effective strategies are implemented.

174. Answer: A) Conducting regular progress reviews and making adjustments as needed

Explanation: Regular reviews ensure goals are aligned with current needs and allow for course corrections to enhance effectiveness.

175. Answer: A) Encouraging staff to propose creative solutions and pilot new initiatives

Explanation: Innovation thrives when staff are empowered to contribute ideas and experiment with new approaches to problem-solving.

176. Answer: A) Identifying strengths and areas for improvement

Explanation: Feedback provides valuable perspectives that help refine and enhance the strategic plan.

177. Answer: A) Conducting training sessions to ensure staff understand the program

Explanation: Training ensures consistency in implementation and helps teachers effectively utilize intervention strategies.

178. Answer: A) To identify student needs and adjust instructional strategies accordingly

Explanation: Formative assessments provide real-time insights into student progress, allowing for tailored instructional support.

179. Answer: A) Pairing new teachers with mentors who model effective management strategies

Explanation: Mentorship provides ongoing guidance and practical examples, helping new teachers build confidence and competence.

180. Answer: A) To support teachers' professional growth and improve instructional practices

Explanation: Constructive feedback fosters professional development and helps teachers refine their instructional strategies.

181. Answer: A) Facilitating cultural competence training and promoting open dialogue

Explanation: Training and dialogue foster understanding and respect, reducing tensions and creating a more inclusive workplace.

182. Answer: A) Modeling respectful behavior and setting clear expectations for interactions

Explanation: Leaders set the tone for respectful interactions by demonstrating positive behavior and establishing clear norms.

183. Answer: A) Establishing team-building activities and shared planning time

Explanation: Opportunities for collaboration build trust and encourage teamwork, improving overall staff dynamics.

184. Answer: A) Empowering students to have a voice in school decisions

Explanation: Advisory councils provide students with opportunities to contribute ideas and take ownership of school initiatives.

185. Answer: A) Refuse the request and explain the importance of accurate records

Explanation: Ethical leadership requires maintaining accurate records and upholding fairness and integrity.

186. Answer: A) Establishing a clear code of ethics and providing regular training

Explanation: A well-defined code of ethics and ongoing education help ensure consistent and ethical behavior among staff.

187. Answer: A) Address the issue privately with the teacher and reinforce confidentiality policies
Explanation: Ethical leadership involves addressing breaches privately while ensuring staff understand and adhere to policies.

188. Answer: A) Investigate the complaint thoroughly and confidentially
Explanation: Ethical leadership requires addressing discrimination complaints promptly and ensuring a fair resolution.

189. Answer: A) Assessing staff needs and aligning training with school goals
Explanation: Needs assessments ensure professional development is relevant and supports the school's objectives.

190. Answer: A) Using multiple communication channels to share updates and gather feedback
Explanation: Clear, consistent communication ensures staff understand and support operational changes.

191. Answer: A) Conducting a thorough audit to identify inefficiencies and areas for improvement
Explanation: Audits provide data to guide decisions and ensure resources are allocated effectively.

192. Answer: A) Involving staff in identifying inefficiencies and proposing solutions
Explanation: Staff input ensures operational changes address real challenges and improve workflow.

193. Answer: A) Collaborating on projects that benefit both students and businesses
Explanation: Collaborative projects enhance student learning and strengthen community ties.

194. Answer: A) Providing translation services and multilingual materials
Explanation: Accessible communication ensures all families can participate fully in their children's education.

195. Answer: A) Hosting focus groups to gather input and discuss strategies
Explanation: Focus groups provide families with opportunities to contribute ideas and support school improvement efforts.

196. Answer: A) Building trust through open dialogue and transparency
Explanation: Town hall meetings foster trust by encouraging open communication and collaboration with the school community.

197. Answer: A) Aligning them with the school's strategic goals and mission
Explanation: Priorities must support the school's overarching goals and mission to ensure a cohesive and effective approach to improvement.

198. Answer: A) Clearly communicating the initiative's purpose and involving stakeholders in the planning process
Explanation: Open communication and collaboration build trust and ensure stakeholders are invested in the success of the initiative.

199. Answer: A) Using data to measure progress and identify areas for improvement
Explanation: Data-driven evaluations provide objective insights into the success of strategic goals and inform necessary adjustments.

200. Answer: A) To provide a clear and inspiring direction for the school's future
Explanation: A vision statement articulates the school's long-term aspirations and serves as a guiding framework for all stakeholders.

TEST-TAKING STRATEGIES

Preparing for and taking the **Praxis Educational Leadership: Administration and Supervision (5412)** exam can feel overwhelming, but with the right strategies and mindset, you can approach test day with confidence. This section provides actionable tips for managing your time, answering questions effectively, and overcoming test anxiety.

Test-Taking Strategies

1. Understand the Exam Format

- Familiarize yourself with the structure of the Praxis 5412 exam:
  - **120 questions in 120 minutes** means approximately **1 minute per question**.
  - Questions are multiple-choice and based on six leadership domains.
- Practice with full-length tests to get comfortable with the timing and format.

2. Prioritize Time Management

- **Budget Your Time:** Allocate no more than 1 minute per question to ensure you complete the test.

- **Use the Mark-and-Review Feature:** If you're unsure about a question, skip it, mark it, and return later.

- **Monitor Your Progress:** At regular intervals (e.g., every 30 minutes), check how many questions you've answered to stay on track.

3. Read Questions Carefully

- Pay close attention to key terms like **"best," "most effective,"** or **"least likely."**

- Identify the **context** of the question by noting phrases that hint at specific leadership domains.

- Eliminate obvious wrong answers to improve your chances of selecting the correct one.

4. Use the Process of Elimination

- Narrow your choices by identifying answers that are clearly incorrect.

- Even if unsure of the correct answer, reducing options increases the odds of guessing correctly.

5. Look for Keywords

- Focus on terms like **"data-driven," "stakeholder input,"** or **"equity"** to guide your decision-making.

- Praxis questions often reward answers that reflect ethical practices, inclusivity, and evidence-based decisions.

6. Avoid Overthinking

- Go with your initial instinct unless you find a strong reason to change your answer.

- Don't dwell too long on difficult questions—move on and come back later with a fresh perspective.

7. Double-Check Your Work

- If you finish early, review your answers for flagged or skipped questions.

- Ensure you've answered every question, as unanswered questions automatically count as incorrect.

Overcoming Test Anxiety

1. Prepare Thoroughly

- Confidence comes from preparation. Follow the **study schedules** in this guide and practice with realistic test simulations.

- Familiarity with the content reduces uncertainty and boosts self-assurance.

2. Adopt Relaxation Techniques

- Practice deep breathing exercises: Inhale for 4 seconds, hold for 4 seconds, and exhale for 4 seconds to calm your nerves.

- Try progressive muscle relaxation: Tense and release different muscle groups to release physical tension.

3. Visualize Success

- Spend a few minutes each day imagining yourself confidently answering questions and completing the exam.

- Positive visualization can help reduce anxiety and build a success-oriented mindset.

4. Stay Focused on the Present

- Avoid worrying about past preparation or future outcomes. Focus solely on the question at hand.

- If your mind starts to wander, take a deep breath and refocus.

5. Use Positive Self-Talk

- Replace negative thoughts like "I can't do this" with affirmations like "I've prepared for this, and I can succeed."

- Remind yourself that it's normal to feel a little anxious, but you are in control.

6. Practice Mindfulness

- Engage in mindfulness activities such as meditation or yoga during your preparation period.

- On test day, take a moment to center yourself before starting the exam.

7. Manage Your Environment

- **Before the Test:**
  - Get a good night's sleep before the exam.
  - Eat a light, balanced meal to avoid fatigue or hunger.
  - Arrive at the testing center early to settle in and reduce stress.

- **During the Test:**
  - Avoid distractions by focusing only on your screen and materials.
  - Use provided scratch paper to jot down quick notes or calculations.

Test Day Checklist

Here's a quick checklist to ensure you're ready for test day:

Bring a valid photo ID and your admission ticket (if required).
Dress comfortably and bring layers in case the testing room is too warm or cold.
Arrive 30 minutes early to allow time for check-in.
Leave personal items like phones and bags at home or in designated lockers.

Motivational Tips

- **Remember Your "Why":** Keep your goals in mind—becoming a school leader and making a difference in education.

- **One Question at a Time:** The exam is just a series of questions, each of which you're prepared to tackle.

- **You Are Ready:** Trust in your preparation, follow your strategies, and stay focused.

By mastering these test-taking strategies and techniques for managing anxiety, you'll approach the Praxis 5412 exam with confidence and poise. You've got this!

Additional Resources

Recommended Online Resources and Academic Materials

Preparing for the **Praxis Educational Leadership: Administration and Supervision (5412)** exam requires a robust foundation of knowledge and supplemental resources to ensure you are fully equipped. This section lists trusted online tools and academic materials to deepen your understanding and support your preparation.

Recommended Online Resources

1. ETS Official Website

- **Website:** ETS Praxis Educational Leadership (5412)
- **Why Use It:**
    - Access the **official Praxis 5412 Study Companion**, sample questions, and test preparation videos.
    - Register for the exam and review state-specific certification requirements.

2. National Association of Secondary School Principals (NASSP)

- **Website:** www.nassp.org

- **Why Use It:**
  - Explore articles, tools, and resources for aspiring principals and school leaders.
  - Gain insights into leadership trends and best practices in education.

3. Edutopia: Leadership Resources

- **Website:** www.edutopia.org
- **Why Use It:**
  - Offers practical articles and videos on instructional leadership, school culture, and professional development.
  - Provides case studies and real-world examples relevant to the exam's domains.

4. Education Week Leadership Blog

- **Website:** www.edweek.org/leadership
- **Why Use It:**
  - Covers current issues in educational leadership, such as equity, policy changes, and instructional strategies.
  - Helps connect theoretical knowledge with current educational challenges.

5. Khan Academy Leadership Courses

- **Website:** www.khanacademy.org

- **Why Use It:**
  - Offers free courses on topics like leadership strategies, organizational management, and ethics.
  - Ideal for brushing up on foundational leadership concepts.

6. School Leadership Resources on ASCD

- **Website:** www.ascd.org

- **Why Use It:**
  - Provides access to leadership guides, webinars, and research-based practices.
  - Focuses on instructional improvement and equity-driven leadership.

7. State Education Agency Websites

- **Why Use Them:**
  - Review state-specific educational leadership standards and policies.
  - Access free resources and frameworks to understand leadership expectations in your state.

Recommended Academic Materials

1. Praxis Prep Books by ETS

- **Title:** *Praxis Educational Leadership Study Companion*
- **Why Use It:**
  - Published by ETS, this resource is aligned with the actual test specifications.
  - Includes sample questions and test-taking tips.

2. *The Principalship: A Reflective Practice Perspective*

- **Author:** Thomas J. Sergiovanni
- **Why Use It:**
  - A foundational book on school leadership, focusing on practical and ethical aspects of the principal's role.
  - Relevant to domains like strategic leadership and ethical leadership.

3. *Educational Administration: Theory, Research, and Practice*

- **Authors:** Wayne K. Hoy and Cecil G. Miskel
- **Why Use It:**
  - A comprehensive resource covering key theories and practices in educational leadership.
  - Provides research-backed strategies applicable to the Praxis exam.

4. *Data-Driven Leadership*

- **Authors:** Amanda Datnow and Vicki Park

- **Why Use It:**

  - Explains how to use data effectively to inform decision-making and improve student outcomes.

  - Essential for mastering instructional and organizational leadership.

5. *School Leadership That Works: From Research to Results*

- **Authors:** Robert J. Marzano, Timothy Waters, and Brian A. McNulty

- **Why Use It:**

  - Focuses on practical strategies for creating effective school leadership.

  - Ideal for domains like strategic leadership and community engagement.

6. *Transformative Leadership in Education: Equitable Change in an Uncertain and Complex World*

- **Author:** Carolyn M. Shields

- **Why Use It:**

  - Explores equity-focused leadership and fostering inclusive school environments.

  - Aligns with climate and cultural leadership as well as ethical leadership.

7. Professional Journals and Articles

- **Examples:**
  - *Educational Leadership* (ASCD)
  - *The Journal of Educational Administration*
  - *Leadership and Policy in Schools*

- **Why Use Them:**
  - Stay updated on the latest research and trends in educational leadership.
  - Use articles for real-world examples to connect theory with practice.

How to Use These Resources

1. **Supplement Core Study Material:**
   Use these resources to deepen your understanding of challenging topics covered in this guide.

2. **Stay Updated:**
   Refer to websites like EdWeek and NASSP for insights into current issues in educational leadership, which may be reflected in exam scenarios.

3. **Diversify Learning Methods:**
   Combine reading academic materials with interactive resources like videos and webinars to reinforce concepts.

4. **Practice and Revise:**
   Use ETS resources and other test-specific materials for additional prac-

tice questions and revision.

By integrating these recommended resources into your study plan, you'll gain a well-rounded perspective on the key topics tested in the Praxis 5412 exam and enhance your preparation for a successful outcome.

Final Words

Congratulations on taking the important step of preparing for the **Praxis Educational Leadership: Administration and Supervision (5412)** exam! Your dedication to advancing your career in educational leadership demonstrates a deep commitment to making a positive impact on schools, students, and communities.

A Journey Worth Taking

Leadership in education is not just a role—it's a calling. As an educational leader, you have the unique opportunity to shape the future by fostering inclusive school environments, supporting teachers, and helping students thrive. This journey requires perseverance, adaptability, and vision. Preparing for the Praxis 5412 exam is one part of that journey, but it's a significant milestone that showcases your readiness to lead.

Keep These Truths in Mind

1. You Are Prepared

Through diligent study, practice, and self-reflection, you've built the knowledge and skills to succeed. Trust in your preparation, rely on the strategies you've learned, and approach the exam with confidence.

2. Challenges Are Opportunities

Every question, scenario, or concept you encounter on this exam is an opportunity to demonstrate your ability to think critically, lead effectively, and solve problems creatively. These challenges are stepping stones to becoming the leader you aspire to be.

3. Focus on Your "Why"

Remember the reason you started this journey. Whether it's to create a better future for students, support teachers in their professional growth, or lead schools to excellence, your "why" will keep you motivated.

Motivational Tips for Test Day

- **Stay Positive:** Even if some questions feel difficult, keep moving forward. You've worked hard to get here, and you are ready.

- **Take Deep Breaths:** Calm your mind and focus on one question at a time. You've got this.

- **Visualize Success:** Picture yourself finishing the exam confidently and celebrating your achievement.

What's Next?

After passing the Praxis 5412 exam, you'll be one step closer to achieving your dream of becoming a transformative educational leader. The knowledge and skills you've honed during this process will serve you well in your future roles. Leadership is a journey of lifelong learning, and this exam is just the beginning of many successes to come.

Words of Encouragement

- **"Great leaders don't set out to be leaders; they set out to make a difference. It's never about the role—always about the goal."**
  As you prepare to lead, remember that your vision, integrity, and dedication will guide you to make meaningful changes in the lives of those you serve.

- **"The future belongs to those who believe in the beauty of their dreams."**
  Believe in your ability to succeed. You've put in the effort, and you're on the path to greatness.

A Final Thank You

Thank you for allowing this study guide to be part of your journey. At **Test Treasure Publication**, we are honored to support you in achieving your professional goals. We wish you immense success on the Praxis 5412 exam and in your future endeavors as an educational leader.

Good luck, and go make a difference!

EXPLORE OUR RANGE OF STUDY GUIDES

At Test Treasure Publication, we understand that academic success requires more than just raw intelligence or tireless effort—it requires targeted preparation. That's why we offer an extensive range of study guides, meticulously designed to help you excel in various exams across the USA.

Our Offerings

- **Medical Exams:** Conquer the MCAT, USMLE, and more with our comprehensive study guides, complete with practice questions and diagnostic tests.

- **Law Exams:** Get a leg up on the LSAT and bar exams with our tailored resources, offering theoretical insights and practical exercises.

- **Business and Management Tests:** Ace the GMAT and other business exams with our incisive guides, equipped with real-world examples and scenarios.

- **Engineering & Technical Exams:** Prep for the FE, PE, and other technical exams with our specialized guides, which delve into both fundamentals and complexities.

- **High School Exams:** Be it the SAT, ACT, or AP tests, our high school range is designed to give you a competitive edge.

- **State-Specific Exams:** Tailored resources to help you with exams unique to specific states, whether it's teacher qualification exams or state civil service exams.

Why Choose Test Treasure Publication?

- **Comprehensive Coverage:** Each guide covers all essential topics in detail.

- **Quality Material:** Crafted by experts in each field.

- **Interactive Tools:** Flashcards, online quizzes, and downloadable resources to complement your study.

- **Customizable Learning:** Personalize your prep journey by focusing on areas where you need the most help.

- **Community Support:** Access to online forums where you can discuss concerns, seek guidance, and share success stories.

Contact Us

For inquiries about our study guides, or to provide feedback, please email us at support@testtreasure.com.

Order Now

Ready to elevate your preparation to the next level? Visit our website www.testtreasure.com to browse our complete range of study guides and make your purchase.

Made in the USA
Coppell, TX
01 March 2025